TRIPLE OVERTIME

TRIPLE OVERTIME

STEPHEN COLE

A TOUCHSTONE BOOK
PUBLISHED BY SIMON & SCHUSTER
NEW YORK   LONDON   TORONTO   SYDNEY   NEW DELHI

Touchstone
A Division of Simon & Schuster, Inc.
1230 Avenue of the Americas
New York, NY 10020

First Touchstone export edition October 2012

TOUCHSTONE and colophon are registered trademarks of Simon & Schuster, Inc.

For information about special discounts for bulk purchases, please contact Simon & Schuster Special Sales at 1-800-268-3216 or CustomerService@simonandschuster.ca.

Designed by Diana Sullada

Manufactured in the United States of America

10   9   8   7   6   5   4   3   2   1

ISBN 978-1-4516-7558-0

To Harry and Lewis, fans of the Buffalo Sabres and Atlanta Thrashers-Winnipeg Jets

CONTENTS

FOREWORD

I'm writing this in an Ottawa train station after the plucky Senators were eliminated by New York Rangers in the 2012 playoffs. The 10-year-old kid fidgeting across from me is still wearing Senator tattoos everywhere — bright, splotchy Roman generals all up his arms; two more frowning commanders on his cheeks. When I say I like his decorations, his mom makes a face.

"They're gone before bedtime tonight, right, Tiger?" she says.

Maybe not, if Tiger stays up to watch tonight's games. We had 16 overtime contests in the first round of the 2012 playoffs. With playoff hockey, there is no such thing as regular bedtime.

I love these long night's journeys into day. I saw the Ottawa-Rangers game on television with an old friend, a nervous Sens fan who shouted *ooh, eeh, ah* throughout, as if he was crossing a hot beach in bare feet.

We weren't the only ones watching. Yeah, you were there, too. But there were also ghosts in our TV machines — glorious apparitions that showed up in the CBC *Hockey Night in Canada* feed of the Ottawa–New York game and the TSN broadcast of the deliciously tense, seventh-game double-overtime match between Florida and New Jersey.

Boy, was it good to see Mark Messier and Glen Sather (chewing an unlit Sgt. Fury cigar) observing the Ottawa-New York game from on high — Ranger brass, yes, but also coach and captain of so many Edmonton Oilers championship teams. And in the Jersey-Florida

game, which I watched into the wee hours back at my parents' house, there was Panthers GM Dale Tallon sitting next to — *Where had we seen that bow tie?* — Bill Torrey, architect of the great Islanders teams of the early 1980s.

Paul MacLean, an old Winnipeg Jet, hockey's most durable moustache, was behind Ottawa's bench. Larry Robinson, Montreal's Big Bird, gray as an Arctic owl these days, shouted advice to New Jersey defensemen. Key on-ice personnel included Devils goalie Marty Brodeur, the Panthers' John Madden (performing with a reassembled face after a ghastly collision) and senior Senator Daniel Alfredsson.

All Jack Benny's age — 39.

Still, the best players last night were Ottawa's suddenly spectacular Erik Karlsson and Jersey's Adam Henrique, both 22.

That's one of the great things about hockey: there always seems to be four generations in the fray — ulcerous coaches sharing gum and strategy with former teammate/assistants behind the bench, while on the ice you have grizzled veterans, today's stars and peppy young recruits.

Follow the game long enough and you watch players go through every stage. I remember seeing Messier as a teenager with the Oilers in 1980, never getting into the game, but ventilating the Montreal Forum during intermission, flying around the boards so fast the fans cheered when the then-shaggy whirl-wind hopped off the ice.

In putting together *Triple Overtime*, I've tried to present hockey the way I see it — as a fluid space-time continuum that exists simultaneously in the past and present. And so, in this volume you will find stories on the 2009 and 1961 Stanley Cup finals, on Edmonton Oiler boy band stars Nugent-Hopkins-Eberle-Hall, along with Drew Doughty, Tyler Seguin, David Backes, P.K. Subban and Carey Price. But looking over their shoulder we also have Glenn Hall, Bill Mosienko and . . . well, let's leave *some* surprises, shall we?

I'm delighted to add that this volume also includes a photo of someone related (at least in spirit) to Tiger, the kid sitting across from me here in the train station. That would be Simon (and his dad), another Ottawa kid wearing the exact same Roman general war paint (see page 144).

In fact, most of the 249 photos in this book are either of or by fans. Flip through the book. Look at the very cool photo a Buffalo Sabres fan took of himself wandering around his TV room watching the Sabres play (see page 24). *Talk about a fluid space-time continuum.* All the photos in some chapters, even the action shots, are taken by fans.

This is by design. The Overtime series (this is the second volume) is intended to be a fan-based pop-culture celebration of all things hockey. The phrase "I couldn't have done it without you" is, in this instance, literally true. This book would not have been possible without the generosity of the many fans who allowed us to use their photos. So thanks.

A couple of other big shout outs: the first to Brendan May at Simon & Schuster Canada, who coordinated the book's photographic efforts. And I have to say thank you once again to my tireless researcher and fellow hockey lifer, Paul Patskou. Almost all of these chapters emerged from back-and-forth discussions/arguments/harangues we had about hockey in the last year.

These discussions never really ended. Nor are they yet resolved. It's now your turn to complete the conversation.

Stephen Cole, April 27, 2012, Ottawa

ANAHEIM DUCKS

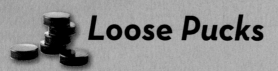 ## *Loose Pucks*

RECORD: "Bro Hymn" by the California band Pennywise is played after every home goal. The band played the song, a tribute to friends who perished in a car crash, during the Ducks' Cup victory rally.

RECORDS

MOST HAT TRICKS, CAREER: Teemu Selanne, 13

MOST POWER PLAY GOALS IN A SEASON: Teemu Selanne, 25, 1998–99 and 2006–07

MOST SHORT-HANDED GOALS, CAREER: Paul Kariya, 16

MOST PENALTY MINUTES, CAREER: George Parros, 812

BEST PLUS/MINUS, CAREER: Teemu Selanne, +122

50-GOAL CLUB: Teemu Selanne, 52, 1997–98; Selanne, 51, 1996–97; Paul Kariya, 50, 1995–96; Corey Perry, 50, 2010–11

WORKING OVERTIME: It was the biggest game in Ducks playoff history: game five of the 2007 semis against Detroit. The series was tied 2-2, with the Wings seemingly in control. Then Teemu Selanne stole the puck in front of Dominik Hasek, gave him a juke, and backhanded a pop-the-water-bottle game-winner. The Ducks breezed through the rest of the playoffs for their first Cup.

DRAFT-SCHMAFT

TOP-10 PICKS, 1993–2009: 9

PLAYERS DRAFTED WHO PLAYED IN 300 NHL GAMES: 21

IMPACT PLAYERS: Paul Kariya, 4th, 1993; Ilya Bryzgalov, 44th, 2000; Ryan Getzlaf, 19th, 2003; Corey Perry, 28th, 2003; Bobby Ryan, 2nd, 2005.

DRAFT-SCHMAFT RANKING: 10th

LINE CHANGES

The Ducks' most famous line, The Kid or PPG Line of Corey Perry, Dustin Penner, and Ryan Getzlaf, led the Ducks to the Stanley Cup in 2007. Penner was 25 and Perry and Getzlaf 22 at the time.

"This is the only thing that has seen more parties than us." — Aerosmith singer Steven Tyler, admiring the Stanley Cup after the Ducks' win.

"That's so when I forget how to spell my name, I can still find my %&^# clothes." — Stu Grimson, explaining why he kept a color photo of himself above his locker.

"I hate kids. They're barely human." — Coach Bombay (Emilio Estevez) in *The Mighty Ducks* movie (1992).

SKATE THAT ONE PAST ME AGAIN: In 2007, high-flying Duck/animal activist Scott Niedermayer wrote a letter to Chicago City Council asking that they uphold a ban on foie gras: "As an Anaheim Duck, I hate to

Anaheim Ducks linemates Ryan Getzlaf (left) and Bobby Ryan (right) surround 2011 Hart Trophy winner Corey Perry. Perry also won the Rocket Richard Trophy for being the league's top goal scorer. After the awards ceremony, the Ducks reportedly stayed in formation until 6 a.m.

see real ducks tortured so that a handful of wealthy chefs can serve their diseased organs."

BRING ON THE ZAMBONI

CELEBRITY FANS: Milo Ventimiglia (*Gilmore Girls*) and Snoop Dogg.

STUMP THE SCHWAB: The Anaheim Ducks are one of three NHL teams with their nicknames scripted on their jerseys. Name the other two. Answer: New York Rangers and Washington Capitals.

Ducks in a ROW

One of the NHL's top lines — Ryan-Getzlaf-Perry — almost never happened. The Ducks had two late picks (19th and 28th) in the 2003 draft, with which they grabbed Getzlaf and, later, Perry. Figuring the latter was expendable, they then traded Perry to Edmonton for Mike Comrie. But the deal was never consummated because of a dispute over bonus money. Lucky Ducks: as he proved in junior, where he led the London Knights to a Memorial Cup, Perry keeps on playing bigger and better. He arrived in London at 5′9″, left at 6′2″. He could always score and was mean as a hangover — great ingredients for a power forward. But the knock on Corey was he didn't have fast feet. Speed-skating lessons every morning took care of that. And Perry always had determination. In the 2005 Memorial Cup final, against Sidney Crosby's team, he was concussed early on, but played through, setting up an important goal. On the bench, he kept asking "What's the score?" in a game his London Knights were winning handily, 4-0. Afterward, he was named tournament MVP. Perry, skating beside Getzlaf, led the Ducks to a Stanley Cup in 2007 and an Olympic gold medal for Canada in 2010. His Ducks linemate, Bobby Ryan, was on the silver-winning American team. Ryan also played against Perry in junior, so knows about his mood swings. "What I've learned is that when he's having a bad day, just leave him be," Ryan says.

"He could always score and was mean as a hangover."

VERTIGO

"There is no position in sports as noble as that of goal-tending," Russian master Vladimir Tretiak once said. But the position is dangerous. And potentially humiliating.

"The goalie is like the guy on the minefield," goalie Arturs Irbe observed. "He discovers the mines and destroys them. If you make a mistake, somebody gets blown up." Meanwhile, Hall of Famer Jacques Plante lamented: "How would you like it if every time you made a small mistake, a red light went on over your desk and 15,000 people stood up and yelled at you?"

The story of hockey's first great goalie, Georges Vezina, is a tale of suffering. A pensive loner, Georges first skated between the pipes for the Montreal Canadiens in 1910, and showed up for every subsequent game for 15 seasons, playing through injury and turmoil. The oft-repeated story that he fathered 24 children, of whom 20 died in childbirth, is a folk legend, an exaggeration of real tragedy — in fact, the Vezinas had nine offspring, of whom only three lived long enough to be baptized. Two were alive when Vezina died, the third having perished after living only a few months.

When Vezina reported to camp in 1925, he was sick, and 35 pounds underweight. Prior to the first game of the season, the goalie had a fever of 102°F, but played, shutting out the opposition for 20 minutes. In the dressing room, he vomited blood and then skated out for the second period. A few minutes in, Vezina performed an awkward dance, stepping sideways, looked up half-turning, and then collapsed to the ice.

He was dead from tuberculosis four months later. Goalies live with trouble. Getting shot at is not a healthy job description. Look at Vezina's Montreal descendants: George Hainsworth, first winner of the Vezina Trophy, died prematurely in a car accident; his successor, Lorne Chabot, fell to Bright's disease at age 46; Habs goalies of the '40s Gerry McNeil and Bill

FAN-tastic

(Top) George Parros gets the finger. (Middle left) Corey Perry joins the Blue Man Group. (Middle right) Two fans in their Ducky pajamas. (Bottom) The Ducks' Jonas Hiller helps a kid buckle up.

Durnan quit the game with bad nerves.

We'll get to Jacques Plante later and skip on to Gump Worsley, who was mortally afraid of flying. Once, Gump and Jean Beliveau were together on a plane that dropped from the sky as a hostess filled Beliveau's drink. The beverage spilled across the Montreal captain's jacket.

"I'm sorry," the flight attendant said when turbulence subsided. "We'll look after the dry cleaning."

"What about my shorts?" a still-shaking Worsley inquired.

The Anaheim Ducks' Jonas Hiller would be the last goalie you'd expect to succumb to trauma. The Swiss netminder grew up in a winter-sports family — though not the one you think. His mom played on the Swiss national basketball team.

Jonas prepared for hockey with monastic diligence. He read more than 200 books on goaltending growing up. Everything he could get his eyes on in five different languages (English, German, Italian, Russian, and Czech). Some well-thumbed artifacts were nothing more than accordions of jammed-together papers photocopied from libraries.

At 17, he attended Quebec goalie guru Francois Allaire's Swiss goaltending camps, returning for seven semesters. The NHL lockout of 2004–05 was his ticket to North America. He played with Joe Thornton and Rick Nash for HC Davos, winning the Swiss championship and Spengler Cup.

Word on the butterfly goalie with fast wings spread. Seven NHL teams offered contracts. In 2007, the meticulous, cautious goalie chose Anaheim. Mentor Allaire was the Ducks' goalie coach.

Hiller impressed Anaheim before he even stepped on the ice. He had less than six percent body fat. "He's like a marathoner," GM Brian Burke exclaimed. And the backup goalie approached every contest, even those he wasn't playing, like a seventh playoff game.

Inside a year, Hiller was the starting goalie, replacing Jean-Sebastien Giguere. He performed miracles in the 2009 playoffs, taking eighth-place Anaheim past league-leading San Jose and pushing Detroit to seven games.

No goalie was better prepared. Hiller's pads and

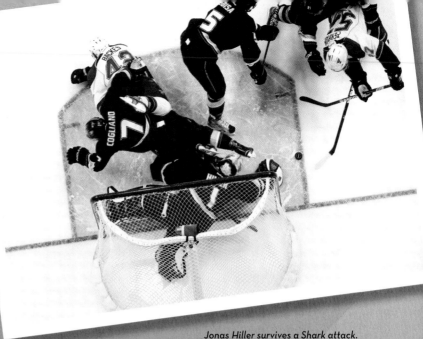

Jonas Hiller survives a Shark attack.

equipment had to be lined up just so. His custom steel skate blades had to be sharpened with one edge higher up front. A car mechanic in Switzerland looked after a special protective cowling attached to the boots. Jonas once flew to the Koho hockey factory in Montreal to supervise the creation of his pads and face mask.

Practice ended with Hiller taking slap shots from the point. Defencemen would let fly from the blue line, and first Corey Perry, then Ryan Getzlaf took turns standing in front of the crease, deflecting incoming missiles — sharpening Hiller's reflexes. Hours later, before games, he'd go into the arena corridor with a tennis ball to play handball.

Throwing the ball faster. Making himself quicker.

Hiller was on top of the hockey world at the halfway point of the 2010–11 NHL season, acclaimed as one of the game's best three or four goalies. He'd been named to the All-Star Game in Raleigh and played well, even if he took a couple of pucks off the mask.

Maybe it was the shots to the head, but he felt different after the All-Star Game — as if, instead of being on top of the world, the world was looking down on him.

Next game, against San Jose, he had trouble following the play and was pulled after letting in three goals. On the bench, he complained he hadn't felt right on the ice — that he was slow, his pads heavy. Days later, the lethargy returned. He felt funny, like when you're walking down a broken escalator.

Jonas Hiller's equipment: Just add goalie and . . . star!

"To me, it just seemed like I couldn't keep up with the game."

Instead of a goalie, Hiller was a professional patient now, visiting every neurologist in southern California. Most had the same diagnosis: vertigo. Hiller's mind and body were out of synch. And no one was sure how or why that happened. They ruled out a concussion. What, then?

Lifestyle fatigue was one theory. The cumulative effect of Hiller's recent travel, the 100 games a year plus practices, the literally thousands of hard, whistling rubber pucks, all the goalmouth collisions, and on top of that, the hundreds of thousands of miles of air travel he'd endured the previous 16 months.

Not to mention the unending pressure of being the last sentinel: the puck stops here. And if it doesn't often enough, your team is out of the playoffs and you're out of a job.

Hiller was suffering from goaltender disease.

The medical consensus was that Jonas had to quit, forget about hockey, about training, being sharp and ready, and get back to where he once belonged — Switzerland. There, he had to stay away from the rink.

Had to un-become a goalie.

Hiller was out almost half a season. Back in his home country, he got better in slow degrees. Some mornings, though, the hangover returned. Aiming a foot into a pant leg took concentration. The trick was not letting that bother him. To remember: I am getting better.

Three months after the vertigo arrived, it began to evaporate. Hiller's head cleared. He felt good again. In the summer of 2011, Francois Allaire returned to Switzerland to host another clinic. And Hiller finally returned to the rink, a goalie once more. He rejoined the Ducks in the fall of 2011, recording a shutout upon returning to Anaheim for the team's first home game.

The good news was that he was an NHL goaltender again. That was the bad news, too.

"To me, it just seemed like I couldn't keep up with the game," Hiller said. "I had trouble tracking the puck. I was just off a little bit. I was always late. It really kind of seemed like instead of a movie in front of my eyes, it was like single pictures.

"For me, there was always information missing. I was always kind of like running behind, catching up because I couldn't see fluid movement. I always saw single pictures. I was always late. I guess goaltending is tough enough without missing a few frames."

MASKING FEAR

A Short Medical History of Goalie Ailments, Real and Imagined

Goalies are a troubled breed. Toronto's Ed Chadwick overcame a club foot to become a puck stopper in the 1950s. Philadelphia Flyer goalie Bruce Gamble had a heart attack in net. Ulcers McCool, who drank milk before games, had a bad stomach. But a better one than Glenn Hall, who emptied his, vomiting before matches. Roger Crozier developed an ulcer in junior. As a pro, playing mostly for Detroit and Buffalo, he endured 30 bouts of pancreatitis and quit hockey for a while at 25 to work as a carpenter. Chicago Hall of Famer Charlie Gardiner played through tonsillitis, never complaining, slumping against the crossbar during lulls in action, laboring through fevers. Weeks after recording a playoff shutout against the Montreal Maroons in 1934, he succumbed to a brain hemorrhage. Tommy Soderstrom suffered from Wolff-Parkinson-White syndrome — an abnormal heart rate. Mark Fitzpatrick was sidelined with eosinophilia-myalgia syndrome, a potentially fatal disease. Evgeny Belosheikin never got over the pressure of being the next Vladislav Tretiak. He committed suicide at age 33.

Then there are the goalies who suffered from feverish imaginations. Here are the top three goalie stars of the malingerer club.

THIRD STAR: Montreal goalie Jacques Plante hated playing in Toronto. Said the air in the Royal York Hotel, where the team stayed, aggravated a bronchial condition. So the team put him up in the nearby Westbury. Before one game, Habs coach Toe Blake found Plante in the dressing room, making a sound like a clogged drain. Maybe he couldn't play. "What's wrong?" Blake demanded. "Didn't you stay at the Westbury?" "I did," Plante responded, "but when I was sleeping, I dreamed I was at the Royal York. When I woke up, I was plugged."

SECOND STAR: New York Ranger goalie Steve Buzinski was bowlegged — tunnel-legged is more like it. He let in so many pucks during the 1942–43 season that he earned the nickname "The Puck Goes-inski" Buzinski. GM Lester Patrick took him out of the net and made him team publicist. One day, the Rangers need a practice goalie. Patrick asked Buzinski to return to the cage. Can't, he said. Too many letters to write. The Puck Goes-inski was sent home to Saskatchewan the next day.

FIRST STAR: Nicknamed "The Cat," Gilles Gratton had more than nine lives. He believed in reincarnation. While playing goalie for New York Rangers in the '70s he told coach John Ferguson he couldn't play one night — bad leg. "How'd it happen?" his coach inquired. "I was a soldier in the Franco-Russian War of 1870 and was wounded in the leg. Still bothers me sometimes."

Plante replica mask (top); Gilles "The Cat" Gratton's mask (right)

BOSTON BRUINS

Loose Pucks

RECORD: Way back in 1967, Bruins TV station WSBK decided to cross-promote hockey and a broadcast of the Nutcracker Suite. Killing two birds with one guitar riff, they produced an ad using a rock-instrumental take on Tchaikovsky's ballet. The Ventures' "Nutty" led off Bruins broadcasts for years and can still be heard at the TD Garden. So can "Dirty Water," a down-and-dirty 1966 garage-rock anthem by the Standells. Songwriter Ed Cobb wrote the song, played after every Bruin win, in response to being mugged near the Charles River. (The Standells were from L.A. — what did they expect?) More recently, the Dropkick Murphys wrote the Bruins' rally cry "Time to Go." Inspirational verse: *"Top corner, five hole, off the post and in / On a quest for the Cup and we're ready to win."*

RECORDS:

MOST HAT TRICKS, CAREER: Phil Esposito, 28,

MOST GOALS, ONE SEASON: Phil Esposito, 76, 1970–71

MOST POINTS BY A DEFENSEMAN, ONE SEASON: Bobby Orr, 139, 1970–71 (NHL record)

MOST GOALS, CAREER: Johnny Bucyk, 545; Phil Esposito, 459; Rick Middleton, 402

BEST PLUS-MINUS, CAREER: Bobby Orr, +589; Ray Bourque, +494; Dallas Smith, +366

MOST SHUTOUTS, CAREER: Tiny Thompson, 74; Frank Brimsek, 35

50-GOAL CLUB: Phil Esposito, 76, 1970–71; Esposito, 68, 1973–74; Esposito, 66, 1971–72; Esposito, 61, 1974–75; Esposito, 55, 1972–73; Cam Neely, 55, 1989–90; John Bucyk, 51, 1970–71; Rick Middleton, 51, 1981–82; Neely, 51, 1990–91; Ken Hodge, 50, 1973–74; Neely, 50, 1993–94

Tiny Thompson — actually, he was 5' 10" — small for a goalie today, but growing up in Calgary, Cecil Thompson was the biggest player on the team and the guys razzed him with the ironic nickname. Still, which you rather be called: Tiny or Cecil? Tough call.

The Bruins' Zdeno Chara and Penguins' Chris Conner chase the puck.

WORKING OVERTIME: There are several playoff overtime heroes in Bruin history — Mel "Sudden Death" Hill scored three overtime goals in a seven-game series against New York in 1939, helping Boston to their second Stanley Cup. Nathan Horton collected two OT goals and an assist against Montreal on way to the team's 2011 Cup, their sixth championship. Bobby Orr won the Bruins' fourth Cup, firing an overtime winner against St. Louis while flying through the air.

DRAFT-SCHMAFT
TOP-10 PICKS, 1989–2009: 7

PLAYERS DRAFTED WHO PLAYED 300 NHL GAMES: 30

IMPACT PLAYERS: Glen Murray, 18th, 1991; Joe Thornton, 1st, 1997; Patrice Bergeron, 45th, 2003; David Krejci, 63rd, 2004; Phil Kessel, 5th, 2006; Milan Lucic, 50th, 2006; Tyler Seguin 2nd, 2010

DRAFT-SCHMAFT RANKING: 11th

LINE CHANGES
THE DYNAMITE LINE: Cooney Weiland, Dutch Gainor, and Dit Clapper, 1928–33

THE KRAUT LINE: Milt Schmidt, Woody Dumart, and Bobby Bauer, 1936-42, 1945-47

THE UKE LINE: Bronco Horvath, Johnny Bucyk, and Vic Stasiuk, 1957–61

THE ESPO LINE: Wayne Cashman, Phil Esposito, and Ken Hodge, 1967–75

THE KHL LINE: David Krejci, Nathan Horton, and Milan Lucic, 2010–

"Just putting on those ****ing skates." — Gordie Howe when asked to name Bobby Orr's best move.

"I've been gifted. The world is full of people who not only haven't been gifted, but have had something taken away from them. All I have to do is see one of them, some little girl who can't walk, and then I don't think I'm such a hero anymore. I think that compared to them, I'm a very small article." — Bobby Orr

SKATE THAT ONE PAST ME AGAIN: Andrew Ference bought teammates a free tattoo after the team won the 2011 Cup. Brad Marchand — "Nose Face Killah" to fans — chose "Stanley Cup Champion." Nice, simple. Except the tattooist spelled it "Stanley Cup Champian."

BRING ON THE ZAMBONI
CELEBRITY FANS: Actor-comedian Denis Leary. Dropkick Murphys singer Ken Casey says the first two words his Boston grandfather taught him to say were "Bobby Orr."

STUMP THE SCHWAB: What was Bobby Orr's number in junior? What was his first number with the Bruins? Answer: Orr was number 2 for the Oshawa Generals, and number 27 in his first pre-season (1966). Once he made the team, the Bruins gave him number 4 (because 2 had been retired with Eddie Shore).

FAN-tastic

(Top) Bobby's girls: Bruin fans at Orr shrine. (Bottom) Tim Thomas and Zdeno Chara wave to the crowd at the Bruins' 2011 Stanley Cup parade.

The TRADE

So, who won the trade? In September 2009, Boston sent Phil Kessel, a 21-year-old goal scorer who wanted tons of money, to Toronto for draft picks that would include the number 2 pick in the 2010 draft, Tyler Seguin. Scouts called Seguin the next Steve Yzerman. Mind you, they once figured Kessel, a 176-goal scorer his first year in bantam, for Sidney Crosby. But Kessel did nothing in the 2006 World Junior Championships, and months later fell to number 5 in the 2006 draft. That's Phil — up and down like a yo-yo. In 2011–12, he was NHL player of the month in October with 10 goals in 11 games. Turn the calendar a page and. . .

Tyler Seguin

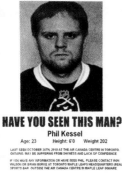

Tyler Seguin, meanwhile, gets better every shift. A bench student much of his rookie year, the teenager replaced the injured Patrice Bergeron in the playoffs and collected three goals and as many assists his first two games — the best teenage playoff debut in NHL history. In 2011-12, Seguin became a complete, two-way center. Good in his own end, a workhorse, a Bruin. Fans love him. So the Bruins won the trade, right? Kessel, whose father, Phil Sr., was a college quarterback (University of Northern Michigan), lacks grit. The Bruins are a hockey team of tackles and tight ends, anyway. But wait — just because Boston won the trade doesn't mean the Leafs lost. The Wisconsin forward may lack emotional presence, may be the man who stepped out of an empty car, but Kessel could be just what the psychiatrist ordered for a franchise like Toronto. Carefree and untroubled by adversity, Kessel is perfect for a hockey city subject to bipolar mood swings. Do you remember him sitting there, waiting to be chosen for one of the teams at the 2011 All-Star Game — and, as it turned out, the last guy picked? Any other NHLer would've been mortified. Phil just sat there, thinking about whatever. Like a guy waiting for a bus on his day off. And Kessel was brilliant more often than not in 2011-12. So who won the trade? Boston, probably, but get back to us in five years.

Boston PATRIOT

Maybe you heard about the party the Bruins had after the team won the 2011 Stanley Cup. It was held in Connecticut at the Foxwoods Shrine Nightclub. Very swanky. At one point, the Stanley Cup faced off against a 100-pound torpedo of Armand de Brignac champagne, Jay-Z's mouthwash of choice.

Even Zdeno Chara couldn't open the great, shiny, metallic brute — which, according to the *Wall Street Journal*, resembled C3PO after 18 months at Gold's Gym.

The Bruins' bar tab for the evening: $156,000. In addition to champers, the Bruins gargled down 35 Jägerbombs (alcohol and Red Bull), 136 Bud Lights, and one conspicuously lonesome $6 Corona.

Here's betting Tim Thomas, MVP of the 2011 Stanley Cup and working class hero of Flint, Michigan, had the Corona. Ordinarily, we'd say Bud... but Bud Light?

What a season Thomas had in 2010-11. What a career until now! If Thomas trusted Hollywood, his life story would make a great movie. The goalie grew up in Michigan, adoring hockey at a time when the world stopped loving Detroit automobiles. His father, a car dealer, moved around, trying to make ends meet. It wasn't easy. Tim's first year in organized hockey, what with equipment and tournaments all over Michigan and Ontario, cost Tim Sr. and Kathy Thomas $8,000. They hocked their wedding rings to pay for travel to one tournament.

The goalie played for the University of Vermont, where he was an All-American and teammate of Marty St. Louis. He went late — 217th — in the 1994 draft to the Quebec Nordiques (a portent of coming cultural intrigue). But Thomas never got a whiff of the NHL. For a decade, only his passport got a major league workout.

"I thought of quitting sometimes."

Tortoise Tim Thomas in 2012 all-star race. Hares, including Alexander Ovechkin, laugh it up on the bench.

Tyler Seguin

Only Thomas's story is better. Unlike Rocky with his sad spaniel eyes, Thomas is perpetually cheerful, a joy to watch. They put a mic on him during one NHL All-Star Game and we watched our guy yak it up with other players, laughing, slapping passersby on the fanny with his paddle, asking referees for help.

He made pro hockey seem as much fun as we dreamed it might be.

Thomas soon became hockey's Everyman hero. An athlete who did us the favor of appearing to understand how lucky he was — a guy making $5 million per, working at a job he loved. With America's economy in near ruin, Thomas won the Vezina in 2009. It felt great to see a working stiff on top of the world.

The story got better, more dramatic, two seasons later. Thomas led Boston to a stirring playoff charge — three game-seven wins, four shutouts, the last a seventh-game clincher against Vancouver (Boston's first-ever road victory in a game seven).

He beat Tampa Bay and Montreal with a highlight reel of toe stabs, arm lunges, and body tosses. Every play around the Boston net seemed to end with Thomas hurling himself through traffic, sliding on his belly to jump on a live grenade — the puck.

Reflex goalies get a crowd going. They enliven the drama. They attack the puck. Get caught out of position sometimes. You figure they can be had. And they can, when they guess wrong or aren't on their game. But against Vancouver — all through the playoffs, really — Thomas was in the moment. Always on. He made goaltending seem like a thrilling offensive position. The battle-fly goalie got into a fight with Alex Burrows. Plowed Henrik Sedin, bowling him over.

And nothing got by him. Thomas let in six goals in seven games against Vancouver. He wore the Canucks out. He wore *us* out. And when it was over, when he finally removed his mask to accept the Conn Smythe Trophy, a big smile split his playoff beard. At 37, Thomas was the oldest guy ever to win the award.

He said all the right things afterwards. "You've been waiting for it a long time, but you got it," Tim pro-

That's because he didn't conform to a classic goaltending style. He was neither a standup nor a butterfly goalie. Tim was *really* old school: a reflex goalie. Aggressive, charge out of the net, throw any limb available at the puck.

Thanks to the spectacular Quebec butterfly, Patrick Roy, goaltending was turning into an exact science in the 1990s. Ball hockey goalies needed not apply. Thomas didn't project to be a big-league pro. Just didn't look like one. Mind you, neither did Curtis Joseph and Eddie Belfour, two other reflex netminders who weren't even drafted and, like Tim, fought their way to the NHL for memorable careers.

Thomas began his professional hockey life in Helsinki and played next in Alabama. Talk about shifting gears. After that, he was a Detroit Viper. Back to Europe — Thomas played for teams in Stockholm, Sweden, and Oulu, Finland. Next up was Providence, Rhode Island, and Finland again — Helsinki — before the goalie finally won a job in the NHL, at age 31, with the NHL Boston Bruins.

"I thought of quitting sometimes," Thomas said of his decade in the wilderness, "but then I'd ask myself, 'Do you enjoy going to practice?' And I always enjoyed going to practice, and that's why I never quit. I still enjoyed playing."

Besides, it's not as though there were all kinds of jobs to be had back in Flint.

Tim Thomas's career is a variation on *Rocky* — the gallant underdog hangs in there to become champ.

"You wanted it, you got it. We're bringing it home."

claimed, looking into the camera back at New England. "You wanted it, you got it. We're bringing it home."

Thomas's gracious sentiments confirmed his solidarity with fans. Did they also presage his coming political career? Dan Shaugnessy in the *Boston Globe* picked up on the goalie's populist message with a lovely Tom Joad bit in the next day's paper:

"[The Bruins] won it for every New England mom and dad who ever woke up to drive kids to the rink at 6 a.m., and drank hot chocolate while they waited in the cold.

"They won it for the Revere girls with the big hair and O'Reilly sweaters; for the shot-and-beer guys who pour every dollar of expendable income into the hockey budget.

"They won it to avenge losing Bobby Orr to Chicago, too many men on the ice in Montreal, free agents never signed, trades that went bad, unspeakable injuries, and game 7 disappointments.

"They won it for you."

Tim Thomas's is a great story that we helped edit and write. Who noticed when he sulked after the Bruins shopped the injured goalie around in 2010? In response, Thomas removed the Bruins' black and gold colors from his pads and took the team crest off his mask. And all we did was laugh when our guy indulged in a little star vanity. Thomas enjoyed a playoff ritual of an English muffin with peanut butter and jam before games. And so the team packed his favorite food and regular toaster for every away game in the 2011 playoffs.

No biggie, but Roberto Luongo, who attracts bad press like a black jacket gathers lint, might've been toasted for doing the same.

Then the hero of the people formalized his job title, turning crusader. Maybe the transformation came when he brought the Stanley Cup back to Michigan and Davison High. Standing in the middle of a jammed football field, he told a crowd of 2,500 (almost half the town): "You can do whatever you want if you're willing to work long enough and hard enough at it. It's kind of the American dream, so to speak, but a lot of people have kind of given up on that."

What was that last part about?

He opted out of a White House visit and later attacked President Barack Obama, writing, "I stand with the Catholics in the fight for Religious Freedom," on Facebook, comparing the American President to Hitler by quoting German anti-Nazi theologian Martin Niemöller: "First they came for the communists, and I didn't speak out because I wasn't a communist. Then they came after the trade unionists. . ."

This wasn't the first time a Boston sports figure, or even a hockey player, had dissed a head of state. Boston Red Sox GM Theo Epstein didn't show up to shake hands with George W. Bush after the Red Sox won the World Series in 2007. And San Jose Shark captain Owen Nolan, born in Northern Ireland, begged off an exhibition game in 2002 against Vancouver that would have required his taking a ceremonial faceoff from Queen Elizabeth.

But those were silent rebukes. Thomas made his opposition public, and in doing so exposed the rhetorical dangers of a reflex goalie talking politics out loud. Manifestos with a lot of upper-case shouting — "This was a choice I had to make as an INDIVIDUAL" — generally make for disappointing reading. And much of what Tim had to shout demanded follow-up questions he refused to answer.

Like what Catholics would Thomas be standing with? Recent polls suggest 98 percent of American Catholics, including probably 100 per cent of Revere girls with big hair and O'Reilly sweaters, practice birth control, which is where Obama and the Church part ways. And would Tim and his followers really stand in the way if American governments came after trade unionists? If so, they've had their chance in plenty of states right now.

Oh well, celebrities creating a stir in social media, telling everyone what they know (and don't know), must be considered the cost of doing business in today's marketplace of ideas.

Still, Tim Thomas's angry winter of 2012 was a dispiriting turn for many fans. *Tim was supposed to be happy for us.* Yet there he was with a Stanley Cup, millions pouring in, attending Armand de Brignac champagne parties. And evidently bitter, complaining.

Geez, what is it about Davison High? The only other celebrity from the Michigan school is perpetually agitated soapbox jumper Michael Moore, the liberal activist filmmaker. Wouldn't it be wonderful if both of them were to go out on the porch and work things out? Or maybe hit the road and make a movie: *Tim & You & Me.*

BUFFALO SABRES

Loose Pucks

RECORD: Sabres defenseman and donut salesman Jim Schoenfeld recorded two pop albums in the '70s: *Schony* and *The Key Is Love.*

RECORDS

MOST HAT TRICKS, CAREER: Rick Martin, 21; Gil Perreault, 18; Danny Gare, 10; Alexander Mogilny, 10; Dave Andreychuk, 9

MOST GOALS IN A GAME: 5, Dave Andreychuk, February 8, 1986, vs. Boston

BEST PLUS/MINUS, CAREER: Craig Ramsay, +328; Bill Hajt, +321

50-GOAL CLUB: Alexander Mogilny, 76, 1992-93; Danny Gare, 56, 1979-80; Pat LaFontaine, 53, 1992-93; Rick Martin, 52, 1973-74; Martin, 52, 1974-75; Gare, 50, 1975-76

WORKING OVERTIME: Encil "Porky" Palmer, former goalie for the AHL Buffalo Bisons, later drove the Zamboni at Sabres games. Porky sat behind the Zamboni door behind the opposition net and kicked the door out when the puck slid toward him. Once, he slapped it past goalie Greg Millen, who had gone behind the net to retrieve the puck. Seconds later, the disk was in the net. The goal counted.

DRAFT-SCHMAFT

TOP-10 PICKS, 1989–2009: 2

PLAYERS DRAFTED WHO PLAYED 300 NHL GAMES: 36

IMPACT PLAYERS: Brian Campbell, 156th, 1997; Ryan Miller, 138th, 1999; Derek Roy, 32nd, 2001; Thomas Vanek, 3rd, 2003

DRAFT-SCHMAFT RANKING: 8th

LINE CHANGES

Buffalo's French Connection, with Gilbert Perreault, Rene Robert, and Richard Martin, was the most exciting line in hockey in the mid-'70s. The club's 2003-04 sequel — French Connection 2? — starred two Quebecers, Jean-Pierre Dumont and Danny Briere. But there was a German, too — Jochen Hecht — so it was called the Maginot Line, a reference to the ineffective French concrete fortification that faced Germany prior to World War II. The Sabres didn't make the playoffs that year, so we never found out how the Maginot Line might've fared against cross-border rival Toronto.

"Only in America." — Miroslav Satan's response to the question, "Is this really your name?"

"When he's not injured or acting like a self-centered little dink, he's a very good player." — Mike Milbury's scouting report on the Sabres' Tim Connolly for NESN.

SKATE THAT ONE PAST ME AGAIN: Upset that the 1974 NHL draft was going on forever, coach and GM Punch Imlach drafted a fictional Japanese player, Taro

Czech mate: The Flyers' Jakub Voracek takes Nathan Gerbe ice-water skiing.

Tsujimoto of the Tokyo Katanas. No such team or player existed. (A katana is a traditional sword worn by the samurai.) The NHL later omitted Tsujimoto from the official records. Score would later give him an honorary hockey card.

BRING ON THE ZAMBONI

CELEBRITY FANS: Actress Noreen DeWulf, wife of goalie Ryan Miller.

STUMP THE SCHWAB: This Buffalo Sabre forward began and ended his career with two-goal games. Answer: Rob Ray.

RUFF'n It!

Lindy Ruff was born on an Alberta farm. Dad Leeson drove a school bus and grew oats, wheat, barley, and hockey players. Sons Randy, Lindy, Marty, and Brent all played junior. Summers were hard, winters harder. Marty, a first-round pick for St. Louis in 1981, blew a knee coming out of junior. Brent died in a bus accident that killed four Swift Current Broncos. Lindy broke his thighbone at 18. The Sabres took a chance on him anyway. He made the team as a teenager and lasted 10 seasons, playing every shift as if it were his last. Lindy Ruff took the game, but never himself, seriously. And he loved a challenge — trying

"Lindy would take the underdog kids and try to make winners of them."

to outsmart and outwork the other guy. Even choosing teams at school, "Lindy would take the underdog kids and try to make winners of them," his dad said. Sounds like the perfect coach for try-harder Buffalo, a small-market team that routinely sees players go to money-green pastures.[1] Ruff's Sabres have authored a number of memorable playoff upsets — specializing in pissing off teams from neighboring Ontario, surprising fat-cat Toronto in 1999 and superstar-rich Ottawa in 2006. The team's coach since 1997, Ruff drives his teams hard, but lets them blow off steam. Once, he donned goalie pads in practice and let everyone blast away at him.

1 Sabre stars who've left the team over money include Dominik Hasek, Michael Peca, Chris Drury, Danny Briere, and Brian Campbell.

Small TALK

Too many hockey families have seen it happen: their boy, Player A, leads the team in scoring one year, skating on a line with another kid, Player B, who is trying his best, but clearly isn't as effective. Player A wins the team MVP award. Player B shakes his hand.

The following season brings tryouts for the next hockey tier. Players A and B again skate out to compete. Player A demonstrates his superiority once more. A couple of practice sessions later, the coach decides on his team — Player B wins a spot. Player A shakes his head. One of the best players in every league he's played, he's somehow been cut.

Why? Because Player B is bigger — he projects better. The coach has visions of Eric Staal or Ryan Getzlaf. The presumption being that size itself is a talent — *you can't teach being big!* Player A has simply come up, well, short.

The puzzled, angry father of Player A approaches the coach, who sags at the sight of him. *Here we go again . . . parents!* "How is my boy too small?" the dad asks. Sidney Crosby, Patrick Kane, Wayne Gretzky, Steve Yzerman, and Marcel Dionne — they all went into the NHL as small guys. Gretzky, Yzerman, and Kane weighed 165 pounds. So does what's-his-name, that new kid — Ryan Nugent-Hopkins.

The coach offers an indulgent smile. As if to say, "Your boy isn't Wayne Gretzky or Patrick Kane."

No, but is Player B necessarily Ryan Getzlaf?

Go big or go home was too often the thinking in the NHL until recently. Marty St. Louis, at 5′8″ and 170 pounds, was never drafted. He was the NHL's MVP in 2006 and runner-up in 2011, at age 35. Doug Gilmour, at 5′10″, was passed over in his first year of eligibility. Former Sabre and current Philadelphia star Danny Briere still keeps a clipping from *Le Journal de Montréal* saying he was too short (5′9″) to make it big in the NHL.

Hey, maybe Briere is a star today because he was a little guy with something to prove. Ever think of that?

FAN-tastic

(Top) Five alive: Time-lapse sequence of a Sabres fan on his way to the fridge for a cold one. (Middle) Sabres fans making out okay in Boston. (Bottom) Bobblehead of the late, great Rick Martin.

Get back here! Nathan Gerbe looks to cut Zdeno Chara down to size.

An argument might be made that being undersized can be a competitive advantage. Always being told you're not big enough builds, in some athletes, a stomach-churning need to prove the world wrong. Some kids are big for their size. Terrible Teddy Lindsay, who stood 5′8″, weighed 160 pounds, and would record 379 goals and 1,808 penalty minutes in a 17-year career, grazed on a feedbag of resentment. Five-foot, six-inch Theo Fleury was the same way, decades later.

If the NHL failed for many years to understand that there was a place for undersized players, it got the message after the 2005 lockout. Players returned in 2006 with new rules — no hooking, no holding. No more waterskiing, players joked. Speed and shiftiness suddenly became more valuable.

In the following NHL draft, Patrick Kane, a forward who could shift and feint like a leaf in the wind, went first overall. "I probably wouldn't have been drafted as high as I was if they hadn't changed the rules," Kane said. "Smaller guys are starting to play."

Hello, Jeff Skinner and Chad LaRose in Carolina, Zach Parise in New Jersey, Mike Cammalleri and Brian Gionta in Montreal — mighty mites every one. In the 2011 NHL draft, 11 of the first 13 picks weighed less than 200 pounds, with five, including first-overall Ryan Nugent-Hopkins, at 175 or under.[2]

The rest of the league was finally catching up with Buffalo, where a smaller player has always had a chance. Five-foot-nine Danny Gare twice broke the 50-goal barrier with the Sabres in the '70s. A Buffalo kid, Patrick Kane grew up watching diminutive Pat LaFontaine, Danny Briere, Chris Drury, and Derek Roy flash and dash. Running back Thurman Thomas (5′10″) and special-teams ace Steve Tasker (5′9″, 180 pounds) owned the Queen City in the 1990s.

Buffalo doesn't know the meaning of the expression "coming up short."

2 Nugent-Hopkins and Jonathan Huberdeau, taken third overall by Florida, weighed 171; Mark Scheifele (seventh, Winnipeg), Jonas Brodin (12th, Minnesota), and Ryan Murphy (13th, Carolina), tipped the scales at 175.

At 5'9" and 155 pounds, middle-sized white boy Tyler Ennis led the Sabres with a plus-11 in the 2011–12 season.

and Jeff played hockey. Sisters Danielle, Breanne, and Shannon figure skated and played soccer and volleyball. Jeff didn't play organized hockey until he was eight, when his brothers, both of whom would play junior, told his parents that the little guy had finally outgrown the frozen pond in the woods.

"I just remember how, when he was five and six and seven, he kept begging and begging to play," remembered his mother, Terrie Gerbe. "He would come off of the pond and follow me into the kitchen. 'I can do it,' he would say. 'I can do it.'"

What impressed the brothers was Nathan's competitiveness. That old Ted Lindsay, gotta-win-to-stay-alive spirit. "What I remember is how [Nathan] hates to lose," Joey said. How after a defeat, "when our friends came over, he wouldn't speak to us."

"It creates a lot of character in the house," Gerbe said of growing up last in a big sports family. "You're always fighting over things, always complaining, someone's always crying, especially in sports. We're all competitive. Going out on the pond to play hockey. . . you just don't want to lose against your siblings. I think that's where you create your competitive nature."

But it was more than needing to win. Joey and Jeff Gerbe noticed how Nathan was so happy riding along in the car with them to tournament games,

None of which was lost on the Sabres' latest Little Big Man, Nathan Gerbe, currently the most wind-resistant player in the NHL at 5'5" and 155 pounds. Upon being drafted by the Sabres in 2003, the Boston College star considered himself fortunate. "They've got a lot of small guys, and they're not afraid to give them a shot," Gerbe said. "It's definitely a lucky chance for me. They have a good system there, and they do well to develop players."

Gerbe has always had to scrap to get ahead. He was the runt of the litter, the youngest of six kids growing up in Oxford, Michigan, a small town (what else?) 40 miles northwest of Detroit. Brothers Joey

"Thank God there's a sport for middle-sized white boys."

belting out country songs in the back seat. The kid wouldn't shut up. Hockey made him come alive.

Upon being given a chance, Nathan was like an arrow that had been pulled back for years and then suddenly let fly. *Fwww* — he just took off. He was a goal-scoring machine, feet racing every minute. At 15, Nathan left home, moving in with a family in Omaha to play for the River City Lancers. He was younger than everyone else and so not getting any ice time, but whenever coach Mike Hastings looked down the bench, he saw two eyes burning like glowing coals. That was Nathan, worried that he was running out of time.

One game, the coach finally threw him out on the ice. "Sure enough, the puck goes into the corner and there goes Nathan, along with a kid who was about 6′3″," Hastings remembers. "Next thing you know, there's a fight. Later, I'm like, 'Listen, Nathan, you don't need to prove anything to us. We know how tough you are. We don't need you to fight. We need you to play.'"

That he did, joining the U.S. National Development Team closer to home in Ann Arbor, Michigan, where he played with Kane and Phil Kessel. "He's my favorite guy I've ever played with," reported Kessel. "He skates unbelievable. He has great skills. He makes great passes. For me, he was the easiest guy to read off of."

Gerbe's speeding career went into overdrive when he went to Boston College, leading all of college hockey in scoring as a junior (68 points in 43 games), helping the Eagles to an NCAA Frozen Four title in 2008. Buffalo liked what they saw. Not just the goals, but how he competed — like he was always trying to outrace time.

"He's a fearless player. He's not a big player, but he's a little like the Energizer Bunny. He gets knocked down, he gets up, he keeps going," said Sabres GM Darcy Regier.

In Buffalo, the Energizer Bunny evolved into a more dangerous species, earning the nickname Tasmanian Devil. On January 21, 2011, the left winger outraced the clock, giving defenseman Jack Hillen "the old how do you do," in TV color man Harry Neale's words, before snapping a shot in off the post past Kevin Poulin. Seconds later, he stripped another defender and snapped his second goal in five seconds — a team record.

"You want little Nathan Gerbe, you got a little more Nathan Gerbe," shouted play-by-play man Rick Jeanneret.

Yeah, go ahead. Make jokes. The little guy has the record for shortest time. "I've heard it all my life, that I'm too small," said Gerbe. "I use that to my advantage. I do that for all the people who told me I couldn't do this."

But people should understand — especially coaches with young teams — that there has always been a place in hockey for smaller players. Gretzky has all the scoring records. And the Pocket Rocket, five-foot seven-inch Henri Richard, has the record everyone should be aiming for in a team game: most Stanley Cup wins (11).

Remember the immortal words of Derek Sutton (played by Patrick Swayze) in the 1986 hockey film *Youngblood*: "Thank God there's a sport for middle-sized white boys."

CALGARY FLAMES

Loose Pucks

RECORD: AC/DC's tub-thumping, guitar-slinging, grammatically incorrect "Shot Down in Flames" (*"Ain't it a shame / To be shot down in flames?"*)

RECORDS:
Most hat tricks, career: Theoren Fleury, 13; Kent Nilsson, 13; Jarome Iginla, 12

Most points in a season: Kent "Magic Man" Nilsson, 131, 1980-81

Most power-play goals in a season: Joe Nieuwendyk, 31, 1987-88

Most assists, career: Al MacInnis, 609

Best plus/minus, career: Al MacInnis, +241

50-goal club: Lanny McDonald, 66, 1982-83; Gary Roberts, 53, 1991-92; Jarome Iginla, 52, 2001-02; Theoren Fleury, 51, 1990-91; Joe Mullen, 51, 1988-89; Joe Nieuwendyk, 51, 1988-89; Nieuwendyk, 51, 1987-88; Hakan Loob, 50, 1987-88; Iginla, 50, 2007-08; Guy Chouinard, 50, 1978-79 (with Atlanta)

Working overtime: Alex Tanguay holds the NHL record for most shootout goals in one season, with 10 in 2010-11.

DRAFT-SCHMAFT
Top-10 picks, 1989-2009: 6

Players drafted who played 300 NHL games: 31

Impact players: Dion Phaneuf, 8th, 2003

Draft-schmaft ranking: 23rd (tied with Florida)

LINE CHANGES
"Getting cut in the face is a pain in the butt."
— Theoren Fleury

Skate that one past me again: Coach and part-time rancher Darryl Sutter once ended a conversation about how small his Flames were with the classic line, "It's not the size of the bull, it's how he's hung."

BRING ON THE ZAMBONI
Celebrity fans: Super secret agent MacGyver (Richard Dean Anderson) often wore a Flames hat in the ABC-TV series of the same name (1985-92).

Stump the Schwab: This Flame was the first Russian player ever to play in the NHL. Answer: Sergei Priakin.

Jarome Iginla projected on a building wall during the Winter Olympics in Vancouver, 2010

Answering
THE CALL

Jarome Arthur-Leigh Adekunle Tig Junior Elvis Iginla was born outside Edmonton on Canada Day, July 1, 1977. His father is a Nigerian Christian lawyer; his mom, a Buddhist music teacher from Oregon. Jarome has twice reconfirmed his citizenship in dramatic fashion. In 2002, the then 23-year-old scored twice in Canada's 5–2 Olympic win over the U.S. The goals demonstrated his qualifications as the best power forward of his generation. To score the first, he shrugged off a bear hug by Gary Suter to tip in a lovely goalmouth feed from Joe Sakic. (Iginla means "big tree" in Yoruba, his father's native language.) In the second, he let go a powerful one-timer that broke through goalie's Mike Richter's glove and trickled over the blue line. Eight years later, in Vancouver, number 12 provided one of the most famous assists in Canadian hockey history, chipping the puck blindly to an open space as he fell into the corner. Later, he would say he *heard* that Sidney Crosby was in the clear. "He was yelling pretty urgently," Iginla

> "There are different pitches of yell, and he was screaming."

recalled. "There are different pitches of yell, and he was screaming." Upon finding the puck on his stick, Crosby cradled and fired it along the ice between Ryan Miller's legs to give Canada its second Olympic gold medal in eight years.

FAN-tastic

(Top right) A Calgary farmer thrashes an Oiler. (Top left) Local girls on their way to a game. (Middle and bottom right) All thumbs: Calgary buddies celebrate their favorite team. (Bottom left) Fan wearing an Iginla T-shirt.

For Once, A Happy SPRING

The thing was that it wasn't just the Battle of Alberta. Not just Edmonton's Oilers and Eskimos, who won — *it was unbelievable!* — a combined 11 Stanley and Grey Cups between 1978 and 1990. Other parts of Canada broke Calgary's heart, too. In May of '86, the Calgary Flames upset Edmonton in the playoffs with the miraculous Steve Smith flub,[1] only to be subdued by rookie goalie Patrick Roy and the snail-sucking Montreal Canadiens in the Stanley Cup finals.

The Flames were better the next year, third overall in the NHL, but stumbled on Dale Hawerchuk and the Winnipeg Jets in the first playoff round.

The following season, the Flames won the Presidents' Trophy, were the top team in the NHL. Scored almost 400 goals. Had two 50-goal men — rookie Joe Nieuwendyk and Hakan Loob — and a record four 40-goal scorers (throw in Joey Mullen and Mike Bullard). *The Hockey News*'s playoff cover shouted out to the world, "Take the Flames."

And that's exactly what Edmonton did — took Calgary four straight in the second round of the playoffs. Game two was harder to swallow than an anvil: in overtime, with Paul Coffey in Pittsburgh and Mark Messier in the penalty box, you-know-who, number 99, sailed down the left side, Flame Gary Suter poking uselessly alongside him, and wired the perfect shot — *how many times did Flame fans hear that?* — over Mike Vernon's glove hand.

A shorthanded goal. *In overtime!* Beaten by Edmonton again, like in the playoffs of 1983 and '84. Like the Eskimos beat the Stamps in the 1987 CFL playoffs.

1 From behind his own net, Smith pinballed a clearing shot off the back of goalie Grant Fuhr's leg for the winning goal.

Okay, now it's 1989, and the Flames are again the best team in the NHL, with two more 50-goal men in Mullen and Nieuwendyk. Plus, GM Cliff Fletcher bolstered the team for the playoffs, sending away chubby phenom Brett Hull for Rob Ramage (talk about a great name for a defenseman!) and acquiring Doug Gilmour and Brian MacLellan in separate deals.

The Flames also brought up 20-year-old pepperpot Thereon Fleury from Salt Lake City. "Which one is Fleury?" kids asked Flames coach Terry Crisp in an airport early in the playoffs. "He's here somewhere — look around for someone your size," the coach said.

Gilmour and Fleury gave the team more speed. And, along with MacLellan, more playoff grit.

Still, here we were again: first round, seventh game, overtime, even with Vancouver — tied with the Canucks! The Canucks, who finished 47 points south of Calgary in the regular season. Inexplicably, the Flames were caught on a sluggish line change. *In overtime!* Stan Smyl, the Canuck captain, walked in alone on the right side. Top sliver of the net was open. He fired the puck.

Right into Vernon's glove.

A few minutes earlier, the Calgary-born goalie had made a better save, sprouting from 5'9" to 5'10" to kick away a one-timer by Petri Skriko. Later, he stabbed a Tony Tanti blast that could've sent the Flames whimpering out of the playoffs.

Calgary was reeling. But then, late in the first overtime, a couple of big guys saved the night, as Jim Peplinski chimed one off Joel Otto's fat boot past Canuck goalie Kirk McLean. The top playoff seed survived the first round. Barely.

The Flames still weren't right for the first game of the next series, against Gretzky's Los Angeles Kings. Vernon fanned on a shot from the blue line in the second period. The Kings were up late in the third. But Gary Roberts tied it up. And early in overtime, Gilmour hooked Marty McSorley as he pulled out from behind his own net (it was called forechecking in 1989), then, seconds later, tipped in a Colin Patterson shot.

With that, Calgary snapped into peak form, burning past Los Angeles and Chicago in nine games. Vernon looked good. The league's best power play was humming, as wheelmen Loob and Gilmour had the freedom to choose between Nieuwendyk — with his extra-long reach — in the slot or Al MacInnis, with the league's best slap shot, at the point.

MacInnis developed the strength and dexterity for hockey's most dangerous weapon as a kid growing up in Port Hood, Nova Scotia, lifting lobster crates in the morning. Then, in the afternoon, painting a barn with black rubber, firing hundreds of pucks off a plywood launch pad.

Day after day, until his shot disappeared.

"Right now, in practice, I get the feeling that he can blow it by me at will," Flames backup goalie Rick Wamsley told reporters. "With Al, you get no feeling, no anticipation. So you start spreading out and hope it hits you. . . . Thank God he's saving it for games. . . or I'd get killed."

The last part wasn't an idle comment. Goalie Mike Liut once said of the Calgary point man's shot, "There's hard and then there's Al MacInnis hard. I tried to get out of the way. If it happens too often, you have to sit down and re-evaluate what you're doing with your life."

Mike Vernon

In the first game of the Stanley Cup finals, at home against Montreal, MacInnis scored twice in the opening period, the first on a windmilling blast from the point that had Patrick Roy talking to the posts. *Guys, you're on your own tonight.*

Nevertheless, it took a Fleury breakaway midway into the second to give Calgary an opening-game win. No team with Roy in nets was ever out of the game. And this defense-first edition of the Canadiens could check, with Bob Gainey and "Guy, Guy" Carbonneau shadowing opposition forwards. Big Larry Robinson, finally wearing a helmet, and Chris Chelios patrolled the blue line.

In game two, the Flames outchanced Montreal 21–14, yet somehow lost 4–2. In the first game in *la belle province*, Calgary again dominated, but took a too-slim 3–2 lead late into the third. And then the Forum, the haunted home of 23 NHL championships, began to emanate a mysterious, disruptive force field. With Roy gone from the net, the short-sleeved crowd made the sound of a jet taking off. Mullen, who'd scored two difficult goals this night, somehow missed an empty-netter. Seconds later, the normally reliable defenseman Brad McCrimmon seemingly had an easy chance to clear. But the puck was bouncing and dribbled off his stick.

It was still rolling when Mats Naslund golfed a rainbow around Vernon's trapper. "It was going wide, but it curved in — a knuckleball," Mats marveled after the game.

Hmm.

A disgusted Gilmour broke his stick on the crossbar. Coach Crisp elbowed the glass behind Calgary's bench. Tie game. Almost two periods of overtime ensued. Late in the second period of extra time, Roberts broke through the Montreal defense like a gunslinger banging through saloon doors. Roy made an awkward save. Mark Hunter collected the rebound. He had an empty net, but backhanded the puck off the outside of the post.

Same shift, a frustrated Hunter forcibly escorted Shayne Corson into the boards in the neutral zone. Referee Kerry Fraser's hand jumped in the air — the first power play in four periods. A shudder of anticipation rippled through the Forum.

But the Canadiens could do nothing with the advantage. The penalty was almost over with a faceoff in Calgary's zone. "Hit the net and I'll be there," center Ryan Walter told Stephane Richer. Seconds later, Richer stripped Nieuwendyk of the puck on the left boards, swerved and cut wide, centering to Walter, who croqueted the puck through Vernon's collapsing pads.

Montreal won! *"Na-na-na-na, na-na-na-na, hey-hey-hey, goodbye."* A few Flames chased after referee Fraser, who, his arms folded, would only shake his Brylcreemed conk. *The game is over, boys.*

Coach Crisp shoe-skied across the ice, paused to stare at the empty Canadiens goal, perhaps looking for evidence of an invisible shield, then grimly trundled on. *What just happened?* Calgary had not lost a game when leading after two periods all year. Naslund's late goal came on Montreal's 17th shot of the game. Their lowest total all season.

Still, Calgary lost. *"Na-na-na-na, na-na-na-na, hey-hey-hey, goodbye."*

That night on sports-talk radio and the next day in the newspapers, there would be stories about how Calgary didn't have it. That they were a spectacularly equipped heavyweight with a glass jaw — looked good until someone caught them with a solid punch.

The Flames didn't buy it. MacInnis was seething in the dressing room. The '89 playoffs' leading scorer had collected another assist. Played more than 50 minutes, scaring everyone with his big shot. But maybe his biggest blast of the postseason came in the dressing room after this disappointing loss. Invited to comment on Fraser's questionable call or how Montreal was getting all the bounces, the normally reserved 25-year-old defenseman piped up in a voice loud enough for everyone to hear: "Listen, we can be disappointed. And we can mope and dwell on it. Or we can pick ourselves up and show what we're made of."

Next day, everyone on the Flames was singing from the same songbook. "If you want to get ticked off, look in the goddamned mirror," Crisp told his players. "We could be leading 3–0, we could be up 2–1, instead we're down 2–1. We've got a job to do.... Why are we going to feel sorry for ourselves? It's a waste of time."

Then Crispy threw in one of his classic non sequiturs. "There's probably 80 million Chinese who don't know that we're down 2–1."

"Show what we're made of," MacInnis had said. Yes, it was show-and-tell time. And here, in the third week of May 1989, down and written off, presumably lost in a crater of despair, the Flames finally became a championship team. They were an unusual bunch, for sure, starting with Coach Crisp. When MacInnis ended a game against the Blackhawks with a slap shot earlier in the playoffs, Crisp surprised everyone, particularly the Flames' brass, by leaning over the glass and kissing assistant general manager Al MacNeil's wife.

Calgary always had great characters. Wayne Gretzky called Kent "Magic Man" Nilsson hockey's best player. All Magic lacked was ambition. Once, he scored four goals in the first period. "You're going to break the record," coach Bob Johnson, Crisp's predecessor, exclaimed. "No I'm not," Nilsson replied.

And he didn't. Another time, with Flames down 6–1, Nilsson lost the puck on the point, then waved at a forechecker who raced down to score. "Seex–one, seven–one, what's the difference?" the Magic Swede later told reporters.

Mostly, though, these Flames cared too much. In 1986, Flames assistant coach Doug Risebrough was still playing and threw himself at Oilers big guy Marty McSorley — a mismatch for sure. Risebrough took a beating, but found himself in the penalty box with McSorley's sweater in his trembling hands. So he threw it to the floor, stomping on the blue and orange jersey with his razor-sharp skates.

When the tantrum was over, the Flames forward threw a handful of used-car-lot ribbons back out on the ice.

This tired-of-losing team also had character: little guys like Joey Mullen, who'd learned to skate on roller skates in Hell's Kitchen in Manhattan. Then you had always-on-fire Fleury and Nilsson's replacement, Loob, more dependable if not as creative as Magic Man. Doug Gilmour was the era's best middleweight. Moving up a weight division, the Flames had the elegant, supremely talented Nieuwendyk and childhood pal Roberts, power forwards extraordinaires. For muscle, there was Peplinski, centerman Otto (great on draws), and hatchet-faced Tim Hunter. Strongmen, bullies when necessary, who could kick snow in your face and make you like it.

Defense was provided by the Big Ms — MacInnis, Murzyn (great in the final series), Macoun, and McCrimmon — along with all-star Gary Suter (hurt), Ramage, and Ric Nattress.

The talent went on forever. Mustachioed Lanny McDonald, who once scored 66 goals for Calgary, sat in the press box, nervously twirling his Klondike moustache — a healthy scratch.

The Flames knew they were good. Better than Montreal. Vernon and the defense corps, particularly MacInnis, were playing great. But the forwards, a group that included six 50-goal scorers — McDonald, Loob, Mullen, Nieuwendyk, Roberts, and Fleury — still hadn't found that extra forward gear that great teams somehow access in now-or-never time.

Until now. Down two games to one, in enemy territory, the Flames came out with their best game of the playoffs, outshooting Montreal 13–3 in the first period. Early in the second, Gilmour snuck out of the penalty

"Everybody in hockey was watching. They knew it was Calgary's time."

box to intercept a Bobby Smith pass to open the scoring. MacInnis again loaded up from the point to swell the lead to 2–0. Another power-play missile. Russ Courtnall halved the lead on an assist from the Forum boards that kicked the puck out at an odd angle past a startled Vernon.

There was more Forum funny business in the third. The Canadiens' Claude "The Fraud" Lemieux, who had replaced the Flyers' Bill Barber as the NHL's high-diving champ, took a swing at Jamie Macoun. The Calgary defender rapped Lemieux with his stick. Up went referee Andy Van Hellemond's hand. Nattress complained and was given a misconduct.

Uh-oh. Montreal fans began to whoop and holler. Sensing what was next, Crisp wisely called a timeout, aborting the séance. "The fans were on a roll and the whole building was rocking," the coach later explained. The Flames killed off the penalty and, minutes later, MacInnis — who else? — blew another slapper past Roy: 3–1, Calgary. There was one more paranormal act. Montreal again pulled its goalie with time running out. Mullen had another empty net, but hit the post. *Ping!* Montreal raced back to score. Lemieux! But with seconds to go, little Joey was sent in alone on an empty net and skated right into the crease, burying a ghostbuster in the center of the net.

Calgary limited Montreal to fewer than 20 shots in tying the series. Back in Calgary, the Flames again charged ahead early. They were leading 2–1 late in the first. Power play. Calgary circulated the puck until MacInnis worked free and golfed his fifth shot of the finals past Roy. The Montreal goalie left the net with his arms raised. *Please God . . . Doug Harvey . . . somebody . . . anybody check that guy.*

The Canadiens came back, outplayed Calgary in the game's last 30 minutes, but could only muster a single goal past Vernon. The series was going back to Montreal with the Flames up three games to two, ready to finally win the Stanley Cup.

It had been a great decade for the Flames, one that started with the team still in Georgia.[2] In fact, a number of Atlanta alumni watched Calgary's play-off progress from the comfort of former Flame Tim Ecclestone's Atlanta sports bar. Willi Plett, Curt Bennett, Eric Vail, even former Flames coach Boom Boom Geoffrion dropped by to cheer their old team on.

Everybody in hockey was watching. They knew it was Calgary's time. Even though a foreign army had never won a Stanley Cup in Montreal (going zero for seven in the process), they knew. Coach Crisp, who didn't sleep a wink before game six, knew. As a player, he'd been a healthy scratch in a Stanley Cup–deciding game for Philadelphia. Knew what he'd have given to play. How hard he'd work.

Half an hour before the game, Crisp passed Lanny McDonald's dressing room stall and said, "You're playing."

Lanny knew, too. Lacing on his skates, he told teammates, "You know I scored my first goal NHL here 16 years ago. Wouldn't it be great if I got my last one here?" To Joel Otto, he promised, "Otts, I'll be the best I ever was."

"Be better," the center replied.

They were ready. They knew. Montreal was ready, too. The teams went skate boot to skate boot in the opening period, Montreal outchancing Calgary. Skating hard. Vernon was ready, though. Then, late in the first, Murzyn swatted a clearing puck at Chelios. A hurrying Colin Patterson smartly swatted the rebound past Roy.

Montreal came back unexpectedly in the second when Lemieux fired a slap shot from the blue line that crawled over Vernon's shoulder and into the net, like a spooked cat running out of its owners arms out the door. It was a bad goal — one of those suspicious accidents that befell opposition goalies in the Forum.

McDonald, trying too hard, was then called for a penalty. Montreal pressed, but didn't hear Roy's beaver-tail warnings — *whaack! whaack!* — with his stick at the end of the power play. They were overcommitted offensively when Lanny hopped back on the ice, racing four on two on Montreal's defense.

2 The Atlanta Flames moved to Calgary in the fall of 1980, changing the A on the front of their jerseys to a C.

Loob, swerving left at the blue line, slipped the puck to Nieuwendyk. He then feathered a perfect rinkwide pass to McDonald, who waited for Roy to fall into his signature butterfly pose before snapping a hard shot high above his left shoulder.

Hockey Night in Canada color man Harry Neale got it right. "[There's a] 26-year-old shot from a 36-year-old man," he said.

After that, both teams played well, with Montreal applying the desperate pressure that was called for. But Calgary knew. All they had to do was play no-mistake hockey. And they did. Midway through the third, Russ Courtnall, an unlikely heavy, bowled Vernon over behind the net. Old Testament shinny wisdom had it that somebody had to now thump Courtnall. Ric Nattress had the little forward in his mitts. Cocked a fist.

Then let him go. Not now. Seconds later, on a power play, Gilmour (the best forward in the series) took a pass from MacInnis (the best player) and flew in on Roy. Took a shot off the goalie's big pads and knocked the rebound out of the air between his legs.

Three–one. Surely now it was over. . . No, wait: a minute later, Rick Green lobbed a shot at the net. Easy save for Vernon, except that Lemieux, circling from behind the net, slew-footed the Calgary goalie. He was in midair, a flightless, flapping bird, when the puck sailed in where he should have been.

Incredibly, referee Denis Morel didn't see the play. Three–two. A minute later, Bobby Smith repeated Lemieux's trick, kicking Vernon's skates out from under him. Again, no call. It was like in wrestling, when the referee is always facing the wrong way when a scoundrel strikes.

Montreal continued attacking. But Calgary was imperturbable. With a minute left and Roy on the bench, Gilmour traveled down the left side and calmly fired the clincher into the middle of the net.

The Calgary bench exploded. But Coach Crisp kept his head in the game. No climbing the glass

looking for friendly, foreign lips tonight. "There's a minute left," he shouted to players. "A minute left," he repeated, pushing his players down on the bench.

But they knew. Everybody did. After a decade of trying hard, the Flames had finally won the Stanley Cup. Minutes later, Al MacInnis responded to a question by *HNIC*'s Ron MacLean by howling, "Port Hood, Cape Breton, I love ya — woo-whooo."

Yes, they were whooping it up in the Admiral Beverage Room in Port Hood. Same with T.J.'s in Atlanta, where Tim Ecclestone and Eric Vail were behind the bar. Inside the 30 or so bars on Electric Avenue in Calgary, of course, it was bedlam. *We did it! We did it!*

Reporters all asked Lanny McDonald what it finally felt like. The pride of Hanna, Alberta, a mostly grown farm boy who once traveled to a playoff game through a blizzard on a neighbor's tractor, told everyone the same thing. "It's the most peaceful feeling I've ever experienced in hockey."

Like a warming zephyr slipping through the Rockies in winter, bathing everything in a warm glow. For once, Calgary experienced a happy hockey spring.

Even Montreal's fans, hockey's most educated constituency, understood and appreciated the Flames' victory, giving the visitors a respectful, prolonged ovation.

"Harry, that's a good hockey team," Montreal broadcaster Dick Irvin advised Harry Neale as the game ended.

"Indeed."

Then Irvin corrected himself: "A *great* team," he said.

CAROLINA HURRICANES

Loose Pucks

RECORD: Jack Say's big-band "Brass Bonanza" was the Hartford Whalers' song forever. Sounded pretty snazzy, like a '70s TV detective show theme, though some ardent Whaler fans used it as wedding music. The Whalers (born in '72) became the Hurricanes in 1997. The Canes' signature song is "Rock You Like a Hurricane," by the Scorpions.

RECORDS

MOST HAT TRICKS, CAREER: Eric Staal, 12[1]

FASTEST HAT TRICK: Ray Whitney, one minute, 42 seconds, February 8, 2007, vs. Boston

MOST POINTS, ONE SEASON: Mike Rogers, 105, 1979–80 and 1980–81

MOST POINTS, ONE SEASON, DEFENSE: Mark Howe, 80, 1979–80

MOST GOALS, ONE SEASON: Blaine Stoughton, 56, 1979–80

BEST PLUS/MINUS, CAREER: Ulf Samuelsson, +70; John Anderson, +39

1 Still active

MOST SHUTOUTS, CAREER: Cam Ward, 21[1]

50-GOAL CLUB: Blaine Stoughton, 56, 1979–80; Stoughton, 52, 1981–82

WORKING OVERTIME: Eric Staal led all NHL scorers in the 2006 postseason, scoring 9 goals and adding 19 assists for 28 points. Teammate Cory Stillman was second, with 26 points.

DRAFT-SCHMAFT

TOP-10 PICKS, 1989–2009: 8

PLAYERS DRAFTED WHO PLAYED 300 NHL GAMES: 22

IMPACT PLAYERS: Bobby Holik, 10th, 1989; Chris Pronger, 2nd, 1993; Jean-Sebastian Giguere, 13, 1995; Erik Cole, 71st, 1998; Cam Ward, 25th, 2002; Eric Staal, 2nd, 2003; Jack Johnson, 3rd, 2005

DRAFT-SCHMAFT RANKING: 18th

LINE CHANGES

THE JET LINE: Fast-moving Jeff Skinner, Erik Cole, and Tuomo Ruutu, 2010–11

THE FTD LINE ("THEY ALWAYS DELIVERED"): Ron Francis, Sylvain Turgeon, and Kevin Dineen, late 1980s

Eric the Red: Hurricane captain Eric Staal looks for a pass.

SKATE THAT ONE PAST ME AGAIN: The NHL's only father-and-son team, Gordie and sons Mark and Marty Howe, played for the Hartford Whalers in 1979–80. Gordie turned 52 during the season.

BRING IN THE ZAMBONI
CELEBRITY FANS: Connecticut-based rock band the Zambonis frequently appear in Hartford Whalers garb. Check out their album *More Songs About Hockey . . . and Buildings and Food.*

STUMP THE SCHWAB:
Who holds the record for most goals by the WHA-era (1972–79) New England Whalers? *Answer:* Tom Webster, 220.

"All that time on the ice gave him incredible ease and balance."

He Shoots, He Scores, He Twirls, HE ACTS. . .

The son of lawyers, Toronto-born Jeff Skinner grew up playing hockey while pursuing figure skating and scholastics, drama being a particular interest. He'd change skates in the back seat between figure skating and hockey games. All that time on the ice gave him incredible ease and balance. That, and a unique hockey resume — Skinner is the only top-10 NHL draft pick ever to win a national figure skating medal (bronze) and appear in a Hollywood movie (*Death to Smoochie*). All before the age of 19, mind you. His first year with the Carolina Hurricanes, he won the Calder Trophy as the league's top rookie, displaying a deft scoring touch along with a football wide receiver's ability to break free of coverage. His sophomore season, alas, was shortened by a concussion.

FAN-tastic

(Top left and right) Diehard New England Whaler fans show their colors (the Whalers moved to Carolina in 1997). (Bottom left) 'Canes fans were living high off the hog after defeating Edmonton to win the Stanley Cup in 2006 (bottom right).

Family FEUD

Carolina is the delta where modern hockey's two great hockey rivers meet. The first and longest of these is the Sutter. Two generations of Viking, Albertans (Alberta Vikings would be more apt) have made the NHL. The first wave included Brent, Brian, Darryl, Duane, and twins Rich and Ron, who arrived with a series of loud thumps in the '70s and '80s.

These Viking farm boys were so good and strongly flavored that they became an adjective scouts employ to describe feisty, flinty forwards.

Sut·ter (sə -tər)

1. *marked by readiness to fight or argue, featuring an aggressive and belligerent tone*
2. *(hockey) relating to or engaged in a legally recognized war or warfare*
3. *a lifelong condition (four Sutter brothers — Brian, Duane, Darryl, and Brent — went on to become coaches and general managers)*

The second NHL Sutter tributary includes cousins Brandon and Brett, both of whom play in the Carolina organization. Brandon is assistant captain of the Hurricanes; Brett, captain of their farm team, the Charlotte Checkers.

Come to think of it, "hurricane checkers" could be another Sutter definition.

Then we come to the Staals. There are four of them, all from a sod farm in Thunder Bay, Ontario — Eric, Marc, Jordan, and Jared. Marc plays for the New York Rangers. Jordan, the Pittsburgh Penguins. Eric is Carolina's captain and best player. The youngest Staal, Jared, skates alongside Brett Sutter on the Charlotte Checkers.

The Staals are big — bigger than Sutters — though not as ornery. Maybe that's because, growing up, family games were played on a spacious, handsomely carpentered, 50-by-100-foot front-yard arena, a Rink of Dreams that allowed the Staal kids plenty of space in two-on-two affairs — eldest and youngest, Eric and Jared, against middle kids Marc and Jordan.

The Sutters, on the other hand, played in a 30-by-50-foot barn hayloft — mid-afternoon ball hockey in prairie summer heat. Mornings were for chores: every Sutter was driving a tractor by the time the time he was 10. After work, war — three-on-three in cramped, sweltering quarters. "Cripes, did we take it seriously," Duane Sutter (Brett's dad) remembered. "Losers wouldn't speak to winners for days. I can remember a few times when things got so hot in the barn games that our dad would take the tennis balls away for a few days until it cooled off."

A question, then, for hockey fans: remember how Jerry and George on *Seinfeld* would argue who would win a superhero fight between Superman and Batman? Well, in the same spirit — hypothetically speaking, allowing for space and time travel to bring the superhero hockey families together at the same age (teenagers, say) — who would emerge victorious in a three-on-three ball hockey or backyard rink match between the Sutters and Staals?

Eric Staal and Cam Ward celebrate a win.

To help you decide, here are the top five reasons the Sutters and Staals might win and claim the. . . let's call it the Allan Stanley Cup. (Allan Stanley being the Hall of Fame defenseman and Tim Horton's blueline partner on the last Toronto team to win the real Stanley Cup, while his uncle Barney was a Vancouver Millionaire and fellow Hall of Famer.)

WHY THE SUTTERS WIN

Sutters never, ever quit. The first hockey Sutter, Brian, set the never-surrender tone for the hockey family when he tried out for the junior Red Deer Rustlers. He was cut, and then wandered Red Deer, Alberta, all day, wondering what to tell his family. Finally, he phoned Viking. "What do you want to do — be a hockey player or come home?" asked his father, Louis, a farmer who chewed wheat instead of gum. A hockey player, Brian said. "Well, you better get your ass back there and talk to someone," the old man suggested. Brian returned to the Rustlers and said he didn't want to go. They sent him to their Junior B team. He made the Rustlers inside a month and was on his way. That's the Sutters: a family who won't quit, even if they're fired.

Sutters are fierce. Brian was eventually a 100-point scorer for the St. Louis Blues. He was joined there by Rich and Ron. Duane and Brent skated for the New York Islanders. One night, the brothers got into a fight — just like back in the barn back home. Referee Ron Wicks waded into a four-Sutter pileup, tried to sort out all the haggling, and then simply shook his head, sighing, "I really feel sorry for your mother."

Sutters are indestructible. In the fall of 2011, Calgary Flames coach Brent Sutter took a puck in the head, courtesy of a wayward shot by Rene Bourque, during practice. Without a care, he went off to get repairs, joking, "Can't get blood out of cement." In the trainer's room, he later gave his assailant a rap across the knuckles. "I can't blame him," Sutter said. "If it was intentional, he couldn't have hit me." *Ouch.*

Brandon Sutter is Brent's boy. And a chip off the same cement block. When Brandon arrived in Carolina, goalie Cam Ward reintroduced himself. He'd played for Brent Sutter with Red Deer in junior and remembered Brandon hanging around the rink. Ward walked away from the reunion, wincing. "Typical Sutter handshake," he said. "He about broke my hand."

"That's the Sutters: a family who won't quit, even if they're fired."

Sutters are sneaky. One night in 2009, Brent Sutter, then a coach with the New Jersey Devils, was in Raleigh to play Brandon's Hurricanes. They scheduled dinner before the game. "Who picks up the check?" a reporter asked Brandon. "I think I'll take him somewhere nice," Brandon said, "and make him pay."

Sutters are lucky. Whatever happened to the seventh Sutter, Gary, the one all the brothers swore was the best hockey player in the family? The one who was invited to play junior, but decided to stay on the farm? He and friends won $10 million in a lottery.

WHY THE STAALS WIN

Staals got off to a faster start. So every Sutter was driving a tractor when they were 10. Hah! That's nothing. Jordan Staal of the Penguins says he and his brothers were driving the tractor on their 500-acre sod farm at age *six*.

Oh yeah, my dad's rink is better than your dad's. It's true that the Sutter family barn had a serviceable hockey aesthetic. The second-floor loft was ribbed with old hockey sticks. But the Staal family rink was a real beauty — almost regulation size, with overhead lights and strong, true boards that the father, Henry Staal, a second-generation Dutch-Canadian, salvaged from cruising around Thunder Bay, making sod deliveries for work. The boys played all night, often with a cousin who lived one farm over. After games, they put their equipment away in personalized, pro-style lockers in the basement. "We were out there all the time," Eric Staal remembered of winter nights at home. "With boards, lights, and mesh on the back, regulation nets, what more could you ask for? We were out there like crazy." Mom Linda would look out the kitchen window, watching them as she made — and later put away — dinner. Father Henry, who played hockey for Lakehead University, had a selfish reason for building a rink so close to home. "That meant I didn't have to drive them somewhere," he's said more than once.

"Oh yeah, my dad's rink is better than your dad's."

Staals, being younger, are more technologically savvy. Once, Henry drove the boys to a minor-hockey tournament in Minnesota. Eric was playing. They watched a pro game, too. Fox TV was experimenting with glowing pucks at the time, and one flew over the boards and under a seat. Marc retrieved it and brought it home to Thunder Bay. The puck worked under Henry's lights, giving off a phosphorescent blush. The boys could find the puck when it flew over the boards and into the snow. So could their dog, however. The family pet eventually took the glow off the Staals' treasured keepsake.

Staals are bigger. Every Staal is 6'4" and over 200 pounds. Duane was the only Sutter to hit six feet and 200. To paraphrase Jerry Seinfeld, if the Staals and Sutters went three on three, the Sutters would fold faster than Superman on laundry day.

Best in show. Brent and Brian Sutter were great, but Eric Staal is the best hockey player of either clan — the kind of big, mobile, two-way, put-him-out-in-the-last-minute-if-you're-up-or-down-a-goal centre scouts go to bed dreaming about. "He's an elite player who has everything going for him," Scotty Bowman once said. Don Cherry calls him "a superstar." With two families this good at playing hockey, you have to go with the old adage: the team with the best player is the best team.

(Top — left to right) Marc, Eric, Jordan and Jared Staal on the Ontario farm where their home rink used to be. (Left) Brandon Sutter and Eric Staal enjoy themselves at a swanky affair.

CHICAGO BLACKHAWKS

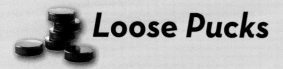 ## *Loose Pucks*

RECORD: The 'Hawks like to play an oldie but goldie, "Here Come the Hawks," a relic of the high-flying Hull–Mikita era, during pre-game interludes. And organist Frank Pellico plays a zippy reprise of the song between periods. It sounds like the Fifth Dimension's "Up, Up and Away" arranged for a Frank Sinatra Jr. recording date. Sample lyrics (start snapping your fingers): *"Here they come movin', weavin', flyin' high and throwin' spray / Blades flashin', sticks crashin', tryin' for the play / And the Blackhawks take control / There's a shot / AND A GOAL!"* And for the kids, the Hawks' playlist in 2011–12 featured Nine Inch Nails, Eminem, and Jay-Z and Kanye bragging about their trip to France.

RECORDS
MOST HAT TRICKS, CAREER: Bobby Hull, 28, Stan Mikita, 18, Denis Savard, 11

MOST GOALS, ONE SEASON: Bobby Hull, 58

MOST GAME-WINNING GOALS, CAREER: Stan Mikita, 67, Bobby Hull, 65, Steve Larmer, 49

MOST POINTS PER GAME, CAREER: Denis Savard, 1.24; Jeremy Roenick, 1.14; Bobby Hull, 1.11; Max Bentley, 1.09

BEST PLUS-MINUS, CAREER: Steve Larmer, +182; Bill White, +176; Keith Magnuson, +170

MOST SHUTOUTS, CAREER: Tony Esposito, 74, Glenn Hall, 51

50-GOAL CLUB: Bobby Hull, 58, 1968–69; Al Secord, 54, 1982–83; Hull, 54, 1965–66; Jeremy Roenick, 53, 1991–92; Hull, 52, 1966–67; Roenick, 50, 1992–93; Hull, 50, 1971–72; Hull, 50, 1961–62

WORKING OVERTIME: The Hawks' Stanley Cup wins in 1961 and 2010 both required overtime labor. Murray Balfour scored in the third period of OT in a pivotal game four against Montreal in the '61 semifinals. Marian Hossa, Dustin Byfuglien, and Patrick Kane scored overtime goals in the 2010 playoff run. Kane's goal against Philadelphia gave the Hawks their fourth Stanley Cup.

DRAFT-SCHMAFT
TOP-10 PICKS, 1989–2009: 8

PLAYERS DRAFTED WHO PLAYED 300 NHL GAMES: 26

IMPACT PLAYERS: Duncan Keith, 54th, 2002; Brent Seabrook, 14th, 2003; Dustin Byfuglien, 245th, 2003; Jonathan Toews, 3rd, 2006; Patrick Kane, 1st, 2007

DRAFT-SCHMAFT RANKING: 22nd

A great Blackhawk fan, unless you're sitting behind him at the game.

LINE CHANGES

THE PONY LINE: Max Bentley, Bill Mosienko, and Doug Bentley, 1940s

THE MILLION-DOLLAR LINE: Bill Hay, Murray Balfour, and Bobby Hull, early 1960s

THE SCOOTER LINE: Ken Wharram, Stan Mikita, and Doug Mohns, 1960s and '70s

"My teeth weren't that good to begin with, so hopefully I can get some better ones." — Chicago defenseman Duncan Keith after he lost several teeth during the 2010 playoffs.

"It must be my body. It's chiseled out of marshmallows." — Tony Amonte on his going more than five seasons without missing a game for Chicago in the 1990s.

SKATE THAT ONE PAST ME AGAIN: Denis Savard, Denis Cyr, and Denis Tremblay were all born on the same day — February 4, 1961 — a couple of blocks away from each other in Montreal. *Les trois Denis* played on the same line from age eight until pro. Savard was a Blackhawk star, of course. Cyr joined him in Chicago in 1983–84.

BRING ON THE ZAMBONI

CELEBRITY FANS: Actors Jim Belushi, John Cusack, and Vince Vaughn, Vice-President Joe Biden, and the rock group Styx.

STUMP THE SCHWAB: How come Blackhawk organist Frank Pellico wears uniform number 61? Answer: No, not because Chicago won the Stanley Cup that year. It's because an organ has 61 keys.

Mos' DEFT

In sports, history can happen when you least expect it. In the last game of the 1951–52 NHL regular season, New York had Chicago in for a game that no one was much interested in. Both teams were out of the playoffs. An icy rain snaked down Broadway. Only 3,254 fans showed up at Madison Square Garden.

FAN-tastic

Ghosts of Christmas past and present: A Stan Mikita figurine (top right) along with Jonathan Toews (middle left) and Patrick Kane tree decorations (middle right). (Bottom left) The pucks stop here: four goalie fans attend a Hawks-Wings game. (Bottom right) *Les deux Denis*: Denis Savard and Denis Cyr.

At least they had empty seats on which to hang drying coats. Rangers were up 5–2 going into the third, and when New York's Ed Slowinski completed a hat trick, fans began to stretch and grab their coats. Who knows how many saw what happened next — a half-minute of hockey that will last in the record book forever. The Black Hawks' Bill Mosienko collected a neat pass at the Ranger blue line, flew around an off-balance defender, and then fooled goalie Lorne Anderson, cutting left and shooting right, catching the inside of the post. As the P.A. system announced, "Chicago goal by Bill Mosienko, assisted by Gus Bodnar. Time: 6:09," Bodnar won the center-ice faceoff, spun, and found Mosienko gathering speed at the Ranger blue line. The right winger split the defense, looked up, and again picked the inside of the right post. "I'm sure Anderson was expecting high shots," Mosienko told *Sports Illustrated*. "Twice before during the game he had stopped high ones." Little Mosienko grabbed the puck from the back of the cage — it was his 30th goal — and sailed to the bench, happy. Coach Ebbie Goodfellow motioned for him to stay on. It was 6–4 now. Bodnar won another faceoff, slapping a pass to left winger George Gee, who found Mosienko again knifing past a defender at the blue line. This time, Anderson came out in a crouch, looking for the low shot. Mosienko fired high over his stabbing trapper. It was his third goal in 21 seconds. The forward fell into a trance. "I wasn't sure what to do until one of our forwards, Jimmy Peters, told me to get the puck. *'That's a record, Mosie,'* he kept yelling." Chicago scored two more to win. In the dressing room, Mosienko was photographed waving hello to the world with three pucks. Indeed, the photo went everywhere. Including, eventually, the outside wall of the Winnipeg bowling alleys Mosie ran in the off-season.

Triple OVERTIME

(Right) A Chicago Stadium ticket stub from 1961; (Below) Reggie Fleming — "Take the Pledge with Reg!"

Although the Chicago Blackhawks played their first game in 1926, the franchise we know and love today — the club whose fans drown out the Stars and Stripes right after "Oh saaay. . ." and celebrate every Hawk goal as if it's New Year's Eve — was born on Sunday, March 26, 1961.

That was the night the "Black Hawks"[1] played their first-ever doubleheader, a triple-overtime playoff game against the champion Montreal Canadiens. Twenty thousand fans showed up in an arena built for 16,666. The most ever, Chicago newspapers reported. Everyone smoked, and it was so hot fans stripped down to short-sleeved shirts. Fortunately, Stadium beer guys never ran out of suds. Even in Prohibition, Chicago never ran out of beer.

Maybe because of all the disappearing ale, the game got louder as it went. Exciting plays were punctuated by boat whistles and cherry bombs. Balloons and paper planes floated on air stained with tobacco smoke. There were fights in the crowd. Rocket Richard, retired now but traveling with the Habs, slugged a fan. Players on the ice fought, too. And when a scrap broke out in the penalty box, organist Al Melgard played "I Love You Truly."

Beginning in the third overtime, he played "Oh, How I Hate to Get Up in the Morning," reminding the thousands of factory workers and students who had spent five hours crammed into the standing-room section way up top that work and school were not far enough away.

It was a night when fans figured their guys had won, and then later were sure they lost — and were wrong both ways. When the game was finally decided, the winning coach screamed goodbye at the ref. And the losing coach marched out on the ice and took a swing at the escaping official. All the remaining cherry bombs exploded, and the fans' boat-whistle orchestra, along with the team's famous 3,663-pipe Chicago Stadium organ, went off all at once.

And right then and there, Chicago fell in love with hockey and the Black Hawks.

Actually, Chicago fans were happy to be in the

1 The Black Hawks became the Blackhawks in 1986.

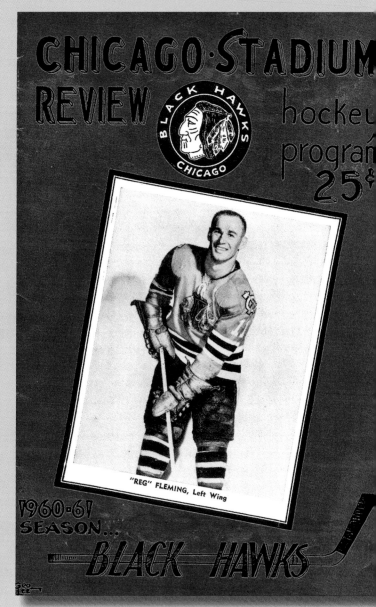

CHICAGO·STADIUM REVIEW hockey program 25¢

"REG" FLEMING, Left Wing

1960·61 SEASON... BLACK HAWKS

playoffs at all in 1961. Between 1945 and 1958, their team made the postseason twice, finishing last nine times. "Chicago was the Siberia of hockey" in the late 1950s, former captain Jack "Tex" Evans remembered. "Four thousand fans showed up some nights.... They played a lot of their home games in Omaha.... When the players tried to put together a union, they were ostracized. They were sent to Chicago as punishment."[2]

Indeed, when NHL players attempted to form a union in 1956–57 in an effort to discover more information about their own pension fund, many leaders — Ted Lindsay (Detroit), Dollard St. Laurent (Montreal), Tod Sloan (Toronto), and Jim Thomson (Toronto) — were traded or sold to Chicago. Goalie Glenn Hall was sentenced to Illinois for telling Detroit GM Jack Adams to perform an anatomically impossible act.

The team chemistry started to change in 1958 when Rudy Pilous, the charismatic, deliberately funny coach of the junior St. Catharines Tee Pees, a man who disliked practice almost as much as players, arrived in Chicago. Pilous kept hockey loose and fun. The first time the team arrived in New York for a game, he took the players aside to issue a warning.

"Now, I don't want you western farm boys to get sunburned on the roofs of your mouths standing out there in the sunshine, staring up at the tops of those tall buildings," he said.

Montreal had won the five previous Stanley Cups and finished first in 1960–61, thanks to strong work from three first-team all-stars, Doug Harvey (Norris Trophy winner), Jean Beliveau, and 50-goal man Boom Boom Geoffrion (Hart Trophy winner). Chicago had nobody among the top 10 scorers, although Hall and Bobby Hull made the second all-star team.

Montreal had easily pushed the Hawks aside in the opening round in the previous two seasons. But this year, with Hull and Stan Mikita coming into their own, and Pilous joking and cajoling, Chicago showed up for the playoffs frisky as colts. Montreal won the first game, 6–2, but not without trouble. It was two-all

2 Chicago played six "home" games at neutral rinks in 1956, performing in Omaha, St. Louis (four games), and St. Paul, Minnesota.

> **"Now, I don't want you western farm boys to get sunburned on the roofs of your mouths standing out there in the sunshine, staring up at the tops of those tall buildings."**

going into the third period. Captain Evans murdered Beliveau along the boards. Geoffrion was hurt, too. The two top scorers in the NHL that season weren't the same after that.

Chicago wasn't afraid of anyone — not even Montreal. Lucky Pierre Pilote once fought and floored Rocket and Henri Richard in the same game. His defense partner, the aptly nicknamed Moose Vasko, was more fortunate still. Moose played 13 seasons in the NHL, sticking his face into all kinds of trouble without losing a tooth.

Chicago shocked Montreal in game two, outshooting (25–19) and outscoring them 4–3 on a late goal by Eddie Litzenberger. The next day, Montreal coach Toe Blake held an exacting practice, going over defensive responsibilities again and again. Then once more after that.

Pilous gave his boys the day off.

When the Black Hawks hit the ice in Chicago on Sunday night, they were surprised by fans waving signs — as if the game were a political convention. "Win with Wharram," read one placard. That was for Kenny Wharram, Mikita's whippet-like winger. "Take the Pledge with Reg," another read — encouragement for rabble-rouser Reggie Fleming. Defenseman Al Arbour had a more specific, gruesome task. "Scalp 'em, Apache Al," his card read.

Chicago had won nine games on the road that season, compared to 20 in their own building. They were homers. "There was no greater place in the league," Hull remembered. "When that guy would sing the national anthem, those people would start roaring. And the puck would drop and they were still roaring. And we'd say, 'Let's get 'em in their end in the first period and not let 'em out.'"

Chicago would indeed come out flying, but the five-time defending champions were ready. Jacques Plante was his old imperturbable self, directing the play with his stick like a traffic cop and going for an occasional skate to break up plays. That was unheard of at the time. As mad as leaving your house with the door wide open. Acrobatic, stay-at-home Hall was just as good at the other end, stylishly pushing aside all Montreal chances.

Liberated by superior goaltending, forwards on both teams went to the attack, pressing to score the one goal that would put their team ahead in the playoffs. *Montreal Star* sportswriter Red Fisher commented, "From the start, the game belonged to Plante and Hall. Breakaways. Scoring chances by both teams from the lip of the crease. One-on-one… two-on-one. Scoring chances in the first period… all turned back by both goaltenders. There were more spectacular stops by Plante and Hall during most of the second period."

Coach Blake, chain-chewing Spearmint gum, scheming every shift, killed one Hawk rally by calling for the hashmarks in Montreal's end to be measured. They looked off. They weren't, and the fans hooted and jeered. Seeing sweating fans set loose squadrons of paper airplanes from the upper balconies, Montreal *Gazette* reporter Dink Carroll pecked, "There wasn't an introvert in the crowd" on his press-box Underwood.

In the middle of the second period, Chicago Stadium crossed over into delirium, exhibiting why it would soon gain the nickname "The Mad House on Madison." Montreal's Billy Hicke and Mikita crossed sticks and then went at it, first on ice, and then in the penalty box. (Incredibly, players sat beside each other in the box at the time.) A Chicago fan became too extroverted with Maurice Richard. The Rocket slugged him.

The game picked up its pace, going back and forth faster than it seemed possible, like when you put your windshield wipers on high in a storm. Everyone was standing now. Then the Million-Dollar Line got into the act.

That would be Hull, Red Hay, and Murray Balfour. "About Christmas time, Bobby was playing with Ron Murphy and Eric Nesterenko and they both got hurt," Hay remembered, years later. "Rudy Pilous put Murray and I on the line with Bobby. We told Bobby how we'll play the game: 'Murray will get the puck out of the corner and bang it around, I'll fool around with it a bit, and you shoot it in the goal. That's as simple as we can make it, Bobby.'"

The trio fell together quickly, with Hay, who warmed the bench early in the season, eventually leading the team in scoring (59 points). Linemates Hull (56) and Balfour (48) finished second and fourth, sandwiching Mikita (53).

This night, the Million-Dollar Line found paydirt pretty much the way Hay had drawn it up at Christmas. The center fooled around with the puck and found Hull, who fired quickly. Plante made the save, but Balfour, a crashing, belligerent winger who, Glenn Hall once said, "never scored a goal standing up," knocked in the rebound as he was being escorted to the ice by a defender.

The way the goalies were playing, that seemed enough. Especially after Montreal's Jean-Guy Talbot was given a minor penalty by referee Dalton McArthur with three minutes to go. Coach Blake exploded behind the Montreal bench. *How could you call a penalty late in a tight playoff game?*

Chicago fans were now jubilant clock-watchers. *We've got this thing won.*

Except, with a minute and twenty seconds left, Red Hay was called for a penalty. Of course, Toe no doubt figured that call was fair — *evened things up. Besides, hey, the guy was holding.*

Blake pulled Plante with under a minute left, and then demonstrated why he was the league's top-paid coach ($18,000). He didn't like the way Beliveau was taking faceoffs, so he stuck the big center on the point in place of injured Boom Boom Geoffrion. A gutsy move. Little Phil Goyette took — and won — the faceoff, passing to Henri Richard, who skimmed the puck past Hall.

Overtime was rare for Chicago. The last two overtime games in Chicago had occurred in 1953 (the

Hawks took that one) and 1944. Both were against the Habs. In the 1944 game, Blake himself had scored, winning Montreal a Stanley Cup.

Maybe that's why the crowd were so jittery, with lots of shrill screaming in the first overtime. This was the first time most of them had been in an OT rollercoaster. Beliveau had a breakaway in the first extra period, but shot wide. Ralph Backstrom flew in alone, but lost the puck. Hall was in Montreal's heads.

At the other end, Hay barged in on Plante, saw a high open corner, and put his shot exactly where he wanted it. But the disk hit the shaft of the Montreal goalie's stick, deflecting high over the net.

Twenty thousand fans let out a deflated vowel sound — *Ohhhhhhhhh*.

And then, in the second overtime — calamity. The Habs had taken the game over. There was a goal-mouth scramble. Montreal's Donnie Marshall bunted a high rebound lazily over a falling Hall into the Chicago net.

Chicago Stadium was quiet, except for 20 or so whooping Montrealers. Time to go home. The crowd stood up. But then there was a stirring. The Canadiens had surrounded referee McArthur, who was making a baseball "safe" signal. He was ruling that Marshall had knocked the puck in with a high stick. No goal.

Montreal fumed. There was a lot of screaming, in both French and English. None of it could be heard, though. Chicago Stadium was again in full, noisy throttle. In the sixth period of play, Chicago got a penalty. Beliveau had another in-close chance. Then Henri. Claude Provost had an open net, but shot wide.

At 11:44, Montreal's Dickie Moore was penalized for tripping. It was the 26th penalty of the game. Both teams now had 13 infractions — even-steven. Chicago's power play came on. The team was tired. They'd had only three shots, all harmless, on Plante this period. Did the Million-Dollar Line have a few bucks left? Pilote shot from the point. There was a scramble. Balfour found the puck on his stick and shot. He was falling as the puck entered the net.

"Twenty thousand fans let out a deflated vowel sound — Ohhhhhhhhhh."

There was a pregnant pause — Was it? Could it really be over? — then Chicago Stadium let out a roar. All the wind instruments — whistles, organs, and voices — joined together in a resounding orchestral climax. The ice was suddenly covered in paper slush — cups and program confetti. Blake, who had been simmering at the back of the Montreal bench since the penalty to Talbot in the third, broke through the clutches of his team and marched onto the ice, reviewing all the injustices the Canadiens had endured: the Moore penalty, all 13 Montreal penalties — *in a playoff game!* — and, oh yes, the disallowed goal.

The disallowed goal!

Still on the ice, Moore felt a shiver seeing Blake's piercing brown eyes. "I thought he was coming for me," he later told Red Fisher. The coach continued as if in a trance, across the ice and along the boards until he got to referee McArthur, who was discussing something, his back turned, with the official scorer. Once there, he threw a punch, catching the referee on the shoulder before being swallowed up by his players.[3]

It was probably the greatest hockey game Chicago fans had ever seen. And one of the most significant. "We knew we were going to win after the Balfour goal," Mikita would say. The Hawks were so sure, in fact, that they took the next home game off, losing 5–2 to a furiously committed Montreal team, despite outshooting the Canadiens 52–19.

It didn't matter. Glenn Hall threw back-to-back 3–0 shutouts. "It was the twilight of the titans," Dink Carroll wrote in the Montreal press box as the Habs relinquished their five-year grip on the Stanley Cup.

After that, the Hawks faced Detroit for

3   Blake received a $2,000 fine for his punch, but was behind the bench the next game. McArthur was fired in the off-season.

Bobby and Stan, back in the day. Hull is wearing number 16 in the photo; he graduated to number 7 and then, in the fall of 1963, the ultimate hockey superstar number: 9.

the Cup. Pilous asked Red Hay, "Do you think you'll be able to check the line of Alex Delvecchio and Gordie Howe?" The center pretended to be offended. "Rudy, you go into their dressing room and ask them if they think they'll be able to check our line," he said.

"They couldn't have stopped us with five all-stars and a tank," Bobby Hull bragged.

Chicago's notoriously parsimonious ownership group weren't nearly as confident as Hay or Hull. The Black Hawks won their first Stanley Cup in two generations on Saturday April 16, 1961, defeating Detroit 5–1 in their own building. There was no champagne or beer on hand to celebrate, however.

"I didn't order champagne," said co-owner Jim Norris, "because I didn't want to jinx the boys."

The Black Hawks found a way to celebrate anyway. Hull was drinking beer out of a teammate's fedora on the bus right about the time the Hawks were told they had to go back. A blizzard had closed the Detroit airport. The team trooped back to their hotel. Somebody found some booze. These guys were from Chicago, right? Several gallons later, the team had somehow manufactured the raucous energy of their home arena, turning the hotel into a block party. Nobody could get any sleep. Well after midnight, puzzled guests emerged from their rooms. What the Hull was that noise?

Anyone who took the elevator down to the first floor to complain would've been greeted by the still-partying Chicago Black Hawks, one of whom was driving a borrowed motorcycle around the lobby.

COLORADO AVALANCHE

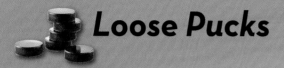

Loose Pucks

RECORD: The Avs play suburban hip-hop/metal during warmups — 2Pac, Lil Wayne's "Snap Yo Fingers," Green Day, Rise Against. . . stuff like that. The team enters to surf guitar — Dick Dale's "Scalped." The party gets loud 'n' proud during games: Joan Jett, Ozzy, Boston, AC/DC. When the home team wins, Colorado fans leave the building snapping their fingers to U2's Beautiful Day" and Kool and the Gang's "Celebration."

RECORDS

MOST HAT TRICKS, CAREER: Peter Stastny, 16; Joe Sakic, 15; Michel Goulet, 13

MOST POINTS, ONE GAME: Anton Stastny and Peter Stastny, 8 each, February 22, 1981, Quebec vs. Washington

MOST CONSECUTIVE HOME SELLOUTS: 487, from November 9, 1995, to October 14, 2006 (NHL record)

BEST PLUS/MINUS, CAREER: Peter Forsberg, +210; Adam Foote, +129

50-GOAL CLUB: Michel Goulet, 57, 1982–83 (Quebec); Goulet, 56, 1983–84 (Que.); Goulet, 55, 1984–85 (Que.); Joe Sakic, 54, 2000–01 (Colorado); Goulet, 53, 1985–86 (Que.); Jacques Richard, 52, 1980–81 (Que.); Sakic, 51, 1995–96 (Colo.); Milan Hejduk, 50, 2002–03 (Colo.)

WORKING OVERTIME: Who has scored the most playoff overtime goals ever? Joe Sakic notched eight while playing with Quebec and Colorado. To put that in perspective, Mark Messier, Gordie Howe, and Mario Lemieux never recorded a single playoff overtime marker.

DRAFT-SCHMAFT
TOP-10 PICKS, 1989–2009: 6

PLAYERS DRAFTED WHO PLAYED 300 NHL GAMES: 41

IMPACT PLAYERS: Mats Sundin, 1st, 1989; Adam Foote, 22nd, 1989; Owen Nolan, 1st, 1990; Eric Lindros, 1st, 1991; Chris Drury, 72nd, 1994; Milan Hejduk, 87th, 1994; Tim Thomas, 217th, 1994; Alex Tanguay, 12th, 1998; Robyn Regehr, 19th, 1998; Paul Stastny, 44th, 2005; Matt Duchene, 3rd, 2009

DRAFT-SCHMAFT RANKING: 1st (tied with Detroit)

LINE CHANGES
THE JAM LINE: Joe Sakic, Alex Tanguay, and Milan Hejduk, 2000s

   "I can't hear what Jeremy says because my ears are blocked with my two Stanley Cup rings." — Patrick Roy responding to an on-ice taunt from Jeremy Roenick.

SKATE THAT ONE PAST ME AGAIN: In the late '80s, Quebec Nordiques defenseman Bryan Fogarty once picked up a teenage girl in a bar, inviting her back to his pad. The girl phoned home at 3 a.m. for a ride, which

Patrick Roy's failed Statue of Liberty play. See story below.

"I can't hear what Jeremy says because my ears are blocked with my two Stanley Cup rings."

is when Fogarty first realized that he'd picked up coach Dave Chambers's daughter.

BRING ON THE ZAMBONI
CELEBRITY FANS: Trey Parker, co-creator of *South Park*, and a Denver boy. The Avs were once depicted in an episode of the series.

STUMP THE SCHWAB: How long did the WHA Quebec Nordiques' first coach last? *Answer:* Two games. The immortal Rocket Richard quit after the team beat the Alberta Oilers 3-0. Wonder what he would have done had they lost?

OOPS!

Colorado has won two Stanley Cups — first in 1996, immediately after their arrival from Quebec City, and again in 2001. The imperturbable, fabulously skillful (and well-upholstered) Patrick Roy was superb both times, winning the Conn Smythe Trophy in 2001. So let's give Saint Patrick a little love before mentioning that his faux pas in the 2002 semis may have cost the team a third Cup.

The Avs were leading the series three games to two and playing the hated Detroit Red Wings at home. Late in the second, there was no score and Roy was invincible. Steve Yzerman, in close, was facing an open net. But no, Roy, flat on his belly, snared the puck. Patrick then decided to put a little mustard on the play — *et voilà!* — lifting the puck in the air to punctuate his larceny. Except, in lifting his chin to strike a noble pose, he left the puck on the ice. Brendan Shanahan swooped in and scored. Colorado was never in the series after that, and the (now chuckling) Wings went on to win the Stanley Cup.

Duchene celebrating

FAN-tastic

The hockey stick is so much fun to hold (and behold!) that it shows up just about everywhere, from an Italian wedding (top left) to a Colorado street (top right).

Stick BOY

Who better to talk sticks and stones than Matt Duchene, Colorado's young center of attraction? Matt grew up in a hockey theme park: Haliburton, Ontario, a small town that can boast more NHL alumni (four) than traffic lights (three). In addition to playing junior hockey (Brampton Batallion — ten-*hut*), Matt had a backyard shooting gallery and could be seen and heard during the summer, firing slap shots and snap-shots at a net, sometimes through a haze of deerflies.

No dummy, Duchene wore a beekeeper's head-gear while working outdoors. Back inside his house, the teenager memorized the tools of his trade on the computer, researching NHL players' equipment. Like a lot of kids at the time, he found hockey sticks interest-ing. No surprise there. Colorado's number 9 grew up in an era when the hockey rifle evolved from something that grew on trees to something closer to one of those super-secret weapons that James Bond's supplier, Q, whipped up in the lab of MI-6.

Here's the sales blurb for Nike/Bauer's Supreme One95 senior hockey stick — "THE POWER PLAYER":

Engineered to deliver explosive one-timers and scoring slap shots, the Supreme One95 stick is built for the strong and powerful. Designed to withstand maximum loading, it delivers pure power in each and every shot. With its low-mid flex, and a torsionally stiff lower third, the overall design creates more energy transfer per shot, resulting in greater velocity.

Hey, wasn't that what all the Bond girls, from Plenty O'Toole to Strawberry Fields, said about 007 — that he had a torsionally stiff lower third? Anyway, Matt's point of entry into the hockey arms race was hockey first one-piece stick.

"Whenever the first Easton Synergy came out . . . I became fascinated with sticks for some reason," he once said. "I guess it was maybe because I was at that young an age. I could tell you each curve on every brand you could get, what flex, everything."

Indeed, when Duchene was on the satellite radio show *NHL Live with Billy Jaffe and Rob Simpson* back in his rookie year (2009-10), the hosts threw a bunch of NHL players' names at him, and Matt identified their sticks — *rat-ta-tat-tat*, one after the other, like he was on a TV quiz show. And it's not as though the guys were throwing him easy names. First up was Manny Malhotra.

"Mmm, I think he uses an Easton."

"Vinny Lecavalier?"

"CCM, square toe."

"Ryan Kesler?"

"Bauer 195, pretty small curve."

"Nik Lidstrom?"

"Warrior. . . pretty long blade, opens up a bit at the toe.

"John Tavares?"

"CCM. He uses a Drury curve."

On he went. Predictably, the talk eventually turned to Duchene's own stick, an A.i9 from Reebok, made out of "Tactile Griptonite" with a "Mid Kick Point," as well as an "XLerated Blade" with an extra layer of carbon and 2:1 "Power Taper Ratio." Duchene customized his weapon, of course, choosing à la carte features from the sticks of reigning hockey superheroes.

"It's a little bit similar to Ovechkin's," he said. "It's a lot smaller, but same idea: it's got a loft on the heel and a then a hook on the toe so you can drag the puck in and really rip it with the heel. I know Crosby uses a really stiff stick, which is good for faceoffs and passing. I use the same flex as him — 115. A short stick like him, as well. My curve is actually pretty similar to Kovalchuk and Sakic's, and those are two great shooters. It hooks up a

little bit and curves at the toe. It's a tool. You want to use the best tools for the job."

For sure. NHL hockey players have been babying their sticks forever. And you wonder whether Matt talked shop with another number 9 after scoring his first-ever goal, snapping a low, 40-foot screamer past Detroit's Chris Osgood on Saturday, October 17, 2009. His parents, Chris and Vince, along with sister Jess were watching from a Detroit luxury suite that night.

Beside them was Old Man Winter, Gordie Howe.

Back in Saskatoon — this was in the 1940s — Gordie spent his summers making money to buy sticks: steam-pressed CCM wood composites. Forty-centers from the hardware store that warped when exposed to moisture or cold, so kids would make sure not to leave their wooden friends outside overnight.

Not when 40 cents was a more than a week's wages for any youngster.

Prairie boy Howe made stick money lying in a barren, early-summer field, killing gophers from 20 paces with a slingshot. Saskatchewan farmers paid a dollar for every 100 severed gopher tails.

In a way, both number 9s spent their summers practicing shots. For sure, Matt would have developed stronger wrists and better hockey form. But maybe Gordie acquired the better shooting eye.

We'll leave it to readers to decide who had more fun.

Matt Duchene gets a wrestling scissors hold from a frustrated Canuck.

COLUMBUS BLUE JACKETS

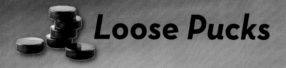

Loose Pucks

RECORD: For the longest time, the team played Godsmack's guitar-riff intro to "The Enemy" when the Blue Jackets hit the ice, then switched to the Hives' "Tick Tick Boom." Bush's "Machinehead" jumps out of the loudspeakers just before the puck is dropped.

RECORDS:

MOST HAT TRICKS, CAREER: Rick Nash, 5

MOST GOALS, ONE GAME: Geoff Sanderson, 4, March 29, 2003, vs. Calgary

MOST POWER-PLAY GOALS, ONE GAME: Bryan Berard, 3

BEST PLUS/MINUS, CAREER: Jan Hejda, +23

50-GOAL CLUB: None. Rick Nash has come closest, scoring 41 as a 19-year-old in 2003–04.

WORKING OVERTIME: Geoff Sanderson scored Columbus's first overtime goal on December 8, 2000, whipping a backhand shot past Peter Skudra to beat Boston 3–2. The Blue Jackets have never scored a playoff overtime goal.

DRAFT-SCHMAFT:

TOP-TEN PICKS 2000-11: 10

PLAYERS DRAFTED WHO PLAYED 300 NHL GAMES: 8

IMPACT PLAYERS: Rick Nash, 1st, 2002

DRAFT-SCHMAFT RANKING: 30th

LINE CHANGES:

In 2006, coach Ken Hitchcock threw together the fast and furious Manny Malhotra, Jason Chimera, and Dan Fritsche as a checking line. Fans liked their spunk. The team made up promotional Speed Team T-shirts to honor the trio.

"I had a player who came into my office and said, 'Doug, I've got a bit of a problem: I hit a parked car last night.' I said, 'No problem, I'll get a lawyer and we'll talk about it.' Then the lawyer came in and said, 'Doug, we have a bit of problem. He hit nine parked cars last night.'" — Former Columbus GM Doug MacLean

SKATE THAT ONE PAST ME AGAIN: Former coach Ken Hitchcock weighed an estimated 475 pounds when he coached junior hockey in British Columbia in 1988.

BRING ON THE ZAMBONI:

CELEBRITY FANS: Napoleon Bonaparte. In 2007, Columbus bought a handmade replica of the 1857 Napoleon cannon. The team shoots the weapon off when the players take the ice, after every Blue Jackets goal, and when the team wins.

STUMP THE SCHWAB: What was the name of the last pro hockey team to represent Columbus before the Blue Jackets joined the NHL? Answer: The Columbus Chill.

Savior or sinkhole? Columbus's Jeff Carter.

Pucked?

A franchise falling off the cliff, Columbus has never won a playoff game in 11 seasons, finishing in the bottom 10 of the league most every year without ever — except for Rick Nash — accumulating much talent. _Good luck, Nikita Filatov, wherever you are. Write when you find work, Rostislav Klesla._ In the talent-rich 2003 draft pool, the team passed on Thomas Vanek, Ryan Suter, Dion Phaneuf, Andrei Kostitsyn, Jeff Carter, Dustin Brown, Brent Seabrook, Zach Parise, Ryan Getzlaf, Corey Perry, Ryan Kesler, Brent Burns, Mike Richards, and Corey Perry to select . . . uh, Nikolai Zherdev. Figuring to erase a past mistake, and very much needing a big center to complement Nash, the Blue Jackets traded their first-round pick in the 2011 draft to Philadelphia for Carter, then a 26-year-old goal scorer in the second season of an 11-year contract worth — Lord have mercy — $58 million. What happens next? Carter disappears for three days upon hearing he's been traded. When the season opens, he reinjures his oft-injured foot. Worse still, the player Philly chose with the Jackets' pick, 18-year-old Sean Couturier, gives evidence of being the big-deal center Columbus has been dreaming about for years. The worst team in the NHL, Columbus appeared to be stuck with one of those contracts that turn general managers

> ## "A franchise falling off the cliff, Columbus has never won a playoff game in 11 seasons."

into TV commentators. But look, GM Scott Howson managed to ship Carter to Los Angeles for perpetual underachiever Jack Johnson and a first-round pick in 2012 at the trading deadline. When that happened, though, Nash decided he wanted out. Rebuilding a perpetually struggling hockey team is like making a bed with insufficiently small sheets — whenever you tuck one corner in, another side is exposed.

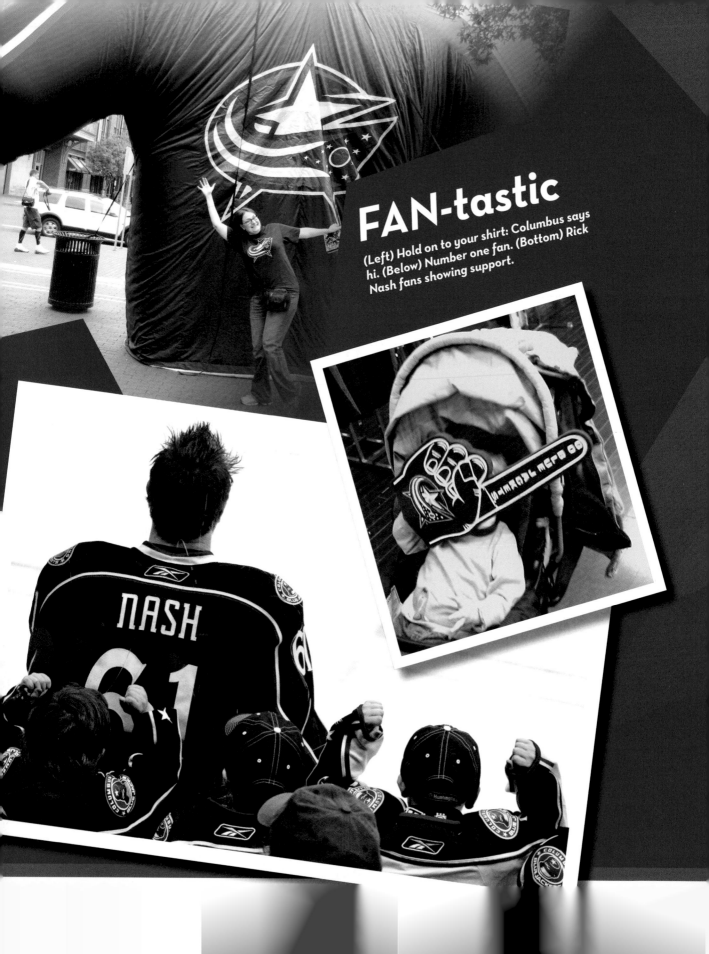

FAN-tastic

(Left) Hold on to your shirt: Columbus says hi. (Below) Number one fan. (Bottom) Rick Nash fans showing support.

NASH
61

One-year WONDER?

No position in hockey is harder to handicap than goal-tending. Calgary fans wince when reminded that their team took Jason Kidd over Marty Brodeur in the 1990 draft. Hey, at least Kidd was a serviceable NHL pro — unlike Muzzatti, Krahn, and Irving. No, that's not a law firm, it's a list of Calgary first-round picks who failed to burst into Flames.

Stop chuckling, Ottawa fans. Your guys used a high draft pick on Mathieu Chouinard — *twice!* The Sens wasted a first-round pick on Mathieu in 1998 (15th overall), couldn't sign him, and then spent a second-rounder on the Quebec junior goalie in 2000. He never did suit up for Ottawa, spending the majority of a short minor-pro career battling rubber for the Grand Rapids Griffins and San Diego Gulls.

Famous first-round goalie flops can be evenly stacked up against superstar netminders who were picked when the custodians were trying to shoo the GMs out of the rink.

Netminding his own business: Steve Mason lost in thought.

LOW-GRADE HIGH PICKS:	HIGH-GRADE LOW PICKS:
Ray Matryniuk #5 pick (Montreal), 1970	**Dominik Hasek** #207 pick (Chicago), 1983
Terry Richardson #11 pick (Detroit), 1973	**Eddie Belfour**, undrafted free agent (Chicago), 1986
Gord Laxton #13 pick (Pittsburgh), 1975	**Curtis Joseph**, undrafted free agent (St. Louis), 1989
Jimmy Waite #8 pick (Chicago), 1987	**Nikolai Khabibulin** #204 pick (Winnipeg), 1992
Patrick DesRochers #14 pick (Phoenix), 1998	**Tim Thomas** #217 pick (Quebec), 1994
Brian Finley #6 pick (Nashville), 1999	**Ryan Miller** #138 pick (Buffalo), 1999
Al Montoya #6 pick (New York Rangers), 2004	**Henrik Lundqvist** #205 (New York Rangers), 2000
Marek Schwartz #17 (St. Louis Blues), 2004	**Pekka Rinne** #258 (Nashville), 2004

But even if a goalie hits it big first thing in the NHL, that's no guarantee of long-term success. Look at the goalies who have won the Calder Trophy as the NHL's top rookie, and you'll find a lot of great netminders, including Hall of Famers Terry Sawchuk, Gump Worsley, Glenn Hall, Tony Esposito, Ken Dryden, Tom Barrasso, and Marty Brodeur. Still, there have been more than a couple of Calder Trophy never-minders: Mike Karakas, Frank McCool, Jack Gelineau, and Andrew Raycroft.

So where do we put the Columbus Blue Jackets' Steve Mason? Mason started off as a world-beater — Ontario Hockey League goalie of the year in his next-to-last year of junior, followed by a season punctuated by a gold medal — and tournament MVP honors — with Team Canada at the 2008 World Junior Championship in the Czech Republic. In 2008–09, he was the best young goalie in the NHL, a 20-year-old Calder Trophy winner with — as they say — a sparkling 2.19 goals-against average, 33 wins, and 10 shutouts in 61 games.

Since then, however, Mason's game has suffered. Seasons two and three in Ohio comprised a prolonged sophomore slump. By the week before Christmas 2010, he had been pulled 12 times in a season and a half, most in the NHL. And his goals-against average ranked 39th — not good in a league with 30 teams.

Making matters worse, the 21-year-old had just signed a two-year, $5.8 million contract.

Blue Jackets goalie coach Dave Rook caught "Mase" sulking one day and grunted, "You're 21, you are a millionaire, you have lots of support — why are you so miserable?"

Later, at dinner, Rook, who worked with Mason in London, told the goalie he needed to improve his fitness level, work ethic, and attitude. The problem, he said, wasn't between the pipes, it was between his ears. His body needed work. So did his body language.

Stop watching Jumbotron replays, shaking your head and getting down on yourself, Rook told Mason. Take a drink of water from the squirt bottle atop the net, forget about the last shot and worry about the next one.

"The whole premise was he was sabotaging himself," Rook later told the Columbus Dispatch. "He was told things he didn't want to hear, but deep down, he knew they were true. . . Part of the process of being a top-end goalie is dealing with issues from the shoulders up. . . Steve has a burning desire to be the best, but sometimes you forget there's a process you must go through to be the best."

And sometimes part of the process is being traded. Columbus began 2011–12 as the worst team in the NHL, with a fuming Mason again being pulled from the nets early many nights.

Perhaps the Calder Trophy–winning goalie he best resembles is Gump Worsley, the fitness-challenged netminder who endured a decade of turmoil for the woeful New York Rangers in the 1950s, only to emerge a Vezina Trophy winner for Montreal the next decade.

"Which team gives you the most trouble?" Worsley was once asked by reporters.

"The New York Rangers," was his famous reply.

A meeting of the minds: Steve Mason and Rick Nash

One-year WONDER BOYS

Here are six goalies who set the world on fire, but only for a short while.

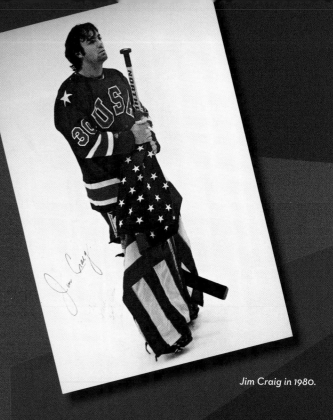

Jim Craig in 1980.

ANDY "THE GLASGOW GOBBLER" AITKENHEAD
This Scottish-born goalie won the Stanley Cup for the New York Rangers as a rookie in 1932, throwing an overtime shutout against Toronto in the deciding game. Two seasons later, he was no longer in the NHL. His problem was nerves, not ability. His successor in New York, Dave Kerr, said of Aitkenhead: "He'd lock himself in his room after a game and play the game over and over. By the time the next game rolled around, he'd played 48 games in that room."

JIM CRAIG
It's a great folk story: a Massachusetts kid with two shamrocks on his mask fights through the grief of his mom passing away to lead David (American college kids) over battle-proven Goliath (Russia) in the 1980 Winter Olympics. The Miracle Worker goes to the NHL's Atlanta Flames, where he leads his team to a 4–1 win in his first game. He would succumb to ulcers and self-doubt. But for a year, anyway, Jim Craig stood atop the mountain.

BLAINE LACHER
Lacher gave up his final year of eligibility at Lake Superior State University to join the Boston Bruins in 1994, where he was stellar, recording four shutouts with a 2.41 goals-against average. In the playoffs, he was almost as good as Marty Brodeur. In the pivotal fourth game, Boston and New Jersey were tied 0–0 in overtime, when a Boston defender lost the puck while circling around the net. Randy McKay whacked it into the net. And with that, the career of Blaine Lacher, "The Net Monster," was pretty well over. He played 12 more games in the NHL.

JIM CAREY
Nicknamed "The Net Detective," "Ace," and "The Mask" because he started his netminding career around the same time as film comedian Jim Carrey. The goalie won the Vezina Trophy in 1995 with Washington Capitals, posting a team-record 2.13 goals-against average. He was almost as good the next two seasons, but his game mysteriously fell apart at age 23. He was gone from hockey two seasons later.

STEVE PENNEY
Came out of nowhere (okay, the AHL's Nova Scotia Voyageurs) to lead Montreal to nine straight playoff wins, including three shutouts, in the 1984 playoffs, before losing to the Stanley Cup–winning New York Islanders. The Ste. Foy native (a francophone) was great the next season, too. Then another Ste. Foy goalie arrived in Montreal. What was his name again? That's right... Patrick Roy.

ANDREW RAYCROFT
A Calder Trophy–winning sensation for the Boston Bruins in 2003-04, but a solid, career backup goalie four years later.

DALLAS STARS

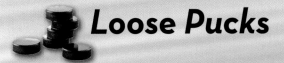

Loose Pucks

RECORD: "Timebomb" by Dallas band (and hockey fans) the Old 97's, played during Stars' games. When the Stars took the Stanley Cup in 1999, a commemorative album, featuring songs by Lynyrd Skynyrd, Twisted Sister, and guess what song by Pat Benatar ("Hit Me with Your Best Shot") was released.

RECORDS

MOST HAT TRICKS, CAREER: Dino Ciccarelli, 16

MOST POWER-PLAY GOALS, CAREER: Brian Bellows, 134

MOST GAME-WINNING GOALS, CAREER: Mike Modano, 71

BEST PLUS/MINUS, CAREER: Jere Lehtinen, +176; Mike Modano, +118

MOST PENALTY MINUTES, CAREER: Shane "Churlish," 1,883

50-COAL CLUB: Brian Bellows, 55, 1989–90; Dino Ciccarelli, 55, 1981–82; Ciccarelli, 52, 1986–87; Modano, 50, 1993–94

WORKING OVERTIME: In the what-a-difference-a-year-makes department: on June 19, 1999, the Stars' Brett Hull scored in triple OT to clinch the Stanley Cup against Buffalo. Yayyyy! On June 10, 2000, Jason Arnott scored on Ed Belfour in double OT to give New Jersey the Stanley Cup over Dallas. *Unhhhhh.*

DRAFT-SCHMAFT

TOP-10 PICKS, 1989–2009: 6

PLAYERS DRAFTED WHO PLAYED 300 NHL GAMES: 22

IMPACT PLAYERS: Derian Hatcher, 8th, 1992; Jere Lehtinen, 82nd, 1992; Marty Turco, 124th, 1994; Jarome Iginla, 11th, 1995; Brenden Morrow, 25th, 1997; Loui Eriksson, 33rd, 2003

DRAFT-SCHMAFT RANKING: 19th

LINE CHANGES

STARS BILLBOARD CAMPAIGN SLOGANS:

"The only thing our refs shave is the ice."

"The ticket covers the hockey. The boxing is a bonus."

"One game in a week? Is the N in NFL for Nancy?"

"At 32 degrees water freezes and blood boils."

"Watch people fight at work."

"Maybe baseball should stop using the word sacrifice."

SKATE THAT ONE PAST ME AGAIN: The deep-in-the-heart-of-Texas Stars are French. Kinda. The team was originally the Minnesota North Stars, who took their name from the state motto, "*L'étoile du Nord*" — French for "the star of the North."

Loui Eriksson finds the net against Los Angeles.

BRING ON THE ZAMBONI

CELEBRITY FANS: Alt-country/rock band the Old 97's. Thrash-metal band Pantera, authors of the tune "Puck Off." Singer-songwriter Willa Ford.

STUMP THE SCHWAB: Name every member of the Pony Express who comprised the Minnesota North Stars' head coaching brigade between 1977 and 1979. Answer: Ted Harris, Andre Beaulieu, Lou Nanne, Harry Howell, and Glen Sonmor.

Loui, Loui

Quiet as a light bulb and appreciated only by those lucky to pick him up cheap in hockey pools, Loui Eriksson is a quicksilver Swedish forward with a gift for goal scoring. In the 2010–11 season he was named the most underrated player in the NHL by his peers. He had four points in the 2011 NHL All-Star Game, including the game-winner. Loui has averaged over 30 goals a year between 2008–09 and 2011–12.

> "A quicksilver Swedish forward with a gift for goal scoring."

FAN-tastic

(Left) A super-cool Dallas fan invites a photographer to his crib. (Middle right and bottom left) Sign language from disgruntled fans. (Bare bottom right) A guy looks surprisingly happy to lose a bet.

KINGS AVERY JERSEY $225.00
RANGERS AVERY JERSEY $195.00
STARS AVERY JERSEY $225.00
BEING AN AVERY FAN-PRICELESS

ANNOYING STARS FAN 1

Sweater GIRLS

Once upon a time, hockey players married into the business, reproducing with a sense of genetic purpose. Montreal great Boom Boom Geoffrion married Marlene Morenz, the figure-skating daughter of Montreal even-greater Howie. Bobby Hull wed a figure skater, Joanne, who begat former Star Brett Hull, whose son Jude is a Minnesota high school goaltender.

Lots of NHLers have moms who were competitive figure skaters. — Dion Phaneuf's mother skated for Prince Edward Island, while Scott and Rob Niedermayer's mom, Saskatchewan.

Doug Gilmour married a Maple Leaf Gardens usherette. San Jose Sharks analyst Bret Hedican, a former player, wed gold medal Olympian Kristi Yamaguchi. Current TSN hockey commentator and one-time NHL star Ray Ferraro hooked up with Team USA women's team captain Cammi Granato. Philadelphia Flyer goalie Ron Hextall, grandson of Bryan, the guy whose overtime goal won the 1940 Stanley Cup for New York Rangers, married Diane Ogilowski, a figure skater. Their kid Brett is currently on Phoenix's top farm team.

If Brett makes the NHL, he'll be the second fourth-generation player in NHL history, after Nashville's Blake Geoffrion — that's right, the great-great grandson of Howie Morenz. See how it used to work?

Even on the Dallas Stars, we have evidence of love in a cold climate. Captain Brenden Morrow married former teammate and coach Guy Carbonneau's daughter, Anne-Marie. Still, in Dallas and elsewhere, we have more examples of hockey players skating on thin ice, hooking up with actresses, singers, and — uh-oh — models.

Pretty soon, the NHL will be handing out a Heart Trophy for hottest hockey wives. In which case, Dallas would lead the league. The quarterback of the 2011-12 power play is Sheldon Souray, a point man with a slap shot timed at 106.7 miles an hour (that's fast) and a wife who once starred on *Baywatch* (that's faster).

Some like it cold: Hockey wives (left to right) Brandy Blake (Mrs. Rob Blake), Angelica Bridges (Mrs. Sheldon Souray), Willa Ford (Mrs. Mike Modano) and Rachel Hunter (Jarret Stoll's fiancée).

The franchise's greatest player, Mike Modano, a Star from 1989 to 2010, married Willa Ford, a singer and former Lingerie Super Bowl competitor. Sean Avery, a Star for a few games in 2008, dated actresses Rachel Hunter and Elisha Cuthbert.

How did this happen? Face guards? Maybe Don Cherry is right. Players start wearing plastic protection and forget what a hockey player's mouth is for — swearing and spitting out teeth.

Here, for those who can stand it and need to know, is a travelogue of how hockey evolved into a glamour profession, if not an outright erogenous zone.

THE LAP DANCE. The New York Rangers hit Broadway in 1926. Swells and showgirls show up. Hollywood's "Blonde Bonfire," Lana Turner, appears rinkside with actor friends in the late 1930s. Ranger Neil Colville spots her and makes like a boiling kettle. "Bump me over the boards into her lap," he tells a teammate. Returning to the bench, Colville looks deflated. "How'd it go?" his pal asks. "Fine, if you happen to be crazy about Edward G. Robinson," Colville responds, brushing off Little Caesar's cigar ashes. Didn't matter: hockey had made the scene in Manhattan. Perhaps not coincidentally, in 1946 the Rangers were the first NHL team to televise home games.

LEAF IN WOLVES' CLOTHING. In the 1930s, the University of Southern California beat UCLA in hockey, using imported Canadians. The USC Trojans evolved into the Hollywood Wolves of the Southern California Hockey League, led by Edmonton center Harry Black,[1] who helped the Wolves to an amateur championship in 1944 over the Boston Olympics, a Bruins farm team. Later, future Maple Leaf hero Bill Barilko launched his pro career with the Wolves and was routinely decorated with starlets in publicity shots. Wolves games were televised on KTLA in Los Angeles. When the Leafs called him up, Bill's sister figured he'd been demoted.

1 Harry Black's son, Harry "Bud" Black, later pitched and coached in baseball's major leagues.

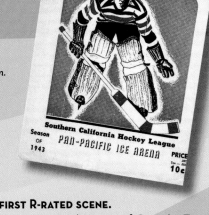

A Hollywood Wolves program.

HOCKEY'S FIRST R-RATED SCENE.
Hugh MacLennan wrote the story of Canada, *Two Solitudes*, in 1945. A sign that hockey was getting hotter: MacLennan's book included the first hockey pillow talk ever published:

There was a scar on his left thigh and another on his chest; when he rolled onto his stomach another appeared on the lower part of his back. She traced it with her finger. "How did you get that?"

"Hockey."

"All of them?"

"Yes."

"It's a good thing you stopped playing."

"That's not why I stopped playing."

"Why did you, then?"

"It took too much out of me." He rolled over on his back again. "After every game I was like a limp rag. And before every game I'd have to tighten myself up. You're useless unless you start nervous."

"You love hockey, don't you Paul?"

"I used to."

Hockey is a sexy, bred-in-the-bone Canadian specific, to paraphrase Al Purdy. MacLennan, a Nova Scotian who thrived in Montreal (like hockey itself), theorizes the sport is the necessary counterpoint to Canadian self-restraint: "To spectator and player alike," he writes, "hockey gives the release that strong liquor gives a repressed man."

TWO SOLITARY DUDES. Two number nines emerged in the 1940s, exciting an epic blood feud. Maurice Richard was the French 9 — the Rocket, a glory-or-shame competitor who exploded in vengeance. Gordie Howe was the English 9 — a graceful hulk with a propensity

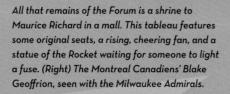

All that remains of the Forum is a shrine to Maurice Richard in a mall. This tableau features some original seats, a rising, cheering fan, and a statue of the Rocket waiting for someone to light a fuse. (Right) The Montreal Canadiens' Blake Geoffrion, seen with the Milwaukee Admirals.

for (galling to the other side) Pearl Harbor sneak attacks. Howe and Richard helped turn hockey into a civil war zone.

BLACK AND WHITE BLACKHAWKS. The Chicago Blackhawks televised home games on WBKB, in 1946–47.

BOOM TIMES. Eddie Martin of the all-black Halifax Eurekas reportedly employed a slap shot as far back as 1905. Historian James Duplacey figures the first mention of hockey's most glamorous weapon is a 1924 *New York Times* article describing how Minnesota's Moose Goheen beat a Boston club with a "slap shot." The New York Rangers' Bun Cook performed slappers in practice and taught the maneuver to teammate Alex Shibicky, who used it in an NHL game in 1937. But it doesn't matter where the shot came from: the guy who popularized windmilling the puck at goalies was hockey's Mr. Onomatopoeia — Boom Boom Geoffrion. As a junior, Geoffrion grew frustrated with his wrist shot in practice and slapped at the puck. Hmmmm. The thing really took off. He spent years honing his

discovery, blasting shots at the boards, earning the nickname "Boom Boom" from Montreal Star reporter Charlie Boire. The Boomer joined the Canadians in 1950. Hockey had the nuclear bomb.

COLD WARS. Hockey came to Canadian TV in the fall of 1952. One week, the country would gets the Habs; the next, the Leafs, accentuating an already uncivil hockey war. TVs were soon a mandatory household appliance. A 1955 edition of *Canadian Broadcaster & Telecaster* reported a besieged retailer in Rimouski delivering TVs to isolated customers by snowmobile prior to the playoffs.

THERE'S A RIOT GOIN' ON. On St. Patrick's Day 1955, NHL president Clarence Campbell suspended Rocket Richard for the playoffs for bopping a ref. Canada's family feud turned ugly. A Montreal bus driver, stunned by the news of the suspension, had a heart attack and veered off the road. Montreal erupted that night during a Habs–Wings game, as spilled Rocket fuel ignited the city. The next morning, rivers of broken

(Background) Jacques Plante dons a mask.
(Foreground) Gerry Cheevers' DIY scream.

glass and charred storefronts extended for miles in every direction from the Montreal Forum. Many say the Richard Riot marked the beginning of Quebec's Quiet Revolution.

LOVE POTION NUMBER 9. Hockey's first sex symbol, Bobby Hull, broke into the NHL with Chicago in 1957 at age 18. He was first given number 16, then 7, before donning the mythical 9. Movie-star handsome and built like Tarzan, Hull could fly. And his untraceable slap shots scared a generation of goalies into wearing masks. The Golden Jet helped win Chicago a Stanley Cup in 1961, and in '66 broke hockey's equivalent of the four-minute mile, the 50-goal plateau. On TV and in magazines, he was everywhere, unleashing a glad mercenary smile — selling hair tonic, swimsuits, and fast times.

HOCKEY HORROR PICTURE SHOW. On November 1, 1959, Montreal goalie Jacques Plante threw out a hip behind the net, sending Ranger Andy Bathgate into the Madison Square Garden boards. In retaliation, Bathgate shot a puck at Plante's bare head, spreading his nose flat against his face. Plante returned wearing what looked like a Halloween mask. Fitting, given it's the day after All Hallows Eve. Within a decade, virtually all goalies were wearing masks.

HALLOWEEN, PART 2. In 1968, Boston goalie Gerry Cheevers got hit in the mask during practice, so he returned to the dressing room. Coach Harry Sinden found his goalie smoking, presumably unhurt, so he yelled at him to get back on the ice. Using a felt-tip pen, Cheevers marked stitches on his mask. *See? I am hurt*. Hockey now had a lurid, thrilling accessory: the designer hockey mask.

BOSS TOWN. The 1960s didn't arrive in North American sports until late in the decade, when the Boston Bruins emerged as the most thrilling, of-the-moment team around. The Bruins wore their hair long while everyone else still sported the military cadet look. And talk about anti-hero cool: Boston dressed in bad-guy black (Phil Esposito even wore an inky turtleneck, like Steve McQueen in *Bullitt*). Derek Sanderson appeared on *The Tonight Show*, waving a cigarette and complaining about "chicks" in Niagara Falls, his hometown.

Once, Bobby Orr arrived at Massachusetts General dressed as a surgeon, then hustled his fallen comrade Esposito's bed into an elevator: "Emergency, doctors coming through!" The team skated Espo down icy Boston streets. "Left turn, stick out your hand," Orr told the patient. Inside a bar, the Bruins inserted a ripe provolone in Esposito's lap and a beer in each hand. The fun-loving Bruins won Stanley Cups in 1970 and 1972.

Orr was a compelling contradiction — a shy virtuoso who wove his way through the entire opposing team — sometimes twice! — before scoring, and then returned to the bench, head down, humbled by his ambition. Suddenly, everyone wanted to be a Boston Bruin. Dr. Charles Sanderson of Passaic, New Jersey, names his son Derek Sanderson Jeter in 1974. For inspiration, basketballer Larry Bird stared up at Orr's Boston Garden banner during pregame anthems in the 1980s. Espo was name-checked on New England bumper stickers ("Jesus saves, but Esposito scores on the rebound") and later in a song by hip-hop's Fun

Lovin' Criminals ("Check that ass like Phil Esposito, the guido, UPS next day back to Toledo.")

The Orr-Esposito Bruins were Boston's team. Before long, hockey players would emerge from New England — Tom Barrasso, Tony Amonte, Bobby Carpenter, Rod Langway, John LeClair, Brian Leetch, and Jeremy Roenick all donned blades while Orr was a Bruin. Intellectuals, goofballs, dark princes — everyone loved the Bruins. George Plimpton, editor of the *Paris Review*, wrote a book about playing goal for them (*Open Net*). Comedian Denis Leary, star of the TV series *Rescue Me*, and the filmmaking Farrelly brothers stocked their works with Bruins.

Cam Neely, former Bruins star and current team president, appeared in Rescue Me and the Farrellys' *Dumb and Dumber, Me, Myself and Irene*, and *Stuck on You*. Neely also dated actress Glenn Close.

Rapper Lil Wayne is — what else? — a Bruins fan.

THE INTERNATIONAL AFFAIR. A team of Canadian NHL all-stars played the Soviet Union's best in the fall of 1972. The West vs. Eastern Europe. . . capitalism vs. communism. . . beer against vodka. Pennants and sweaters turned into flags. Hockey was now more important — a militaristic thrill. The West/capitalism/beer won. Barely.

Saints preserve us: (Left) Derek Sanderson on a Boston magazine cover. (Right) A stained-glass messiah, Bobby Orr on the window of John Harvard's Brew House in Cambridge, Massachusetts.

Boston January 1971 75¢
The Beatification of Derek Sanderson

THE BEST HOCKEY SONGS YOU CAN NAME. New Brunswick–born singer-songwriter Stompin' Tom Connors wrote "The Hockey Song" in 1972. "Hello out there, we're on the air, it's hockey night tonight. . . The goalie jumps and the players bump and the fans all go insane. Someone roars, 'Bobby scores!' at the good old hockey game." Alberta-born singer-songwriter Joni Mitchell wrote *Raised on Robbery* a year later: "He was sitting in the lounge of the Empire Hotel . . . Little money riding on the Maple Leafs / Along comes a lady in lacy sleeves." Hockey could now be played on guitar.

BOBBY III. Bigger and badder than the Big Bad Boston Bruins, the Philadelphia Flyers gave Pennsylvania two Stanley Cups in 1974 and '75 — and provided hockey with a necessary dramatic component: a company of villains dressed in Halloween orange. Their leader was Bart Simpson under a Shirley Temple wig: Bobby Clarke.

(Above) A hockey 10: Ranger Ron "Doogy" Duguay

GIVE ME DANGER, LITTLE RANGER. The New York Rangers became hot on Broadway in the late '70s. Phil Esposito (traded from Boston), boyishly handsome Ron Duguay, Dave Maloney, and Anders Hedberg appeared in TV commercials for Sasson jeans. Duguay was romantically linked to Cher, Farrah Fawcett, supermodel Cheryl Tiegs, and Bianca Jagger in Manhattan gossip pages. Eventually, he married supermodel Robin Bobo and, later, Kim Alexis. Hockey players were now officially chick magnets.

RULES OF THE GAME. Writer Nancy Dowd had her minor-league hockey-playing brother tape-record between-game bus trips, then turned overheard conversations of the North American Hockey League's Johnstown Jets into a touching, frequently hilarious Peter Puck/Peter Pan comedy about young (and not so young) men who were afraid of growing old and leaving their toys behind. Paul Newman, the star skater in the 1977 movie *Slap Shot*, was 52 at the time. The "retarded," toy car–playing Hanson brothers,[2] were in their late 20s. Loved everywhere, particularly in Quebec (where it was dubbed into *joual*), the film included the classic hockey lesson, given by Quebecois goalie Denis Lemieux to an American broadcaster.

CARR: Hi, Jim Carr again. Denis, I know that some in our audience don't know the finer points of hockey. Could you tell them, for example, what is icing?
LEMIEUX: Well, um, icing happen when the puck come down, bang, you know, before the other guys, you know. Nobody there, you know. My arm go *comme ça* (raises it) and then the game stop, then start up.
CARR: I see. What is high-sticking?
LEMIEUX: High-sticking happen when the guy take the stick, you know, and he go like that . . . you know?
CARR: Uhh [*recovering*] . . . you don't do that?
LEMIEUX: Against the rule. You know, you're stupid when you do that. Just some English pig with no brains, you know.

2 The Hanson Brothers were played by Steve and Jeff Carlson and David Hanson. Steve Carlson and Hanson would play in the NHL.

"Two minutes, by yourself, you know, and you feel shame, you know. And then you get free."

CARR: Uh, what is slashing?

LEMIEUX: Slashing is, um, like that . . . you know.

CARR: Uhh [*recovering*]. . . And there's a penalty for that?

LEMIEUX: Yeah, and for the trip also, you know, like that. . . And for hook, like this. . . And for spear, you know, like that. [*Jim Carr takes a beating.*] You do that, you go to the box, you know. Two minutes, by yourself, you know, and you feel shame, you know. And then you get free.

BLUE ANGELS. The St. Louis Blues introduced cheerleaders to hockey in 1978–79. Give me an F, give me an E, give me a D, E, R, K, and O. What's that spell? *Federko!*

ROCKY ON ICE. A team of U.S. palookas upset the mighty Red Army in 1980. Following hockey is now a patriotic act in America, Canada, Scandinavia, and Eastern Europe.

DOG SOLDIERS. Red-white-and-blue Snoopy doghouses began sprouting up in the hometown of Peanuts creator Charles Schulz after America's 1980 gold medal win.

HALLOWEEN, PART III. The script for *Friday the 13th* (1982) called for mad murderer Jason Voorhees to wear a mask. Before filming began, "Jason" needed a lighting check. Special effects supervisor Martin Jay Sadoff was a hockey fan who packed an equipment bag. He gave Jason a Red Wing mask, and a pop culture icon was born. Soon, every Halloween was *Hockey Night in North America*.

ROYAL WEDDINGS. Los Angeles Kings 50-goal scorer Charlie Simmer married Playmate of the Year Terri Welles in 1981 at the We've Only Just Begun Wedding Chapel in Las Vegas. New York Ranger Ron Greschner married supermodel Carol Alt in 1983.

WAYNE'S WORLD. The most exciting hockey team ever assembled, the Wayne Gretzky–Jari Kurri–Mark Messier–Glenn Anderson–Paul Coffey edition of the Edmonton Oilers, took the ice in Alberta in the 1980s, winning five Stanley Cups and setting goal-scoring records that will never be broken. The centers on the Cup champion Toronto Maple Leafs of 1966–67 — Dave Keon, Bob Pulford, and Red Kelly — accumulate a total of 50 goals and 75 assists, for 125 points. In 1985–86, Gretzky tallied 52 goals and 163 assists for 215 points all by his lonesome. Edmonton's provincial rivals, the Calgary Flames, were almost as good. Their rivalry split a province. A bar in Red Deer drew a line down the middle to separate fans. If these two teams had played in New York and Los Angeles, who knows how hot hockey (and hockey players) might have become in the States?

Of course, hockey's bogeymen, the Philadelphia Flyers, have a goalie in their system named Jason — Jason Bacashihua, and, that's right, he wears a mask that pays homage to Jason from Friday the 13th.

Wayne and Janet untie one on.

OILER DISCOVERED IN L.A! Wayne Gretzky married Hollywood starlet Janet Jones in 1989 and was traded to L.A. to play for the Kings. Before long, he was hosting *Saturday Night Live*. Jari Kurri eventually followed suit, marrying a former Miss Finland, Vanessa Forsman.

NEW YORK WINS EDMONTON'S SIXTH STANLEY CUP. Ex-Oilers Messier, Anderson, Adam Graves, Kevin Lowe, Craig MacTavish, Esa Tikkanen, and Jeff Beukeboom help New York win the Stanley Cup in 1994. Millions watch the Stanley Cup float down Broadway, then turn up, with Mark Messier, on David Letterman's show. Bring on the girls!

SEE JANE SCORE. In 1998, Rachel Gibson began her *New York Times*–bestselling hockey romance series with the novel *Simply Irresistible*. Deirdre Martin made the bestseller lists with *Body Check* in 2003. Elle Kennedy delivered another *Body Check* for Harlequin in 2009.

FROM RUSSIA WITH LOVE. Pavel Bure married a fashion model upon arriving in North America and signing with the Vancouver Canucks in 1990. Brother Valeri married actress Candace Cameron in 1996 while with Montreal. The Detroit Red Wings' Sergei Fedorov romanced, married and was cross-checked by tennis celebrity Anna Kournikova, the world's most Googled woman, in 2001.

HIT MUSIC. Hockey caught rock and roll fever as the Tragically Hip offered up a powerful hymn to Bill Barilko, "Fifty Mission Cap." Kid Rock showed up at Red Wing games. Alice Cooper in Phoenix. Warren Zevon recorded an ode to Prairie enforcers, "Hit Somebody." Dallas's Old 97's were big Stars fans. The band played in Toronto the night the Stars won the Cup in 1999. "We ended up going on stage at the beginning of the third overtime because the promoters finally came and said, 'Guys, everybody's been waiting for hours,'" recalls singer Rhett Miller. "We didn't get to see Brett Hull kick the [game-winning] puck in. Slobberbone [the opening act] came out with no shirts on and had 'Stars win' written on their chests, and they were jumping around when they finally did win."

Old 97s Rhett Miller and Murray Hammond performing in the American Airlines Center in Dallas.

TOO SEXY FOR NEW YORK AND HELSINKI. In 2006, the Anaheim Ducks' Teemu Selanne was voted the sexiest man in Finland by readers of *Eeva* magazine. That same year, *People* magazine named Henrik Lundqvist one of the world's 100 most beautiful people.

. . . AND NASHVILLE. Mike Fisher of the Ottawa Senators married the reigning queen of country music, Carrie Underwood, in 2010. Next thing, he was traded to Nashville.

MODEL HOCKEY WIFE. No reason to panic, old-school hockey fans. Some NHL wives are trophier than others.

GOING ONE ON ONE. Time to give up. Here's a short list of hockey players and their celebrity girlfriend/wives:

Maxim Afinogenov	Elena Dementieva (tennis player)
Mike Comrie	Hilary Duff (actress)
Tie Domi	Belinda Stronach (politician), Kelly Carlson (actress), Tia Carrere (actress)
Patrik Elias	Petra Volakova (TV hostess)
Ray Emery	Keisha Chanté (singer, actress)
Scott Hartnell	Lisa Hartnell (model)
Nathan Horton	Tammy Plante Horton (model)
Dan Hinote	Amy McCarthy (actress)
Tomas Holmstrom	Annelie Holmstrom (Olympic swimmer)
Cale Hulse	Gena Lee Nolin (*Baywatch* actress)
Jaromir Jagr	Inna Puhajkova, Andrea Veresova, Iva Kubelkova (Czech models)
Eric Lindros	Kate Hudson (actress)
Daniel Marois	Martine Bernier (Playboy model)
Ryan Miller	Noureen DeWulf (actress)
Peter Nedved	Veronika Varekova (supermodel)
Dion Phaneuf	Elisha Cuthbert (actress)
Tomas Plekanec	Lucie Vondrackova (Czech actress-singer)
Ladislav Smid	Amanda Vanderpool (TV hostess)
Jarret Stoll	Rachel Hunter (*Sports Illustrated* swimsuit model)
Scottie Upshall	Melanie Collins (NBA-TV reporter)
Alexei Yashin	Carol Alt (former model)
Henrik Zetterberg	Emma Andersson (Swedish singer)
Dainius Zubrus	Nathalie Sanschagrin (model)

For instance, Bruins forward Nathan Horton's wife, Tammy Plante Horton, onetime *Playboy* coed of the week, is also a great-niece of seven-time Vezina Trophy winner Jacques Plante. The popularizer of the goalie mask also won the Hart Trophy as the league's MVP in 1962.

Mike Modano and Willa Ford — she's the one not wearing a tie.

DETROIT RED WINGS

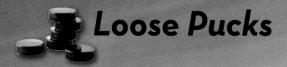

Loose Pucks

RECORD: "Detroit Rock City" by Kiss is played before Red Wing games.

RECORDS:

MOST HAT TRICKS, CAREER: Gordie Howe and Steve Yzerman, 18 each

MOST GOALS, CAREER: Gordie Howe, 786

MOST EVEN-STRENGTH GOALS, CAREER: Steve Yzerman, 440

BEST GOAL-PER-GAME PERCENTAGE, CAREER: Mickey Redmond, 0.56

BEST PLUS/MINUS, CAREER: Nicklas Lidstrom, +450, Sergei Fedorov, +276

50-GOAL CLUB: Steve Yzerman, 65, 1988–89; Yzerman, 62, 1989–90; Yzerman, 58, 1992–93; Sergei Fedorov, 56, 1993–94; John Ogrodnick, 55, 1984–85; Mickey Redmond, 52, 1972–73; Ray Sheppard, 52, 1993–94; Redmond, 51, 1973–74; Yzerman, 51, 1990–91; Yzerman, 50, 1987–88; Danny Grant, 50, 1974–75. . . aw, hell, let's give Gordie some love: 49, 1952–53

WORKING OVERTIME: Sergei Fedorov holds the NHL record for overtime points, with 27 (15 goals, 12 assists).

DRAFT-SCHMAFT

TOP-10 PICKS, 1989–2009: 2

PLAYERS DRAFTED WHO PLAYED 300 NHL GAMES: 27

IMPACT PLAYERS: Nik Lidstrom 53rd, 1989; Sergei Fedorov, 74th, 1989; Vladimir Konstantinov, 221st, 1989; Keith Primeau, 3rd, 1990; Slava Kozlov, 45th, 1990; Chris Osgood, 54th, 1991; Mike Knuble, 76th, 1991; Darren Mc-Carty, 45th, 1992; Tomas Holmstrom, 257th, 1994; Pavel Datsyuk, 171st, 1998; Niklas Kronwall, 29th, 2000; Jimmy Howard, 64th, 2003; Johan Franzen, 97th, 2004

DRAFT-SCHMAFT RANKING: 1st (tied with Colorado)

LINE CHANGES

THE PRODUCTION LINE: Sid Abel, Gordie Howe, and Ted Lindsay, 1947–52

THE HUM LINE: Paul Henderson, Norm Ullman, and Bruce MacGregor, 1960s

THE RUSSIAN FIVE: Sergei Fedorov, Igor Larionov, Vyacheslav Kozlov, Vladimir Konstantinov, and Viacheslav Fetisov, 1990s

"Well, what I did was bring the octopus in a brown paper bag. I always let the people sitting around know what I was going to do. Most of them took the news quite calmly. Once, though, this woman beside me let out a scream. I had leaned over and said to her very quietly, 'Look, I think you should know. I'm the octopus-thrower.' She couldn't take it." — Pete Cusimano, Red Wing fan and Detroit's first mollusk dispenser

Pavel Datsyuk dekes Ilya Bryzgalov, then with the Phoenix Coyotes.

"The Russian sees the game in slow motion, even as he slices between defenders."

"You can always get someone to do your thinking for you." — Gordie Howe, when asked why hockey players in the '60s never wore helmets but always wore jocks.

SKATE THAT ONE PAST ME AGAIN: Gordie scored the last of his 18 NHL hat tricks at age 51.

BRING ON THE ZAMBONI
CELEBRITY FANS: Kid Rock, actor Jeff Daniels, and actress Kristen Bell.

STUMP THE SCHWAB: Former Wing Howie Young played what movie star's double? Answer: Frank Sinatra (*None But the Brave*, 1965)

WINGMAN: Pavel Datsyuk

A cancelled flight prevented another scout from watching Pavel Datsyuk. Going into the 1998 NHL draft, only Detroit had seen him play. And so the Wings got the shy, slight center on the cheap — 171st overall. Growing up in a Sverdlovsk high-rise with no elevators made his legs fast and strong, but Pavel's real genius lies in his creative imagination: the Russian sees the game in slow motion, even as he slices between defenders. And his hands are as nimble as a Vegas croupier's.

Pavel has won four Lady Byng Trophies for his gentlemanly play. One reason: he never gloats over hockey's most YouTube-able goals. His best move is hypnotizing opponents with a head shiver, and then bending, off-balance, around his frozen prey, somehow keeping the puck on his stick. *Bing!* Another goal. Afterward, number 13 sails around the net, head down, stick on the ice, leaving the celebration for Detroit's thankful fans.

FAN-tastic

(Top) High-flying winger: A statue of Amelia Earhart at Harbour Grace, Newfoundland. The American aviatress flew from Harbour Grace in 1932. (Bottom left) Wings fan fiddles around. (Middle center) Months-old fan tries Gretzky's trick of baby-powdering his stick. (Middle right) A really left-wing Detroit fan. (Bottom right) Gallows hockey humor.

WHEN SHE PLAYS THE VIOLIN THE REDWINGS ALWAYS WIN!

Iron Man: Red Wings fans file past the statue of Gordie Howe outside Joe Louis Arena. Veteran fans know not to get close to the business end of Gordie's stick. You never know.

Hey, This Hat DOESN'T FIT

The phrase "Gordie Howe hat trick" entered the public lexicon on December 17, 1989, when *Toronto Star* hockey reporter Frank Orr, writing the game summary of a Maple Leafs loss to the Minnesota North Stars, threw in, late in his story, "Basil McRae, who had what his mates called a Gordie Howe hat trick — a fight, a goal and an assist — gave the Stars a 2-0 lead."

The first time a player bragged of pulling a Gordie to an interested scribe was December 22, 1991, when Brendan Shanahan, then with the Blues, wiggled his way into a piece by Dave Luecking of the *St. Louis Post-Dispatch*, focusing on Brett Hull's conventional, three-goal hat trick against the New York Islanders. "[I got] a *Gordie Howe* hat trick: a goal, an assist and a fight," Shanahan told Luecking. (He'd scored on Steve Weeks and tussled with Rich Pilon.) The expression caught on around 2000. And then caught fire. The saying found its way into 143 English North American newspapers in 2010. You hear it all the time

on sports radio. The term is now one of a slew of catchphrases that entered the hockey lexicon in and around the goal- and fight-clogged years from 1980-81 to 1991-92. Another one? How about going "five hole," or scoring between a goalie's legs — first used in print by Al Strachan in *The Globe and Mail* on May 29, 1985.

Then came the three words that ended Gretzky's Roaring '80s: "neutral zone trap," the practice of lying back, clogging the middle, putting the other team (and sometimes fans) to sleep (John Dellapina, *The Record* [New Jersey], October 3, 1991).

But back to Gordie; how did he come to epitomize a full, ferocious night's hockey work? That's easy, sort of. While playing major pro hockey for 32 seasons (between 1946-47 and 1979-80), a run that spanned the presidencies of Harry Truman and Ronald Reagan, Howe played right wing with consummate skill and occasional savagery. Only Wayne Gretzky surpassed Mr. Hockey's lifetime scoring record of 2,589 points. And big Gordie, for 25 seasons a Detroit Red Wing, spent close to a day and a half in the penalty box — 1,905 minutes.

Howe also won one of hockey's most memorable fights, in 1959, catching reigning NHL heavyweight "Leapin' Lou" Fontinato with a chopping right that bent his nose against his face, rudder left, spilling a bucket of blood.

And so there you have it, right? The Gordie Howe hat trick — a Gordie for short — explained forever.

Except a full look at Howe's career indicates that Howe himself only had two Gordies: one on October 10, 1953, against the Leafs, when he scored, assisted on a Red Kelly goal, and fought defenseman Fern Flaman to a draw, and another the following spring, when he scored, twice set up Ted Lindsay, and fought the Maple Leafs' Teeder Kennedy, again to a no-decision.

Gordie's career tale of the tape consists of 21 fights, including two wins (against Howie Meeker and Fontinato), seven losses (Bill Ezinicki, Fred Shero, Bill Judza, Flaman twice, Tim Horton, and Larry Cahan), and a pile of no-decisions, including a memorable draw against Rocket Richard in 1949.

What are we to make of all that? Not much. There weren't many fights in the NHL way back when. Gordie fought 21 times in 32 seasons. Red Wing forward Bob Probert went at it 40 times his first year in the NHL (1985–86). "Why fight?" Gordie likely reasoned. You could get hurt. In fact, he dislocated a finger and hurt a rib battling Fontinato.

Then there was the pain to your wallet. In an October 20, 1946, fight against the Leafs' Bill Ezinicki, an encounter that the 18-year-old Gordie was losing, referee King Clancy shouted, "Cut it, Ezinicki, or it will cost you $25." That would have seemed a fortune back when gas was 21 cents a gallon and two draft beers went for 15 cents at a tavern.

No, hockey may be murder on ice, as sportswriter Jim Murray wrote, but before games were televised from a dozen prying angles, the killings took place when cops weren't around, with nobody looking. Hockey fights were almost accidents, cases of tempers exploding in front of a referee. And Howe, who had fractured his skull and almost died in a game early in his career, would engage windmilling attackers with limited enthusiasm, like the rope-a-doping Muhammad Ali, caught in a corner by a determined opponent, late in his career.

This is hardly news, by the way. No one back in the day figured Gordie for a big fighter. Nevertheless, he had a reputation for taking care of business. "Despite an even temperament and a real distaste for combat, there is a part of Howe that is calculatingly and primitively savage," Mark Kram wrote in *Sports Illustrated* in 1964. "He is a punishing artist with a hockey stick, slashing, spearing, tripping and high-sticking his way to a comparative degree of solitude on the ice."

Gordie preferred meting out frontier justice on the sly. He was also prepared to bide his time, waiting for just the right moment. One night in 1957, Maple Leafs rookie Bobby Baun caught number 9 skating with his head down. *Oooffff!* Gordie had to be assisted back to the bench for smelling salts. A thousand games later, in 1968, Baun was playing for the white-booted California Golden Seals when Howe swooped down his side of the ice, hoping to score. Or so Baun thought.

Just as Howe raised his stick to shoot, Baun fell to block the puck. After releasing the shot, Gordie let his stick follow through, stabbing the defenseman in the throat. As Baun lay struggling for breath, Howe skated past, bending at the waist to whisper, "Now we're even."

No penalty was called.

Okay, so we've established that Gordie isn't the right guy to wear Detroit's heavyweight hat-trick crown. Historically speaking, then, who is? Ted Lindsay, Gordie's ruffian linemate, liked to fight, right? (His best weapon was a jab to the stomach with a Northland stick.) Nope, Terrible Ted only pulled off a Gordie twice.

Who, then, on the Wings? Think about it. Players would probably have to have played in the modern era, specifically in the 1980s and '90s. And they'd have to have to be scrappers who lined up on the first line. Played on the power play. That simplifies matters. Captain Steve Yzerman was centering the big line back then. Who were his most truculent wingers?

Bingo, you've got the top three Gordie Howe hat tricksters — and, incidentally, the NHL's top two Gordie-getters of all time. Any bets you don't get the first one right?

NUMBER 3: BOB PROBERT (SEVEN GORDIES WITH DETROIT, TWO LATER WITH CHICAGO)

Probie fits the profile: big, tough, with soft hands that balled into hard fists. Number 24 played on Stevie Y's line for much of the late '80s, when most of his Gordies took place. Longtime Detroit fans might figure he would rank higher, but he only scored as many as 20 goals once after his big 1987–88 season when he collected 29 goals, 33 assists, and 398 minutes in penalties.

PROBERT'S RED WING GORDIES

FEBRUARY 8, 1986, VS. MONTREAL — lost a close decision to Chris Nilan, scored a goal against Patrick Roy

MAY 1, 1987, VS. TORONTO — narrow win over Chris Kotsopoulos, goal against Ken Wregget

DECEMBER 4, 1987, VS. CHICAGO — decision over Curt Fraser, scored against Murray Bannerman

DECEMBER 14, 1987, VS. NEW YORK RANGERS — won a bloody battle with Mark Tinordi, goal against Bob Froese

MARCH 28, 1987, VS. PHILADELPHIA — lost a slugfest to Craig Berube, slipped one past Ron Hextall

APRIL 9, 1987, VS. TORONTO — narrow win over Al Iafrate, scored on Ken Wregget

NOVEMBER 13, 1992, VS. PITTSBURGH — took a close decision over Jay Caulfield, two goals against Tom Barrasso

"He is a punishing artist with a hockey stick, slashing, spearing, tripping and high-sticking his way to a comparative degree of solitude on the ice."

NUMBER 2: BRENDAN SHANAHAN (NINE GORDIES WITH DETROIT, EIGHT OTHERS WHILE PLAYING WITH NEW JERSEY, ST. LOUIS, HARTFORD, AND NEW YORK RANGERS)

That's right, our current NHL disciplinarian is the league's all-time Gordie leader, with 17. If Probert had lots of fights (302) and a modest number of goals (178), it was the other way around with Shanahan, whose career totals include 129 brawls and 716 goals. For the record, Shanahan regularly lined up on Yzerman's left wing on the power play and often five on five as well. (Coach Scotty Bowman liked to mix and match wingers.)

SHANAHAN'S RED WING GORDIES

DECEMBER 13, 1996, VS. CHICAGO — clobbered by none other than Bob Probert a minute into the game, goal against Ed Belfour

NOVEMBER 9, 1997, VS. CALGARY — came out even in a fight with Jarome Iginla, scored on Rick Tabaracci

FEBRUARY 9, 1999, VS. NASHVILLE — no-decision vs. Bob Boughner, goal against Mike Dunham

MARCH 21, 1999, VS. PHILADELPHIA — outpointed Luke Richardson, two goals against Ron Hextall

JANUARY 6, 2000, VS. NASHVILLE — beat up Bob Boughner, two goals on Mike Dunham

OCTOBER 10, 2001, VS. CALGARY — draw with Bob Boughner (boy, these guys danced with each other so often it was like they were going steady), scored on Roman Turek

APRIL 1, 2002 VS. TORONTO — lost (with a bad wrist) to Wade Belak, slipped one past Corey Schwab

DECEMBER 31, 2003, VS. ATLANTA — narrow victory over Garnet Exelby, goal against Pasi Nurminen

MARCH 30, 2006, VS. NASHVILLE — decision over Scott Hartnell, scored on Tomas Vokoun

Detroit and Chicago fans wearing Probert pajamas get close to the action of the 2009 Winter Heritage classic played at Wrigley Field.

NUMBER 1: GERARD GALLANT (15 GORDIES WITH DETROIT)

A bit of an eye-opener, but then Gallant's entire NHL career was a heartening surprise. Drafted in the sixth round by Detroit in 1981, the Prince Edward Islander was thought too small (5'10", 186 pounds) and slow to play power forward. An oversized motor under his Red Wing crest kept him on the team's top line nevertheless. From 1986–90, he averaged over 35 goals and 235 penalty minutes a season. Small in stature, he lacked a knockout punch. But as Fred Shero once said, it's not important how many fights you win, but how many you show up for. Gallant was a battler, recording an incredible, never-to-be-broken record of seven Gordies (including 12 goals) in one calendar year (1998).

GALLANT'S DETROIT GORDIES

NOVEMBER 2, 1985, VS. ST. LOUIS — won fight with Mark Reeds, scored on Greg Millen

DECEMBER 31, 1986, VS. CALGARY — no-decision vs. Gary Suter, goal against Mike Vernon

FEBRUARY 20, 1987, VS. QUEBEC (1 GOAL, 2 ASSISTS) — no-decision vs. Gord Donnelly, scored against Clint Malarchuk

MARCH 10, 1987, VS. VANCOUVER — no-decision vs. Dave Lowry, two goals against Richard Brodeur

APRIL 25, 1987, VS. TORONTO — no-decision against Grant Ledyard, potted two on Ken Wregget

OCTOBER 23, 1987, VS. PITTSBURGH — no-decision against Rod Buskas, a goal against Gilles Meloche

NOVEMBER 25, 1987, VS. WINNIPEG — win over Doug Smail, a goal on Pokey Reddick

JANUARY 7, 1988, VS. ST. LOUIS — draw vs. Rob Ramage, scored on Greg Millen

JANUARY 15, 1988, VS. MINNESOTA — draw against Gordie Roberts, goal against Don Beaupre

APRIL 10, 1988, VS. TORONTO (2 GOALS, 1 ASSIST) — lost fight to Todd Gill, two goals against Ken Wregget

APRIL 25, 1988 VS. ST. LOUIS (2 GOALS) — fight with Brian Benning, two goals against Rick Wamsley

NOVEMBER 1, 1988, VS. WASHINGTON — draw with Bob Gould, popped two past Clint Malarchuk

NOVEMBER 6, 1988, VS. EDMONTON (2 GOALS) — no-decision vs. Craig Muni, two goals on Grant Fuhr

NOVEMBER 29, 1988, VS. NEW JERSEY — draw with Jeff Norton, two counters against Billy Smith

FEBRUARY 11, 1989, VS. MINNESOTA — outpointed by Bob Rouse, goal against Mark Fitzpatrick

CONCLUSION

While the Gordie Howe hat trick is a misnomer, it is somehow appropriate that the term is associated with the Detroit Red Wings, as two Wings, Brendan Shanahan and Gerard Gallant, top the NHL's all-time Gordies list. Certainly, Detroit fans enjoy the feat. When Pavel Datsyuk pulled off a Gordie in the first game of the 2010–11 season, scoring on Anaheim's Jonas Hiller, assisting on a marker by Dan Cleary, then, later in the game, throwing himself at big, mean Corey Perry like a kid taking on his big brother, fans at the Joe Louis Arena were ecstatic.

"I'm happy to have Gordie Howe hat trick, but it's not my best dream," Datsyuk said after the game.

For Wings coach Mike Babcock, watching Datsyuk fight was a nightmare. Just as former Detroit coach Tommy Ivan must've sweated it out every time Gordie Howe started throwing lefts and rights.

"He's a real good player and really strong, but I don't need to see Pav fight anymore," Babcock admitted after the game.

DETROIT RED WING POST-GAME SNACK

The Arby's fast-food chain once gave out curly fries to Michigan customers after any Red Wing recorded a three-goal hat trick. Some locations still do, apparently. All customers have to do is bring in a hat trick scorecard and . . . free hot potato!

Cat in the hat trick: Detroit hockey fan enjoys free curly fries after a Nik Lidstrom hat trick.

EDMONTON OILERS

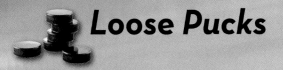

Loose Pucks

RECORD: "The Oil's Back in Town" by the great Corb Lund (go see him if you ever get the chance). Inspirational verse: "*There ain't no louder building than the house of 99 / Got the echoes of the dynasty a-burnin' in their minds / You better cheer 'em on, they're the roughest necks around / Cause it's hockey night in Edmonton / The Oil's back in town.*"

RECORDS:

MOST HAT TRICKS, CAREER: Wayne Gretzky, 43; Glenn Anderson, 20; Jari Kurri, 20

MOST POINTS BY A DEFENSEMAN, ONE SEASON: Paul Coffey, 138, 1985–86

MOST GAME-WINNING GOALS, CAREER: Glenn Anderson, 73; Wayne Gretzky, 61; Jari Kurri, 60

BEST PLUS/MINUS, CAREER: Wayne Gretzky, +551; Jari Kurri, +367

MOST SHUTOUTS, CAREER: Tommy Salo, 23; Curtis Joseph, 14; Grant Fuhr, 9

50-GOAL CLUB: Wayne Gretzky, 92, 1981–82; Gretzky, 74, 1983–84; Gretzky, 73, 1984–85; Gretzky, 71, 1982–83; Jari Kurri, 71, 1984–85; Kurri, 68, 1985–86; Gretzky, 62, 1986–87; Gretzky, 55, 1980–81; Glenn Anderson, 54, 1983–84; Anderson, 54, 1985–86; Kurri, 54, 1986–87; Gretzky, 52, 1985–86; Kurri, 52, 1983–84; Gretzky, 51, 1979–80; Mark Messier, 50, 1981–82

WORKING OVERTIME: In game one of the 1990 Stanley Cup finals, Boston's Ray Bourque scored two late goals to tie the game, then Edmonton and Boston battled through three overtimes and two power outages. Mark Messier missed an open net once. And the lights in Boston Garden went out in the third overtime, causing a half-hour delay. Late in the sixth period of play, Edmonton coach John Muckler threw out Petr Klima, who'd been benched for four periods. Klima ended the game upon touching the puck, snapping a wrist shot between Andy Moog's legs. *Edmonton Sun* reporter Terry Jones would once say of the Czech forward, "Petr Klima is 32 years old, played 12 years in the NHL and has never broken a sweat."

DRAFT-SCHMAFT
TOP-10 PICKS, 1989–2009: 7

PLAYERS DRAFTED WHO PLAYED 300 NHL GAMES: 27

IMPACT PLAYERS: Martin Rucinsky, 20th, 1991; Kirk Maltby, 65th, 1992; Jason Arnott, 7th, 1993; Miroslav Satan, 111th, 1993; Ryan Smyth, 6th, 1994; Tom Poti, 59th, 1996; Shawn Horcoff, 99th, 1998; Mike Comrie, 91st, 1999; Ales Hemsky, 13th, 2001; Jordan Eberle, 22nd, 2008; Taylor Hall, 1st, 2010; Ryan Nugent-Hopkins, 1st, 2011

DRAFT-SCHMAFT RANKING: 6th

LINE CHANGES
CZECHS-MEX LINE: Raffi Torres, Petr Sykora, and Ales Hemsky (2006–07). Torres is Hispanic, while Sykora and Hemsky are Czechs.

Ryan Smith in a practice jersey.

BABY OIL: Current youngsters Taylor Hall, Ryan Nugent-Hopkins, and Jordan Eberle.

"What's next? The goalies stopping for a picnic? Should we put fried chicken and cheese and crackers there too?" — Edmonton coach Glen Sather, seething after goalies started putting water bottles on top of the nets in the early 1980s.

"Part of the learning curve in Edmonton is learning how to hate Calgary." — Steve Smith (who later played in Calgary)

"If you take your eye off Gretzky, he'll bank it off your skate, your back, your helmet or your wife. I could hang a nickel in the net and he'd hit it every time." — Floyd Whitney, Edmonton Oilers practice goalie in the 1980s.

SKATE THAT ONE PAST ME AGAIN: In the book *I'd Trade Him Again*, former Oiler owner Peter Pocklington said he once proposed trading franchises with the woeful Toronto Maple Leafs in the early 1980s. Toronto would've received a team full of future Hall of Famers — Gretzky, Messier, Coffey, Fuhr, and Kurri — and $50 million. Edmonton would've got Ballard and Walt Poddubny.

BRING ON THE ZAMBONI

CELEBRITY FANS: Kobe Bryant and 50 Cent have been seen in Oiler tourist garb. Alt-country rocker Corb Lund is a real fan, as is comic book auteur Todd (*Spawn*) McFarlane, who was once a part owner of the club.

STUMP THE SCHWAB: Name the six goalies who started for the Oilers in their debut NHL season (1979-80). Answer: Eddie Mio, Jim Corsi, Dave Dryden, Ron Low, Don Cutts, and Bob Dupuis.

RYAN the First

Before Ryan-Nugent Hopkins, before Ryan Jones, Ryan Whitney, Ryan Stone, even before Ryan Potulny and Ryan O'Marra, there was Edmonton Oiler original Ryan: Ryan Smyth, a born-in-Alberta Oiler-for-life. The team's stick boy at 11, Ryan didn't even complain when a team member ran him down in a hotel parking lot. Smyth was tying his laces (you have to be careful) when Glenn Anderson backed over him. Hey, sprained ankle, it was nothing. Even as a kid, Smyth had an incredible pain threshold. Once, he broke his left thumb and the doctor designed a cast that allowed him to shoot right-handed. "He scored five or six goals that next game," his dad remembered. Smyth made the Oilers in 1995, playing well enough his second season to tie a Gretzky scoring record (most power-play goals in a season, 20.) He put in 11 exemplary campaigns for Edmonton and cried — wept openly — when sent from the team in 2006. Being traded by the Oilers was the only injury he couldn't abide. There followed five years in the wilderness, during which the power forward did his thing — plowing fearlessly to the net in search of goals. He returned to Edmonton in the fall of 2011, ready to finish out his career, an Oiler forever.

FAN-tastic

(Top) Getting out in summer to catch some blu-rays. (Bottom left) Oil be home for Christmas: Former stars Mark Messier (wearing toque) and Paul Coffey return. (Bottom right) Northern hockey lights.

Boy Band of BROTHERS

The week that 18-year-old Ryan Nugent-Hopkins's mother, Deb, ordered his high school graduation photos, he collected three NHL goals and assists. So did linemate Jordan Eberle, 21. Their regular left wing, Taylor Hall, 20, was hurt and so was kept off the score sheet.

At least in the real world. At home, in an executive apartment overlooking the Edmonton River Valley he shares with "Ebs," who knows how many goals "Hallsy" scored on the roommates' copy of NHL 12.

That's what the roommates do on nights before a game: they sink into a black, L-shaped couch with enough leather to upholster a fleet of Buicks, fire up the game console, and play as themselves while shoveling down a tub of ice cream.

Elsewhere in Edmonton, Nugent-Hopkins lives with teammate Ryan Jones, who tells everyone who asks, "Nuge is a really good roommate. He just sleeps." That's when he isn't hooked up to his own game machine, playing Halo (interstellar war), Call of Duty (regular war), or dreaming about an exploding Rocket. When he was 12, you see, Nugent-Hopkins saw the Maurice Richard biopic *The Rocket* and was instantly transfixed. From then on, he himself was number 9, hero-in-waiting. The Rocket is his favorite player.

The most talented assortment of young guns to draw together since Toronto's Kid

1 Doug Messier played minor-pro hockey, mostly in Edmonton and Portland.

Line (Charlie Conacher, Joe Primeau, and Busher Jackson) way back in the late 1920s, Edmonton's Boy Band of Brothers are still obviously a dreamy bunch. But they do come with impressive pedigrees.

Regina's Jordan Eberle has been killing teams ever since he scored an overtime winner to beat Steve Stamkos's club. Both were 10 at the time, playing in the finals of the 2000 Brick Pee Wee Tournament in Edmonton. Eberle was tournament MVP.

Jordan Eberle also scored one of the biggest goals in junior hockey history, tying Russia with seconds left in the 2009 gold-medal final. Canada won in OT.

Taylor Hall has the royal jelly as well. His Australian-born dad, Steve, played CFL football and was, for 12 years, a member of the Canadian Olympic bobsleigh team. Mom Srba's favorite player growing up was Bobby Orr, which is why Taylor wears number 4. Orr is also Taylor's agent. And if Calgary-born son of a pro Hall's boisterous play is reminiscent of Edmonton-born son of a pro Mark Messier's game, it should also be mentioned that Taylor grew up with a more adventurous home skating surface than Walter Gretzky's Rink of Dreams.

The Hall rink had more pizzazz, circling the house like a frozen moat. (A sturdy, tongue-shaped carpet was thrown out the front door to the street to allow the safe passage of Canada Post.) During practice, Dad would be at one end, clad in goaltender equipment, guarding a net.

The boys in blue: Ryan Nugent-Hopkins (93), Taylor Hall, and Jordan Eberle (14) after a goal at home.

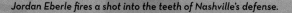

Jordan Eberle fires a shot into the teeth of Nashville's defense.

"GO!" he'd yell out.

Taylor would then kick into high gear, stickhandling with his head up as he made the turn. "Four seconds later, he would be coming around the Lindros Loop and then to the left or the right of the Scott Stevens Tree," Steve told Calgary *Herald* reporter Vicki Hall.

The what and what? The Lindros Loop is a reference to former star Eric Lindros's periodic head-down stroll through the middle of the ice. The Stevens Tree was a poplar the Taylors named after New Jersey Devil crusher Scott Stevens. Years ago, Stevens famously interrupted a Lindros loop with an unforgiving shoulder.

"If you hit [the tree], you were in trouble," goalie Steve elaborated. "You weren't going anywhere."

"You didn't want to hit it," Srba confirmed.

Taylor lived on the family rink in winter and would start playing an hour before school. One night, when Taylor was 13, his dad took him to see *Miracle*, the Kurt Russell movie celebrating America's 1980 Olympic win. The guys returned home at 10 p.m., and Taylor regurgitated the plotline to his barely interested mother. *And then they did this. And then they did that.* Half an hour later, it was time for bed. But what was that sound? *Rssssk-rsssk-rsssk.* Taylor was outside again, practicing the Lindros Loop.

Nobody really expected Ryan Nugent-Hopkins to make the Oilers after the 2011 training camp. Like Hall the season before, he'd arrived in Edmonton as the first-overall pick at 18 years of age. But where speedy, quick-grinning Taylor was a solid 200 pounds and came with regulation, V-shaped NHL shoulders, Nugent-Hopkins

weighed a lot less, by as much as 30 pounds, maybe. Nor was he as fast on his skates. And he looked like. . . well, like someone named Nugent-Hopkins. Like the grocery clerk who carries bags out to your mom's car and then lopes away before she can fish into her purse for a loonie. When Nugent-Hopkins made the team, Hall tweeted, "New equipment guy for the year."

Except the Hyphenated One was an immediate sensation. It didn't matter that he wasn't big or fast or strong; like Gretzky or Duke Ellington long ago in jazz, Nugent-Hopkins's great talent lay not in playing but conducting. On a power play, especially at home, with a thrilled Rexall Centre crowd on the edge of their seats, the teenager spread out a defense with a shift or two of his shoulders, then set up Eberle or Hall with crisp, on-the-tape passes.

As with linemate Hall, there is a backstory that explains his uncanny puck poise. Growing up in Burnaby, outside Vancouver, Nugent-Hopkins's father would spread hockey pucks around the basement. Then Ryan would stickhandle marbles through the maze, his head up the whole time.

He'd do that for 20 minutes at a time, year after year through adolescence, blindly controlling a half-inch marble until his brain, wrists, and hockey stick were one.

Ryan had an agent and trainer at age 14, but make no mistake, none of Nugent-Hopkins, Hall, or Eberle skated trough adolescence on Easy Rink. Roger Nugent, Ryan's dad, battled cancer when his son was nine. The family didn't have enough money for Ryan to compete in pee wee one year.

Dreaming in color: Can Nugent-Hopkins return to Edmonton to Stanley Cup glory?

And all three players battled through junior as hockey protégés, a daunting marathon of games, practice, school, sleep, and tournaments. "The Western Hockey League humbles you," Roger Nugent once said of his son's life. "It's not easy to play three games in four nights in four cities, get home on the team bus at 3 a.m., and go to school the next morning."

In his last weeks of high school, Nugent-Hopkins was training to bulk up to 170 pounds while pushing his English grades over 60. And so he was on the ice before breakfast, then hitting *King Lear* and *Death of a Salesman* after dinner.

He graduated. They all did. Now they're "Halls," "Ebs," and "Nuge," cornerstones of an Edmonton franchise that once got high swilling from the Stanley Cup, winning five times between 1984 and 1990. Can they do it again, even once?

It would be unfair to suggest it's just up to this threesome. The great Edmonton dynasty had enough cornerstones to build a castle. After Gretzky and Messier there were Fuhr, Coffey, Kurri, Anderson, Tikkanen, and Lowe. And the old Oilers had lots of unheralded players come up big in the playoffs. Key contributors to the 1990 Stanley Cup included Adam Graves, Joe Murphy, and goalie Bill Ranford.

Still, Nugent-Hopkins, Hall, and Eberle are going to have to lead the way. They have to become soldiers to a common cause — have to have each other's front, back, and sides.

That probably means they'll have to adopt a few more hyphens — become Nugent-Hopkins-Hall-Eberle. That's not happening quite yet. "We try to hang out with Nuge as much as possible, but for the most part he kind of likes to be off on his own," Hall once told a reporter.

The first evidence that the old Oilers might be something special appeared during the 1981 playoffs, when the boys started singing on the bench while upsetting the top-ranked Montreal Canadiens. And the song went something like this:

"Here we go Oilers, here we go. Here we go Oilers, here we go."

(Left) Hall's summer stick work; (Top right) Ryan Nugent-Hopkins.

FLORIDA PANTHERS

Loose Pucks

RECORD: The Panthers hit the ice to Godfrey Townsend's psychedelic guitar workout, "Gaga Over Raga."

RECORDS:

MOST HAT TRICKS, CAREER: Pavel Bure, 10, Ray Sheppard 5, Ollie Jokinen, 4

MOST GAME-WINNING GOALS, CAREER: Ollie Jokinen, 31

MOST SHUTOUTS, CAREER: Roberto Luongo, 26

BEST PLUS/MINUS, CAREER: Martin Gelinas, +34

50-GOAL CLUB: Pavel Bure, 59, 2000–01; Bure, 58, 1999–2000

WORKING OVERTIME: In 1996, the Panthers reeled off two straight playoff overtime wins, on goals by Dave Lowry and Mike Hough, to upset the Flyers, winning hockey's only Orange Bowl — a series between teams wearing bright orange sweaters. The Cats went all the way to the finals that season, losing to Colorado.

DRAFT-SCHMAFT

TOP-TEN PICKS, 1992–2009: 10

PLAYERS DRAFTED WHO PLAYED IN 300 NHL GAMES: 22

IMPACT PLAYERS: Ed Jovanovski, 1st, 1994; Stephen Weiss, 4th, 2001; Jay Bouwmeester, 3rd, 2002; Nathan Horton, 3rd, 2003

DRAFT-SCHMAFT RANKING: 23rd (tied with Calgary)

SKATE THAT ONE PAST ME AGAIN: The San Antonio Rampage, Florida's AHL affiliate, established a world record for the most dogs ever to attend a sporting event — 854 — at the 2012 edition of the annual Pucks and Paws Game.

BRING ON THE ZAMBONI

CELEBRITY FANS: Supermodel Niki Taylor dated Panther Rob Niedermayer for a while.

STUMP THE SCHWAB: Which former Panther holds the NHL record for most saves in a shutout? Answer: No, not Roberto Luongo, who has the most shutouts (26), but Craig Anderson, who stopped all 53 shots in a March 2, 2008, whitewashing of the New York Islanders. Two nights later he beat Boston 1–0, making 40 stops.

"*Perpetually poor and playoff-less...*"

Kris Versteeg gets ready for some target practice.

What A DIFFERENCE A Day Makes

Perpetually poor and playoff-less — that was a good description of the Florida Panthers in early June 2011. The team that had not won a playoff round since 1996 was $20 million under the league's suddenly enforced salary cap floor ($48.3 million). They'd shed a dozen contracts to get so skinny and needed bodies to fill the team's new (old) red uniforms. GM Dale Tallon went power shopping, trading for Brian Campbell and Tomas Kopecky from Chicago. Two down. On July 1, when NHL free agent agents dangled loose, Tallon and assistant Mike Santos war-roomed up, working the phones, Internet, and Twitter. A TV set playing TSN was left on. Tallon started Canada Day by re-signing Ed Jovanovski, a star for the Panthers

when they had playoff claws in the mid-'90s. Don Meehan was Jovanovski's agent. Santos advised Meehan that the Panthers wanted another of his clients, goalie Jose Theodore. Done. Florida got hold of Scottie Upshall, advising him they'd signed his old partner Jovanovski. Want aboard? Sure. "After Jovo and Scottie, the calls started coming in," Santos remembered. Sean Bergenheim enlisted. Tallon traded two draft picks to Philadelphia for scorer Kris Versteeg. Marcel Goc and Thomas Fleis-chmann were signed. Contracts were all lawyered and signed. Florida had a new hockey team. Most of the $20 million was gone. But Tallon still had enough money to take the Florida war party out to dinner.

ROCKET
Descending

He had greatness in him. Pavel Bure was named after his great-grandfather, watchmaker to Tsar Alexander III. A Swiss ancestor, Eduard Buré, invented the wristwatch. Pavel's father, Vladimir, won four Olympic medals in swimming. Pavel chose hockey and was good enough at 12 to skate with Wayne Gretzky on a Russian TV special. Two years later, he was the star of the Russian juniors, eventually fitting onto a line with Sergei Fedorov and Alexander Mogilny that was expected to push Soviet hockey supremacy into the New Millennium. The Soviet Union itself didn't last past 1991, however, and the line pursued fame and glory in the NHL. Somehow the most spectacular of the trio left the least mark. How was that possible? Pavel electrified his first NHL city, Vancouver. Thousands attended his first practice. The Russian Rocket beat Nicklas Lidstrom, an older player, for rookie of the year. He was the league's quickest player, with a blur-of-the-wrists inside-out move that tortured goalies. He scored 60 goals twice, taking the Canucks to the '94 finals. One playoff game, he stood behind the Toronto net, saw both exits covered, flipped the puck over the goalie's turned head, bolted past a defender, and converted his own pass into a shot on net. He scored five goals for Russia in a game against Finland in the 1998 Winter Olympics and was named the tournament's best forward. He was traded by Vancouver to Florida in 1999 and scored eight goals in his first five games as a Panther. He led the NHL in goals in consecutive seasons, with 58 and 59, despite playing on a weak offensive team. In 2000–01, he scored 29.5 percent of all Florida's goals — the highest percentage in NHL history. Gretzky told Ranger management that he would play another year if they could get Bure on his wing. They couldn't. Pavel was eventually traded to New York. He didn't last long — a chronically injured kneed forced him into retirement. The grandson of a watchmaker ran out of hockey time at age 32, in 2003.

FAN-tastic

Put your cat clothes on: Florida fans sporting every one of the team's recent uniforms

Bure isn't in the Hockey Hall of Fame. He never won a Stanley Cup and left a trail of disappointed fans. He was only really happy scoring goals. In the dressing room, talking to reporters, Pavel was a man in a dentist's chair. He was, as Churchill said of Russia, a riddle wrapped in an enigma. He was a hero in Vancouver until he demanded to be traded — he never said why — sitting out $4 million worth of games before getting his way. Usually, the player who resembled *Home Alone* star Macaulay Culkin was placid on ice. But there were flashes of violence, usually against bigger, tougher opponents. He was thrown out of games for attacking Shane Churla and, in the '94 playoffs, Jay Wells. He was said to have ties to Russian mobsters. He was engaged to sexy tennis star Anna Kournikova, on momentary loan from former linemate Fedorov. He changed his uniform number as often as he changed teams — 10, 96, 10 again, and 9. He once attempted to relaunch the Bure watch line in Russia. He retired in Florida, marrying in Miami in 2009. He occasionally slips into Panther games, where he is seldom noticed.

"He had greatness in him."

LOS ANGELES KINGS

Loose Pucks

RECORD: Dionne and the Puck-Tones (a.k.a. the Kings' Triple Crown Line of Dave Taylor, Charlie Simmer, and Marcel Dionne) in the studio, recording "Please Forgive My Misconduct Last Night."

RECORDS:
MOST HAT TRICKS, CAREER: Marcel Dionne, 24

MOST HAT TRICKS, ONE SEASON: Jimmy Carson, 5, 1987–88

MOST GOALS, ONE GAME: 4, by each of the following: Serge Bernier, Butch Goring, Mike Murphy (twice), Syl Apps Jr., Marcel Dionne (three times, including twice in one week in 1979), Charlie Simmer, Dave Taylor, Ian Turnbull, Bernie Nicholls (twice), Brian MacLellan, Jimmy Carson, and Luc Robitaille (twice)

BEST PLUS/MINUS, CAREER: Dave Taylor, +181, Marcel Dionne, +106

MOST SHUTOUTS, CAREER: Rogie Vachon, 32

50-GOAL CLUB: Bernie Nicholls, 70, 1988–89; Luc Robitaille, 63, 1992–93; Marcel Dionne, 59, 1978–79; Dionne, 58, 1980–81; Charlie Simmer, 56, 1979–80; Simmer, 56, 1980–81; Dionne, 56, 1982–83; Jimmy Carson, 55, 1987–88; Wayne Gretzky, 54, 1988–89; Dionne, 53, 1976–77; Dionne, 53, 1979–80; Robitaille, 53, 1987–88; Robitaille, 52, 1989–90; Dionne, 50, 1981–82

WORKING OVERTIME: On April 10, 1982, the Kings were down 5–0 in the third period of a playoff game to the first-place Edmonton Oilers led by Wayne Gretzky and Mark Messier. With 14 minutes left, Jay Wells clubbed one in from the point. And all of a sudden it was Grant Goals, not Grant Fuhr, in Edmonton's net. Doug Smith, Charlie Simmer, Mark Hardy, and, with five seconds left, Steve Bozek scored to tie it at 5–5. Daryl Evans won it early in overtime, capping the biggest comeback in NHL playoff history. The Kings went on to win the series.

DRAFT-SCHMAFT
TOP-10 PICKS, 1989–2009: 7

PLAYERS DRAFTED WHO PLAYED 300 NHL GAMES: 36

IMPACT PLAYERS: Kimmo Timonen, 250th, 1993; Olli Jokinen, 3rd, 1997; Lubomir Visnovsky, 118th, 2000; Mike Cammalleri, 49th, 2001; Dustin Brown, 13th, 2003; Anze Kopitar, 11th, 2005; Jonathan Quick, 50th, 2005; Drew Doughty, 2nd, 2008

DRAFT-SCHMAFT RANKING: 5th

LINE CHANGES
THE TRIPLE CROWN LINE: Dave Taylor, Charlie Simmer, and Marcel Dionne. Each of them recorded more than 100 points in 1980–81.

Drew Doughty flashes a Hollywood smile.
Not bad for a London, Ontario, boy.

THE LAPD LINE: Jason Allison, Ziggy Palffy, and Adam Deadmarsh, 2001–02.

"When he put out his arms to celebrate, the rest of us skated immediately to the bench and left him there all alone." — Dave Taylor, after Marcel Dionne received death threats

"You miss 100 percent of the shots you never take." — Wayne Gretzky

"I went to a fight the other night and a hockey game broke out." —Rodney Dangerfield

"What are you lookin' at, you hockey puck?" — Mr. Potato Head, _Toy Story_ 1995

SKATE THAT ONE PAST ME AGAIN: The Kings traded away 11 of 15 first-round picks between 1969 and 1983.

BRING ON THE ZAMBONI

CELEBRITY FANS: Jerry Bruckheimer, Sandra Bullock, Elisha Cuthbert, Cuba Gooding Jr., Alyssa Milano, Kurt Russell, Michael Vartan, and Rob Zombie.

STUMP THE SCHWAB: Name eight former Toronto Maple Leafs who coached the L.A. Kings. Answer: Red Kelly, Johnny Wilson, Larry Regan, Bob Pulford, Ron Stewart, Parker MacDonald, Pat Quinn, and Barry Melrose.

Royal ASCENT

Sharks forward Logan Couture slipped by a Kings defender to score in the 2011 playoffs, and then turned to see that he'd beaten his BFF, Drew Doughty. "You ——er!" Doughty shouted. Turns out they were, in fact, only BFUP — best friends until playoffs. In fact, if it weren't for Couture, Doughty might not be an NHL millionaire and marquee player for the Los Angeles Kings. Both loved sports other than hockey when they were growing up in London, Ontario. Couture won two national baseball skills competitions, while Doughty came from a football-soccer family — sister Chelsea is named after the famous UK soccer team, while Drew's mom, a Dallas Cowboys fan, named him after Drew Pearson, the All-Pro receiver. Come winter, however, Doughty and Couture were hockey teammates. At age 14, they had to pick a sport. "I remember [Logan] saying in the dressing room he wasn't going to play baseball anymore, and that when I decided not to play soccer," Doughty told the San Jose _Mercury News_. "I was better at soccer than hockey," he added, "but I knew being a soccer [goalie] in Canada wasn't going to take me far." That's not entirely true. Doughty allows that playing nets in soccer helped him read plays as they developed, a skill that has made him

FAN-tastic

(Middle right) We three Kings fans.
(Bottom left) Royal audience: Wayne
Simmonds with youngsters.

a star of the team he once rooted for. When the Kings' scout visited Doughty's house, the teenager invited him to his room, which featured an L.A. Kings telephone and pillowcase as well as a poster of Wayne Gretzky — Drew's hero for responding to a fan letter, a message that arrived a day before his sixth birthday.

NET Flicks

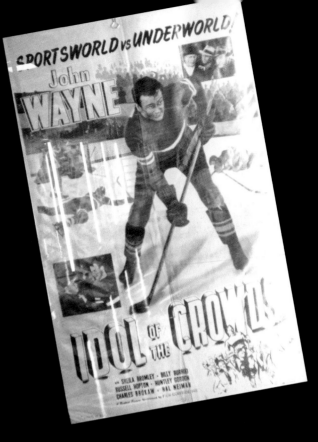

There are lots of differences between United States and Canada. The latter is colder in the winter; the former, hotter during elections. You want to discuss cultural differences between the countries that make up the 30-city NHL? Let's talk hockey movies, which reveal just how differently Canadians and Americans dream in public.

Take winning, for example. In Hollywood hockey movies — like *Miracle*, the story of the U.S. Olympic upset of Russian in 1980, or John Wayne's B-movie crowd-pleaser *Idol of the Crowds* — victory is hero time. Glory, glory, Hallelujah. In Canadian hockey movies, winners take nothing. Or, to quote the trailer for the 1971 Canadian cult hockey film *Face Off*: "[Here is a story] all about fighting your way to the top . . . And finding no one there."

Part of the issue here is temperament. Canadians aren't reserved, but can't help but appear so when standing next to Americans. Still, there is a more obvious reason why Canadian net flicks are shrink-wrapped in gloom: English-Canadian films seldom make it to theaters. When they do, audiences are small. Inevitably, hockey movies reflect the lonely, fruitless pilgrimage of their creators.

Because Hollywood movies are made only to make money, they hope to be entertaining. Because Canadian hockey films are made to secure government funding, they hope to be culturally illuminating.

Canadian hockey movies are *Soul on Ice*. Hollywood hockey movies are the Ice Capades.

But hey, enough of my yakking. What do you say let's look at some hockey movies, comparing three classic Canadian hockey films with their American cousins.

(Bottom) The bleeding, toy-playing Hanson brothers from Slap Shot. (Top) Right wing Duke Wayne in action.

I've been in the league for 12 years.
I've never seen no bylaws!

NHL PRESIDENT CLARENCE CAMPBEL: *They're right here.* [Brandishes a book.]

LINDSAY'S LAWYER: *May I see them, please?*

CAMPBELL: ## They're confidential.

LAWYER: ## How can a bylaw be confidential?

CAMPBELL: *Only the governors are privy to them. It says so right here in the bylaws.*

LAWYER: ## Well, you show me where it says that.

CAMPBELL: *You're prohibited from seeing the bylaws.*
It says so in the bylaw!

FIRST PERIOD

SLAP SHOT (1977). Aging minor leaguer Reggie Dunlop (Paul Newman) tries to save a floundering team, the Charlestown Chiefs, by turning hockey into a burlesque act, beating up every team in sight. His secret weapons: the Hanson Brothers, a forward line who play slot cars in their hotel room by day . . . and demolition-derby hockey at night. The film probably set out to be a dark parable about how the business of sport ruins games, but Reggie and the Hansons would appear to be having too much fun to care. Moviegoers presumed a working-class solidarity with Reggie and the boys. That, along with all the bawdy checks, makes *Slap Shot* an enduring favorite.

PAPERBACK HERO (1973). A gun-wielding hockey star (Keir Dullea), who rules his Prairie hometown like a Wild West sheriff, cracks up when his team folds. The film ends with a shootout at the Not-OK Corral. Shot on location, with a cameo by 1940s NHL star Max Bentley, the Dipsy-Doodle Dandy from Delisle, Saskatchewan. Peter Pearson's film is one of those probing, identity-crisis classics that keep university Canadian Studies courses going. If only students could find the damn thing — there's your identity crisis right there!

INTERMISSION FEATURE: Adam Sandler in **HAPPY GILMORE** (1996). "During high school, I played junior hockey and still hold two league records: most time spent in the penalty box, and I was the only guy to ever take off his skate and try to stab somebody."

SECOND PERIOD

MIRACLE (2004). Kurt Russell is Herb Brooks, the merciless, you'll-thank-me-later general who drove the Americans to victory over the Soviets in the 1980 Olympics. Typical slave-galley patter: "Red line, back. Blue line, back. Far blue line, back. . . Get used to this drill. You'll be doing it a lot. Why? Because legs feed the wolf, gentlemen; I can't promise you we'll be the best team at Lake Placid. . . but we will be the best conditioned." This is the Great Man Theory of history in throbbing CinemaScope, complete with a rah-rah finale that is guaranteed to put a puck in your throat.

CANADA RUSSIA '72 (2006). Skate spray to the face of anyone who believes that The Hockey Fight of Our Lives, the historic first meeting of Canadian pros and Russia's fabled national team, was a simple story of grit and glory. The miniseries depicts Canada's now-canonized hockey standard-bearers — Paul Henderson, Phil Esposito, Ken Dryden, et al — not as hockey heroes, but as frightened POWs who, in slaying the Russian bear, killed part of themselves. Even the miniseries' obligatory climax — Henderson's last-minute series-winning goal — becomes part of a somber, unsettling tableau. Canadian players celebrate the clinching tally on the ice and in the dressing room, as you might expect, but soon return in a trance to the dark cavern that is the now-empty Moscow arena. There, a familiar mosquito-hum guitar stirs alive, followed by the voice of gloom, Leonard Cohen, murmuring, "I stepped into an avalanche; it covered up my soul. . ."

Foiled again: Hanson brothers cruising for a bruising in figurine world.

INTERMISSION FEATURE: A scene from the CBC miniseries *Net Worth* (1995), the story of how the NHL squashed the players' attempt to form an association in the late 1950s.

THIRD PERIOD

IDOL OF THE CROWDS (1937). John Wayne on skates? Yes, and he twirls around like Hal Gill with a pail of beer in him. The film tells the story of Johnny Hanson, a Maine chicken farmer who is lured to the big city by the New York Panthers with the promise of a gaudy, $100-a-week paycheck. There's a crooked gambler, a screwball dame, and a poor kid in a hospital who needs Johnny to win the big game. Does he? Check the title.

SCORE: A HOCKEY MUSICAL (2010): Finally, a feel-good Canadian hockey movie, right? Yes, and it's a singing-dancing-shooting-and-scoring musical, with Olivia Newton-John. Wait a minute — sounds weird? Yes, deliberately so. *Score* insists that you understand you're watching a play-acting movie, a time-warp '30s musical, no less. Hollywood sports films are typically fodder for the crowds — team-building exercises. This Canadian film celebrates oddball integrity. The star, Farley Gordon (Noah Reid), quotes Gandhi: "An eye for an eye only ends up making the world blind."

"Finally, a feel-good Canadian hockey movie, right?"

THIRD STAR: Al Waxman playing fighting-mad Detroit GM Jack Adams in *Net Worth*.

SECOND STAR: Kurt Russell channeling Patton in *Miracle*.

FIRST STAR: Tom McCamus, *Waking Up Wally*.

The Top 30 (Plus One) Hockey Movies

1. **SLAP SHOT** 🍺🍺🍺🍺

2. **PAPERBACK HERO** 🍺🍺🍺🍺

3. **COWARDS BEND AT THE KNEE** (2003). You know from the opening shot, in which we look through a microscope at sperm and see hockey players, that this is primo Canadian Studies stuff. For graduate students only. From Winnipeg Jets fan Guy Maddin. 🍺🍺🍺🍺

4. **THE SWEATER** (1980). The National Film Board's take on Roch Carrier's story about a Quebec kid who receives— gasp! — a Maple Leaf sweater.
The divide between Upper and Lower Canada explained. 🍺🍺🍺🍺

5. **THE ROCKET** (2005). The Maurice Richard story features wondrous recreations of 1930s outdoor hockey. 🍺🍺🍺 ¹/₂

7. **SCORE: A HOCKEY MUSICAL.** 🍺🍺🍺 ¹/₂

8. **MIRACLE.** 🍺🍺🍺 ¹/₂

9. **NET WORTH.** 🍺🍺🍺

10. **MYSTERY, ALASKA** (1999). As preposterous as The *Mighty Ducks*, but almost as much fun as *Slap Shot*. With Russell Crowe (wobbling on skates) and Burt Reynolds. 🍺🍺🍺

11. **WAKING UP WALLY** (2005): Wayne's dad, Walter Gretzky, wakes from a stroke at 53, speaking Ukrainian. The film follows his heroic comeback. Tom McManus is brilliant as Wally. 🍺🍺🍺

12. **LES BOYS** (1997). *Le Slap Shot* du Quebec. Spawned three sequels. 🍺🍺 ¹/₂

13. **FACE OFF.** Cheesy and unrelievedly gloomy — Sid and Nancy on ice. Worth seeing, however, for the great, in-close NHL hockey footage from 1970. 🍺🍺 ¹/₂

14. **YOUNGBLOOD** (1986). Dean Youngblood (Rob Lowe) dreams of making it to the NHL. So does Patrick Swayze and a French-Canadian goalie played by Keanu Reeves (!). Superior schmaltz with lots of unique hockey curses. The best, addressed to a snarling fan: "Hey, go hump your St. Bernard, numb-nuts." 🍺🍺 ¹/₂

"The *Gladiator* of hockey movies."
— Brian D. Johnson, Maclean's Magazine

ROY DUPUIS
THE ROCKET
(MAURICE RICHARD)
A film by CHARLES BINAMÉ

His passion sparked a riot and ignited a legend

Produced by DENISE ROBERT · DANIEL LOUIS
Written by KEN SCOTT

(Right) Lego recreation of a scene from Slap Shot.

15. **BREAKFAST WITH SCOTT** (2007). Mild comedy about a gay hockey player who adopts his brother's stepson. Okay message film. The sermon: Love yourself, live and let live. 🍺🍺 ½

16. **KEEP YOUR HEAD UP: THE DON CHERRY STORY** (2010). Or, 400 *Hockey Blows* — Don Cherry's rough and tumble hockey life. Good performances, in particular by Sarah Manninen as Don's wife, Rose. 🍺🍺 ½

17. **GROSS MISCONDUCT** (1992). Atom Egoyan's autopsy on the short, unhappy career of fallen Leaf Brian Spencer. 🍺🍺 ½

18. **PRAY FOR ME, PAUL HENDERSON** (1989). A TV quiz show plays out during the '72 Russia–Canada hockey series. 🍺🍺 ½

19. **THE MIGHTY DUCKS** (1992). Boys of Teal! 🍺🍺 ½

20. **THE HOUNDS OF NOTRE DAME** (1981). Hockey's Hoosiers. 🍺🍺 ½

21. **HOCKEY NIGHT** (1984). Parry Sound's successor to Bobby Orr is a girl (Megan Follows). With Rick Moranis. 🍺🍺 ½

22. **IDOL OF THE CROWDS.** 🍺🍺

23. **THE LAST SEASON** (1990). CBC drama about a disintegrating hockey player. The Roy MacGregor novel it was based on is better.

24. **THE MIGHTY DUCKS 2** (1993). 🍺🍺 ½

MISSED THE PLAYOFFS

25. **GOON** (2012). A sunny idiot slugs and stammers his way through Maritime arenas, dreaming about a beautiful, unattainable girl. More a sequel to *Of Mice and Men* than Slap Shot.

26. **THE TOOTH FAIRY** (2010). The only hockey movie to star Julie Andrews. 🍺🍺

27. **THE CUTTING EDGE** (1992). 🍺🍺

28. **THE ROOKIES** (1991). 🍺🍺

29. **THE LOVE GURU** (2008). 🍺 ½

30. **SLAP SHOT 2** (2002). 🍺 ½

31. **THE RHINO BROTHERS** (2001). Canadian hockey movie directed by Dwayne Beaver. 🍺 ½

MINNESOTA WILD

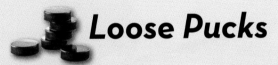

Loose Pucks

RECORD: The Wild have the NHL's best theme song: "State of the Game," a stirring, beer-in-hand sing-along. Inspirational verse: *"We were born with a stick and a pair of skates / On the ice we cut our teeth / We took our knocks in the penalty box / Our mother was the referee / The sport was here before we came / It'll be here before we're gone / The game's in our blood and our blood's in the game / Lay us down under a frozen pond. . ."*

RECORDS

MOST HAT TRICKS, CAREER: Marian Gaborik, 9

MOST GOALS, ONE SEASON: Marian Gaborik, 42, 2007–08

BEST PLUS/MINUS, CAREER: Marian Gaborik, + 54, Keith Carney + 30

MOST SHUTOUTS, CAREER: Nicklas Backstrom, 26; Dwayne Roloson, 15

50-GOAL CLUB: None

WORKING OVERTIME: The best 24 hours in Wild history came in 2003, when they scored consecutive overtime wins against the Colorado Avalanche. Richard Park fired one between Patrick Roy's pads at home in game six. The next night, in Denver, Andrew Brunette closed Colorado out, confusing Roy with an inside-out move, then tucking a backhand past the spinning netminder.

DRAFT-SCHMAFT

TOP-10 PICKS, 2000–2009: 5

PLAYERS DRAFTED WHO PLAYED IN 300 NHL GAMES: 8

IMPACT PLAYERS: Marian Gaborik, 3rd, 2000; Mikko Koivu, 6th, 2001; Brett Burns, 20th, 2003

DRAFT-SCHMAFT RANKING: 29th

LINE CHANGES

The Slovakian Trio: Branko Radivojevic, Pavol Demitra, and Marian Gaborik, 2006–07. Also known as the Super Slovaks and the Trencin Trio.

SKATE THAT ONE PAST ME AGAIN: None of the Trencin Trio won a Cup for Minnesota. Still, the Cup recently made it to Trencin (population 56,000) four years in a row. Bringing it all back home to the Big T were Tomas Kopecky (Detroit, 2008), Mirolsav Satan (Pittsburgh, 2009), Marian Hossa (Chicago, 2010), and Zdeno Chara (Boston, 2011).

BRING ON THE ZAMBONI

CELEBRITY FANS: Minnesota hockey fans. The only number the Wild have retired is 1, dedicated to the team's fans.

Wild goalie Josh Harding's mask includes images of facial ware worn by Jacques Plante, Ken Dryden and Gerry Cheevers.

STUMP THE SCHWAB: Who holds the NHL record for most hits in a season? Answer: Cal Clutterbuck collected 356 body blows in the 2008–09 season — pretty good for a guy Don Cherry called "Buttercup" for fighting with a visor.

The Mask(s)

Wild goalie Josh Harding went to Massachusetts mask artist Mike Myers to create a working tribute to goalie-protection history. The mask includes images of facial wear worn by Jacques Plante (that's Jake the Snake's mask above the right eyebrow), Ken Dryden, Gerry Cheevers, Tony Esposito, Terry Sawchuk, Ed Giacomin, and Pelle Lindbergh. Wait a sec. . . Mike Myers — wasn't he the insane killer from *Halloween* who wore a goalie mask? You don't think. . .?

> "**Pretty good** for a guy Don Cherry called 'Buttercup'"

FAN-tastic

SHOT OF THE GAME

SYLVANIA

A SHARK out of Water

Devin Setoguchi came to, and left, San Jose via trades. The team dispatched three draft picks to the Atlanta Thrashers in 2005 to gain access to the speedy, crash-the-net forward — a perfect match for play-maker Joe Thornton. "Seto" fit the bill from 2008 to 2011, emerging as an energetic, goal-scoring winger who seemed to get bigger in the playoffs.

On a team lacking prime-time players, Setoguchi more often than not came through. In 2011, Devin scored playoff overtime winners against Los Angeles and Detroit (in the latter instance, completing a hat trick).

The Japanese-Canadian forward was immensely popular with San Jose fans and loved playing for the Sharks. His grandmother back in Taber, Alberta, had 150 photos of her favorite Shark on a wall. In late June 2011, Setoguchi formalized his commitment to California, saying "I do" to a three-year, $9 million contract.

The next day, he was divorced, sent packing to Minnesota for defenseman Brett Burns.

Probably, Setoguchi was devastated. He was going from a contender to a rebuilding team. From California to the land of the wind chill factor. Tellingly, he remained in San Jose after the trade, working out with Sharks trainer Mike Potenza. He was in the Sharks' dressing room when his replacement, Burns, waltzed through the door.

"It was a little weird when Burnsie came walking through the double doors and I was standing there, working out," Setoguchi said.

"He's got Wild gear, working out in the Sharks' gym," Burns would say. "[GM] Doug Wilson gave me a tour of the rink, and he said, 'Oh, I think you know Seto.' I thought that was just really cool. I had just never seen that before. When you get traded, you never know, everybody is so nice and you never know if it's because you got traded. You see that, it just shows that that's the way it is."

Yes, that's the way it is. Most players change uniforms before their career is over. Gretzky represented five different cities as a big-league pro. Messier, five. Gordie Howe, three.

But not everyone survives a team change. Messier never fit in in Vancouver. Baseballer Jackie Robinson

refused to accept a trade to the New York Giants, a trip across the East River. And in football, another transfer from California to the Land of Lakes ended badly: Randy Moss sulked when traded from Oakland to Minnesota, but perked up again to become a New England All-Pro.

And Devin Setoguchi wilted in his first year in Minnesota. He was injured. He missed a meeting and was benched for a game against his former team, the Sharks. He missed the net and was demoted to the third line. He never seemed to get it going, and as this was written, the 25-year-old was en route to a sub-20-goal season.

What happened? Well, Minnesota didn't play well and Seto fit right in. A high-energy player, perhaps Seto missed the calamitous Shark tank arena in San Jose as much as he missed center Joe Thornton.

One thing Minnesota fans don't have to worry about, though, is Setoguchi turning into a Randy Moss–style quitter. He comes from resilient stock. His Japanese grandparents on his father's side, Ken and Nancy, were stolen from their Vancouver homes during World War II and transplanted to Taber, Alberta.

The Setoguchis prevailed, building a potato farm that, three generations later, remains the family business. Seto proved that he could endure hardship at age 10 when he was working on the farm and lost the

end of a finger on a conveyor. A week later, he was playing hockey.

Bet on Devin coming back in 2012–13.

NHLERS WHO HAD DIFFICULTY ADJUSTING TO A CHANGE IN SCENERY:

TED LINDSAY was 31 when the high-flying Detroit Wings punished him for his role in trying to start a players' association, trading him to Chicago in 1957. Discouraged, he went from being a 30-goal scorer to 15-goal man. Terrible Teddy bounced back the following season with 22 goals, however.

GILLES MAROTTE was supposed to the Boston's savior. He was a junior all-star who led the Niagara Falls Flyers to a Memorial Cup in 1965. But when an evidently better religious figure (and defenseman), Bobby Orr, arrived, Boston sent Marotte to Chicago in a package for future superstar Phil Esposito. Marotte didn't score in his first season in Chicago and was gone two years later.

After helping Boston to a Stanley Cup in 1972, feisty 26-year-old center **DEREK SANDERSON** signed a $2.5 million contract with the WHA's Philadelphia Blazers. "Day I signed for millions with Philadelphia, I rolled over and went to sleep," he said.

GARY LEEMAN scored 51 goals for Toronto, and two years later — at age 27 — was traded to Calgary in a deal for Doug Gilmour. He would never score as many as 10 goals in a season again.

A great two-way forward with New Jersey, Bobby Holik signed a five-year, $45 million contract with the New York Rangers in 2002. The Rangers bought out his contract two years later.

Florida traded Robert Luongo to Vancouver for **TODD BERTUZZI** in 2006. Their return? One goal in seven games.

A 30-goal man in Anaheim and Edmonton, **DUSTIN PENNER** was dealt to Los Angeles at the 2011 trading deadline. He has never been able to get it going in L.A., and in January 2012 hurt himself eating pancakes — back spasms. Weeks later, a cruel Vancouver hockey fan tried to get him off his game with a bottle of table syrup.

MONTREAL CANADIENS

Loose Pucks

RECORD: *Olé* comes from Spanish bullfighting — crowds shout "*Olé*" when the matador performs a heroic feint. At the 1992 Olympics in Barcelona, Neapolitans sang "*Olé, olé, olé olé, Diego, Diego*" in tribute to Diego Maradona. The first report of Montreal going *Olé* surfaced on April 22, 2003. The baseball Expos returned from opening their season in San Juan, Puerto Rico, and the crowd toasted them with some Spanish soccer caroling. The Expos won that night, 4-0, behind a Japanese pitcher, Tomo Ohka. "*Olé, olé, olé olé . . .*"

RECORDS

MOST TOURS DU CHAPEAU, CAREER: Maurice Richard, 26; Jean Beliveau, 18; Guy Lafleur, 16; Boom Boom Geoffrion, 14

MOST GAME-WINNING GOALS, CAREER: Guy Lafleur, 93; Yvan Cournoyer, 68

MOST GOALS IN ONE GAME: Newsy Lalonde, 6 , January 10, 1920 (Montreal beat the Toronto St. Pats, 14-7 — *Olé, olé, olé olé. . .*)

MOST BLANCHISSAGES, CAREER: George Hainsworth, 75; Jacques Plante, 58; Ken Dryden, 46

MOST STANLEY CUP WINS AS A PLAYER: Henri Richard, 11 (NHL record)

BEST PLUS/MINUS, CAREER: Larry Robinson, +700. Montreal were the first team to collect plus/minus data, starting in the 1950s.

50-GOAL CLUB: Guy Lafleur, 60, 1977-78; Steve Shutt, 60, 1976-77; Lafleur, 56, 1975-76 and 1976-77; Lafleur, 53, 1974-75; Lafleur, 52, 1978-79; Stephane Richer, 51, 1989-90; Richer, 50, 1987-88; Lafleur, 50, 1979-80; Pierre Larouche, 50, 1979-80; Bernie Geoffrion, 50, 1960-61; Maurice Richard, 50, 1944-45

WORKING OVERTIME: The heir to Georges Vezina in the Montreal net, George Hainsworth, once recorded four and a half consecutive hours of shutout hockey in 1930.

DRAFT-SCHMAFT
TOP-10 PICKS, 1989-2009: 4

PLAYERS DRAFTED WHO PLAYED IN 300 NHL GAMES: 31

IMPACT PLAYERS: Patrice Brisebois, 30th, 1989; Saku Koivu, 21st, 1993; Jose Theodore, 44th, 1994; Tomas Vukoun, 225th, 1994; Andrei Markov, 162nd, 1998; Tomas Plekanec, 71st, 2001; Jaroslav Halak, 271st, 2003; Carey Price, 5th, 2005; P.K. Subban, 43rd, 2007

DRAFT-SCHMAFT RANKING: 12th

LINE CHANGES
THE FLYING FRENCHMEN: Didier Pitre, Jack Laviolette, and Newsy Lalonde, 1917-19

THE PUNCH LINE: Toe Blake, Elmer Lach, and Rocket Richard, 1943-48

What a Guy. A woodcut of *Le Blond Demon*.

"Les Canadiens sont là!" — Anonymous

"Go Habs Go!" — Anonymous

"The only two Western institutions that really get ceremony are the House of Windsor and the Montreal Canadiens." — sportswriter Michael Farber

SKATE THAT ONE PAST ME AGAIN: Campbell Soups put out a Rocket Richard soup to lessen the PR damage of NHL president Clarence Campbell's suspension of Maurice Richard in 1955. Campbell had no connection with the soup company. Rocket had a bread named after him in the '50s as well.

BRING ON THE ZAMBONI
CELEBRITY FANS: Sidney Crosby (growing up), author Mordecai Richler, singer Celine Dion, actors Viggo Mortensen and Jay Baruchel, singers Sam Roberts and Robert Charlebois, broadcaster George Stroumboulopoulos

STUMP THE SCHWAB: Which numbers between 1 and 10 have the Canadiens not retired? Answer: six and eight.

A bumper year: Montreal won their last Stanley Cup in 1993.

The Last-Minute Club

"In overtime, you're flipping a coin," Ranger coach Emile Francis sighed after losing a playoff game in extra time. So what are the chances of a flipped coin coming up heads 10 times in a row? One in 1,024, it turns out. Close to impossible. But that's what Montreal did in the 1993 playoffs, reeling off 10 straight overtime wins on their way to their 24th Stanley Cup. Actually, that postseason began horribly for Montreal. In their first game, the Habs were up 2–0 against the hated Quebec Nordiques with minutes left. Quebec pulled their goalie and scored two quickies and finished Montreal off in overtime. After that, though, the Habs were unbeatable in extra time. And it wasn't even close. The 10 overtimes took 94 minutes. Patrick Roy never had to stand on his head. Two games were over in the first minute. There were no lucky bounces, unless you count Montreal's good fortune in facing inferior playoff opponents. After dispensing with Quebec (who finished two points ahead of Montreal with 104), the sixth-seed Canadiens played against .500 teams that had performed playoff miracles — first Buffalo (86), who knocked off Boston (109); then the New York Islanders (87), who had shocked Mario's NHL-best, 119-point Penguins; and finally, the Los Angeles Kings (88), upset winners over Toronto (99). Give

FAN-tastic

To Hab and Hab not: Montreal hockey dream house includes recreation-room lights from the Forum (top right); a bleu-blanc-rouge desk and easy-win chair (middle centre & middle right) along with a mantelpiece for more Habs lore (bottom right). That's a statue of Maurice Richard (bottom left).

them credit: the Habs beat all comers. And they were indeed fabulous in overtime, overwhelming opponents with a hunger for glory that was once the defining characteristic of *les Canadiens*.

For the record, the overtime scorers that magic, improbable spring were, in order, Vincent Damphousse, Kirk Muller, *Guy-Guy-Guy* Carbonneau, Patrice Brisebois, Muller again, Stephane Lebeau, Carbonneau *encore*, Eric Desjardins, and John LeClair, who in the end did in Los Angeles twice in a row.

In Defense of THE REALM

It says in the GM's rebuilding handbook that to succeed in the NHL you need: a) time, b) a great goalie, c) at least one strapping dray workhorse defender, d) a two-way playmaking center, and e) a coach who knows how to draw water from the wells of salvation (your third- and fourth-line pluggers).

How much do the Montreal Canadiens have?

Time? The great Canadien Doug Harvey used to say that Montreal fans are behind you "win or tie." Montreal expects to win. It's in the city's DNA. The Maroons and *les Expos*, the city's old English hockey and baseball teams, aren't here anymore because they didn't. The football Alouettes remain around because they do.

The Canadiens, though, are different. They've already won more than anyone else — 24 Stanley Cups. Toronto is stuck on 13. Detroit has 11. Boston six. Edmonton five. So thanks a lot, Frank Selke; great knowing you, Sam Pollock — the Montreal Canadiens don't need to win a Stanley Cup right away.

But they *do* have to fill out their uniforms with a certain *élan*. Have to look like they're going to win soon. Play attractive hockey. Make Saturday nights at the Bell Centre seem like state occasions. Or the natives will begin gathering fuel (rolled-up sports sections) for the boiling pot to cook the coach and general manager.

How bad is it in Montreal when the team disappoints? Former defenseman Terry Harper says that when the Habs didn't win the Stanley Cup as expected in 1967, losing to Toronto, Henri Richard couldn't bear to show his face in Montreal and so

spent the summer indoors, head down, arms dangling, lost, replaying the playoffs over in his mind.

Going into the 2012 stretch run, *les Glorieux* became *les Miserables*. The preseason began with the disastrous re-signing of oft-injured 33-year-old Andrei Markov to a three-year, $28 million contract — a game of Russian roulette that Montreal seem destined to lose. The team's little men — Cammalleri, Brian Gionta (hurt twice), and Scott Gomez — failed to come up big. Cammalleri was traded. Coach Jacques Martin got the axe. His substitute, Randy Cunneyworth, failed to pass his oral French.

ALL IN ALL: disaster. Mr. Cunneyworth, your bath is bubbling. Grab a couple of carrots on your way in.

Yes, time to start again. To rebuild. . . but around what? Do the Canadiens have their prime-time goalie in Carey Price? Is Pernell Karl Subban your horse on defense? You don't have the big center? Do you trade Subban or even Price to get precious rebuilding assets? What should you look for in a coach?

Leave us explore. First things first: let's look at the scouting reports on Price and Subban. Are they building blocks, or stumbling blocks?

CAREY PRICE

PERSONAL INFORMATION: Carey grew up in Anahim Lake, a small village near the reservations of the Ulkatcho First Nation, 500 kilometers north of Vancouver. Mom Lynda was two-term chief of the Ulkatcho. Dad Jerry is the son of Alberta ranchers. Jerry Price also played goal in junior hockey and was drafted by the Philadelphia Flyers in 1978.

EDUCATION: Carey loved to rodeo growing up. His specialty was calf roping. To allow Carey to compete in minor hockey, his dad bought a small plane — "a lawnmower with wings" — to skip over the 2,400-meter Itcha and Ilgachuz mountains for 640-kilometer roundtrips to Williams Lake. Just father and son with a hockey duffle bag in a four-seat Piper Cherokee. The two made the trip three times a week for practice and games. Yes, the son occasionally drove. "Carey could keep [the plane] flying straight when he was 10," according to Dad.

PROFESSIONAL QUALIFICATIONS AND AWARDS: In 2007, Carey was named the CHL Goaltender of the Year, stole a gold medal for Canada in the World Junior Championships in Sweden, and won the tournament MVP award. That spring, he turned pro, taking the

Carey Price in repose. Shooters never see this much net.

Hamilton Bulldogs to the AHL Calder Cup championship and earning another MVP trophy, this time for the American Hockey League playoffs.

THE SKINNY: Babe Ruth used to say he sometimes felt "hitterish." In the same way, we can say Carey Price looks and seems "goaltendery." Riding rodeo, roping calves, working fast with your hands or else you'll lose a finger — what better physical and mental preparation can a young boy have for the dashing, dangerous work of goaltending?

And all those flights over the Rockies before he was a teenager! "You've just got to keep it in a straight line and go over that mountain. The wind blows you every which way, but you just keep her steady," Carey once said of flying. But he could also be talking about goaltending in the playoffs, right?

As for the spiritual side, Carey's maternal grandmother taught him how to make dreamcatchers — protective charms that filter in good dreams. Like the Stanley Cup, maybe.

ANOTHER TALISMAN: Carey Price was named after a goalie Montreal drafted, Carey Walker. No, he didn't make it, but his brother is a failed goalie who became an Expo star and was National League MVP in 1997. That would be Larry Walker. Carey Price also has two cousins in the NHL — Shane Doan and Keaton Ellerby.

But forget about portents and pedigree. Price has everything you want in a goalie. Here's his 2007 Team Canada junior coach, Corey Hirsch, talking about the 6′3″ netminder: "He's big and he just doesn't open up for you — he doesn't give you any reason to think that you can score on him. You can make a move on him, and he doesn't fall for anything. He's just so technically sound. He's a lot like Patrick [Roy] in that way. They just don't give you anything."

Under Montreal goalie coach Rollie Melanson, Price has developed into a hybrid butterfly/standup goalie. He comes out fast and tall at shooters, expertly cutting down angles, then spreads wide to guard against chances in close. And the transition is flawless. A three-time all-star at age 24, the only two knocks against Carey are that he appears too relaxed at times — he isn't a demonstrative, on-ice leader — and hasn't yet shone in the NHL playoffs.

It's true that Price appears nonchalant. He's not a Tim Thomas type, rolling and tumbling, motivating fans and teammates. Nor is he sociable — again, in contrast to Thomas, who can be seen kibitzing with enemy forwards, joking with referees. Price is tall, dark, and silent. He keeps his own counsel in the dressing room. Reporters don't grab for their notepads upon seeing him, the way they did when the Blessed Trinity — Georges Vezina, Jacques Plante, or Patrick Roy — were around.

No, Price is a blend of Montreal's great Toronto-born goalies. He's got Ken Dryden's height and reach, along with George Hainsworth's implacable calm. You probably know about Ken — the best-selling author (*The Game*) and hero of so many Canadien highlight reels from the '70s. But Hainsworth is the more apt comparison. In the 1928–29 season, Hainsworth recorded 22 shutouts in 44 games. He holds the Montreal record for career shutouts — 75. And hardly anyone remembers him.

"I'm sorry I can't put on a show like some of the other goaltenders," George once said. "I can't look excited because I'm not. I can't shout at other players because that's not my style. I can't dive on easy shots and make them look hard.

"I guess all I can do is stop pucks."

Price is mostly quiet on the ice. But make no mistake, there is fire in his belly. He arrived in Hamilton, a teenager still eligible for junior, to take the Bulldogs to the AHL championship. "The kid hadn't said three words during the playoffs," remembers captain Ajay Baines. But in the second game of the finals against Hershey, the Bulldogs were taking a beating. In the intermission, Price shocked teammates by jumping up and shouting, "Some guys got to ****ing step it up!"

And when Price played poorly for Montreal in his Stanley Cup playoff debut, he did not process defeat easily. After the game, Price turned off his cell phone, jumped in a truck, and began the long, solitary drive home. After a Mexican holiday with boyhood friends and a fishing trip with his dad, he showed up in Calgary to take revenge on his body for letting him down in the playoffs. The Canadiens had suggested he lose "a little" weight.

He lost 28 pounds killing himself in the weight room.

Henri Richard would understand. And be impressed.

Goalies with Carey Price's pedigree show up once every couple of decades. Commentator Mike Milbury says Canadiens traded the wrong goalie when they kept Price and let go of Jaroslav Halak in 2010. But Milbury has been wrong before (see the New York Islanders chapter).

P.K. SUBBAN

PERSONAL INFORMATION: Named after Pernell Roberts, who starred as Adam Cartwright in the '60s TV western *Bonanza* — color TV's first big hit. His dad is a Jamaican immigrant who made good in Canada, growing up in a French-speaking neighborhood in Sudbury, falling in love simultaneously with hockey and *les Habs.* Karl Subban didn't strap on skates until he was 11, but grew (to 6′3″) to do a pretty fair Ken Dryden impersonation, playing nets in corner-rink games. He also played college basketball. He's now a Toronto high school principal. Mother Maria, a bank analyst, was a high school track star in Toronto, winning a provincial gold medal in relay.

EDUCATION: P.K. learned to skate as a tyke at Nathan Phillips Square in Toronto, twirling on a rink built over what was once a Jewish, black, then Chinese neighborhood. He played minor hockey for the Markham Majors, eventually joining the Belleville Bulls of the Ontario Hockey League, where his younger brothers Jordan and Malcolm now play. In 2007, the Canadiens surprised everyone by spending a second-round pick on a player who wasn't ranked in the top 100 North Americans by NHL Central Scouting.

PROFESSIONAL QUALIFICATIONS AND AWARDS: Helped Canada to gold medals in the 2008 and 2009 World Junior Championships, and was named to the tournament all-star team in '09. First-team AHL all-star in 2010 for the Hamilton Bulldogs.

THE SKINNY: If confidence were all it took to be an NHL defenseman, P.K. Subban would be Bobby Orr. When Montreal surprised the hockey world in 2007, taking Subban in the second round, the teenager sprang to the podium and told the Montreal brass, "You guys made the right choice." Minutes later, he spotted a TV hockey commentator he recognized. "Hey, Nick Kypreos, you came to my hockey camp when I was nine."

"No," Kypreos said, taken aback. "You came to *my* camp."

Subban has always believed in himself. His mom, Maria, says the family was watching *Hockey Night in Canada* one Saturday night in 1993 when four-year-old P.K. (his nickname since birth) called out, "Dad, I want to be one of those guys on TV."

He can skate, shoot, and think as well as any defender in hockey. He's also tough and in your face— he has the conceit of a superstar. The 2010 and 2011 playoffs proved all that. Against the Stanley Cup champ Bruins in 2011, he was better than Zdeno Chara. *And only 21!* Go to YouTube and look up his tying goal with a minute left in game seven, where he one-times a blur from the point past Tim Thomas.

P.K. Subban can be fantastic. And the 2010–11 season, which saw the rookie Montreal defenseman pile up 14 goals, produced a highlight reel to savor — scenic goals and hits, great skating and passes, along with a hat trick against the Wild. Then there were all those NBA-style, high- and low-five postgame celebrations with goalie Carey Price.

But after a giddy year-long celebration, there came a marathon hangover. There were games — weeks even — in 2011–12 where

Pernell Karl (P.K.) Subban firing away.

Youppi stalks a Boston fan outside the Bell Centre.

Subban was plainly off. He ran out of ideas on the power play. He fought with a teammate, Tomas Plekanec. He was suspended for slew-footing an opponent. He got yelled at by coaches.

"You've been out here 40 minutes, wake up!" the assistant coach yelled at him in late January. He might have said 40 games.

Francois Gagnon, a respected and astute columnist from *La Presse*, suggested that it was time for the Canadiens to consider trading their second-best asset. As the trade deadline approached, the Internet rumor mill had him going to Edmonton for a raft of draft picks.

That shouldn't, and hopefully won't, happen. Baseball guru Bill James once said bad teams blame their best players for the club's misfortunes. And it could be argued that growing frustrated and dispensing prematurely with a young defenseman is exactly what has made the Montreal Canadiens a bad team.

Who did the Habs take with their first pick in 2007? Ryan McDonagh, a two-way defenseman they traded in a package to New York in order to land Scott Gomez. By 2012, McDonagh was a 25-minute rearguard with the first-place Rangers. And Gomez, an $8 million forward who scored as many goals in the NHL as you did in 2011.

Zero.

Defensemen, like left-handed pitchers in baseball, take time to mature. The Habs' Doug Harvey won the first of his seven Norris Trophies at age 31. So did Nicklas Lidstrom for Detroit, as a matter of fact. Another great Canadien blueliner, Larry Robinson, had his best year at age 34.

Montreal has suffered mightily for foolishly trading away young defensemen, then watching them become stars in other cities: Chris Chelios, Eric Desjardins, Stephane Robidas, Mathieu Schneider, and Ron Hainsey. They also left Mark Streit unprotected in 2008.

In baseball, the Expos traded lefty Randy Johnson away and then watched him become one of the top 10 pitchers of all time.

Only a GM looking to finish his professional career in a broadcasting booth would give up on P.K. Subban at age 23.

The coach?

After Martin was let go, there was a great flap about the need to get a French-speaking coach — a sentiment that gained popularity because, after all, the 2011 Stanley Cup was waged by two francophone generals, Boston's Claude Julien and Vancouver's Alain Vigneault. Quebec premier Jean Charest said the province would not kick in any money to building an NHL-caliber arena for a new NHL team unless the coach could speak French.

Before attacking Quebec for naked tribalism, we should ask how Calgary's fan base would respond to a coach who only spoke French. How would Toronto?

Yes, having a French-speaking coach in Quebec is the sensible thing to do. But maybe, just for good luck, the successful candidate shouldn't be able to *read* French. The only three French-Canadian coaches ever to win a Stanley Cup were Claude Ruel (1969), Jean Perron (1986), and Jacques Demers (1993).

And Demers, though a great, smart leader, happened to be unable to read in any language. That probably helped. Because nowhere is the media pressure on a coach greater than Montreal. Eleven beat writers follow the team. (The Rangers have four.) Then there are the radio and TV guys. "It's too much," former Habs goalie Jose Theodore once said. "Even when there are two days with no game, there are 20 people there looking for a story. That's when they start to stay stuff. I remember players getting booed and wondering, 'Why is he getting booed — the game just started.' And it was about a story."

The perfect Montreal Canadiens coach, then, should be bilingual, unfailing upbeat in good times or bad, equipped with a hide thick enough to weather winter storms, with a charisma that pulls fans smiling and cheering from their seats.

Yes, the new Habs' coach should be their popular mascot, Youppi!

NASHVILLE PREDATORS

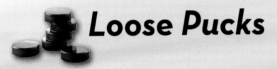
Loose Pucks

Record: When the Preds score, the Bridgestone Arena twangs to life with country singer Tim McGraw's "I Like It, I Love It." Tim serves it up, too, with a hockey-lyric adaptation of his 1995 hit: *"Don't know what it is about the Predators scorin,' but I like it, I love it, I want some more of it."* Lots of Music City artists have entertained or set a spell at Preds games. Carrie Underwood is married to Preds assistant captain Mike Fisher.

RECORDS

Most hat tricks, career: Steve Sullivan, 4

Most goals, one season: Jason Arnott, 33, 2008–09

Most points, one season: Paul Kariya, 85, 2005–06

Most catfish thrown on ice: Four, after Andrew Brunette scored the Preds' first goal on November 13, 1998 (NHL record)

Best plus/minus, career: Shea Weber, +44; Ryan Suter, +43

Most shutouts, career: Pekke Rinne, 25

50-goal club: None

Working overtime: Mike Fisher chatted up future wife Carrie Underwood on the phone for three months before their first date.

DRAFT-SCHMAFT

Top-10 picks, 1998–2009: 5

Players drafted who played in 300 NHL games: 12

Impact players: Scott Hartnell, 6th, 2000; Ryan Suter, 7th, 2003; Shea Weber, 49th, 2003; Pekka Rinne, 258th, 2004

Draft-schmaft ranking: 20th

LINE CHANGES

"We've got a rope, we've got a tree; all we need is a referee." — Nashville crowd's chant in response to a bad call against the Preds.

Skate that one past me again: For her 2009 wedding to Mike Fisher, Carrie Underwood dressed her shivering rat terrier, Ace, in a Swarovski crystal–pink tuxedo. "Mike was like, 'He's in pink! What are you doing?'" the singer told *People* magazine.

BRING ON THE ZAMBONI

Celebrity fans: Just about every female country singer in Nashville, including Carrie Underwood, Amy Grant, Barbara Mandrell, and the Dixie Chicks.

Stump the Schwab: Who played on the Preds' Vowel Line in the 2001–02 season? Answer: Martin Erat, Vladimir Orszagh, and Denis Arkipov.

Ryan Suter (left) and Shea Weber

The GOLD RUSH of '03

In the 2003 NHL draft, Nashville loaded up on defense, selecting blueliners early: Ryan Suter (seventh overall), Kevin Klein (37th), and Shea Weber (49th). All three now excel for Nashville. Suter and Weber are hockey's best defense duo — big and fast with that telepathic bond that defines great blueline partnerships. Weber hits forwards hard and pucks harder — he's Al MacInnis with a dash of Scott Stevens. Suter is more like his smart, sneaky-fast uncle Gary Suter, who, along with MacInnis, once comprised the NHL's premium defense pair. But Ryan is better defensively. "I used to tap Vernie [Flames goaltender Mike Vernon] on the leg a lot and say, 'Thanks,'" Gary once said. Weber (gold) and Suter (silver) tapped a rich vein in the 2010 Olympics, playing for Canada and the U.S., respectively. There's more where that came from in the Suter clan, though. Gary won silver for the U.S. in 2002. Grandfather Bob won gold in 1980. (All three defensemen wore the number 20.) Speaking of gold, the question remains whether Nashville can afford the $22 million or so that would give them the NHL's best defensive triumvirate. The Preds have locked up goalie Pekka Rinne to a seven-year, $49 million contract. Can they also re-sign Suter and Weber? During the 2012 All-Star Game draft, which was televised, Montreal goalkeeper Carey Price turned to Tim Thomas at one point and said of the NHL's hardest shooter, "We were down in Nashville once. He took a slapper from right between the dots. Almost took my head off. Hit the glass before I moved." So you're probably asking: How could Weber have lasted until the 49th pick? Well, Shea was a late bloomer who grew five inches when he was 14 and took another year to figure out how his new chassis worked. But he always had that shot. His dad, a B.C. lumberman, rigged a shooting gallery in the back yard. Tin cans were attached to the four corners of a rusting old net. "I shot out a lot of tin," Weber has said. He and his agent, Jarrett Bousquet, will be aiming for a more precious metal when discussing his next contract.

FAN-tastic

(Left) Preds fans make a snowman. (Bottom left) Basement predator: a fan works on his shot. (Bottom right) Jar-Jar Binks flanked by an anonymous fan (left) and his assistant, Waldo (right).

Hockey-Tonk Masquerade

You read where, in 2010, former Edmonton Oiler Gilbert Brule picked up Bono on a rainy day in West Vancouver and offered the U2 singer a lift. Later, Bono sent Brule a backstage pass to his Edmonton show, giving him an onstage shout-out: "I like ice hockey because people who play ice hockey pick up hitchhikers. I've decided I want to be Gilbert Brule."

Boy, it really must've been really raining that day in Vancouver.

This wasn't the first time a hockey star came to the aid of a civilian. In 1968, Bobby Orr found a fan outside Boston Garden mired in a snowdrift. "I'll give her a push, you drive," Bobby said, leaning into the stalled sedan. Twenty minutes of snow spray later, the car was free.

Then there was the time in 1973 that Gordie Howe cross-checked a Texas thief. Exiting a hotel, Mr. Hockey saw a bad guy grab a woman's purse, jump in a car, and scram. Not so fast. Gordie hopped into his car and sped after the crook, cutting him off, T.J. Hooker style. The frightened purse snatcher tossed the handbag out the window. When Gordie returned it to the woman, her boyfriend asked, "How can I ever thank you?" Ever the professional, Howe said, "Well, I'm a hockey player for Houston Aeros. How about attending some games?"

Or how about Brooks Laich, Washington defenseman. In the spring of 2010, driving home an hour after the Caps' devastating game-seven playoff loss to Montreal, he spotted a woman and her daughter stranded on D.C.'s Theodore Roosevelt Bridge, with a tire as flat as Brooks's heart. Didn't matter. Brooks jumped out and changed the flat. "I was praying," said the stranded driver, Mary Ann Wangemann, a Caps fan. "He was like an angel that night."

"Saskatchewan education," Laich shrugged when asked how he could quickly go from being in a bad mood to a Good Samaritan.

The King loves it when Shea Weber throws a hunk-a hunk-a burning rubber at goalies.

Great stories, but we here at *Triple Overtime* figure there must be more instances where hockey players remain strong and courageous, even after they take off their superhero uniforms. And wouldn't it be great if, as with Brule and Bono, there were a duet or double-celebrity angle?

Of course, no one does duets like Nashville. Think of Johnny Cash and June Carter doing "Jackson." Willie Nelson has teamed up with everyone from B.B. King to Ziggy Marley.

Shea Weber

1 Coach Trotz quotes from Brooks's 1989 single "The Dance": Yes, my life is better left to chance / I could have missed the pain, but I'd have had to miss the dance.

Because NHL hockey only came to Music City in 1998, there aren't yet any country star–hockey player duets. *Can Mike Fisher even sing?* It's only a matter of time, though. Predators coach Barry Trotz is fond of quoting from Garth Brooks's songs in pre-game pep talks.[1]

Until then, to paraphrase the Everly Brothers, all we have to do is dream. Here then, in chronological order, are three wonderful-to-contemplate scenarios where hockey players rescue Nashville or Tennessee musicians from distress, creating true hockey-tonk magic.

THIRD STARS: MAURICE RICHARD AND ELVIS PRESLEY

HOW IT HAPPENED: In August 1955, Maurice Richard and a bunch of *Sports Illustrated* cover heroes appear on Ed Sullivan's *Talk of the Town*. Sullivan isn't a rockabilly fan, so Elvis doesn't show up on Ed Sullivan until the public insists, in September 1956. (Even then, actor Charles Laughton hosts.) But what if Elvis appeared on the same show as The Rocket?

HERO TIME: A few crewcut athletes make derisive remarks about Elvis's glistening pompadour as he exits after performing "I'm Left, You're Right, She's Gone." E.P. is flustered and makes an intemperate remark. The toughs jump up, ready to go. But the Rocket, who liked his coal-back hair landscaped just so and knew what it was like to be picked on, intercedes. The player who was too often called Frog shouts "Enough!" Seeing the lime pits of fury in Rocket's eyes, the bullies disperse. "Thank you, thank you very much," Elvis says.

CONSEQUENCES: Elvis and Rocket become friends. "Colour your hair like me, man," Elvis tells Rocket later in the '60s. "When it comes to growing old, a lot of

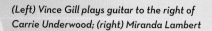
(Left) Vince Gill plays guitar to the right of Carrie Underwood; (right) Miranda Lambert

it is up here," Elvis says, gesturing to his own shoe-polish-black conk. "Think about it, Rock." Because he's a friend of Richard, Elvis is bigger in Quebec than anywhere in North America. Local TV shows in the '70s host ongoing Elvis contests. One winner, a Francophone who believes Elvis is his spiritual father, plays Presley in the 1981 film *This Is Elvis*. After Elvis dies, Richard starts doing hair-colour ads.

Wait, all that stuff about the hair commercials and French Elvis impersonators is true? *Hey, maybe . . .*

SECOND STARS: DON CHERRY AND WILLIE NELSON

How it happened: On May 24, 1979, two weeks after the underdog Bruins lose in the semis to the eventual Stanley Cup champions, the Montreal Canadiens, Boston GM Harry Sinden "releases" coach Don Cherry. Leaving Boston Garden, Cherry finds country star Willie Nelson's tour bus beached in a parking lot. "Out of gas," Nelson advises Cherry. "Geez, I hear ya," the ex-coach says, helping Willie by siphoning gas from a nearby car. "Thanks, friend. Hey, leave some for yourself," Willie says. "Don't worry — my boss's car," Cherry chuckles. A rebel himself, Willie invites Cherry into his bus for a smoke.

Consequences: Willie and Don become friends. "Bud" Cherry quits hockey and enters politics, replacing Flora MacDonald as the NDP member for the riding of Kingston and the Islands.

FIRST STARS: HENRIK AND DANIEL SEDIN AND THE PISTOL ANNIES

How it happened: In early 2011, the Pistol Annies — hellcat Miranda Lambert, Ashley Monroe, and Angeleena Pressley — are recording their fabulous hit album *Hell on Heels*. The girls need a break before tackling "Taking Pills," so Lambert stops in at Jack's Bar-B-Que on Broadway and First for a Country Supper to go — Tennessee pork shoulder, smoked chicken, fresh pole beans, fried green apples, fried corn, slaw, corn bread, and chocolate fudge pie. With three Diet Cokes. Just as she's leaving, a gang of thugs — basketball fans, most likely — grab her purse and high-step it down Broadway.

Hero time: Just then, Henrik and Daniel Sedin, in town for a game against the Preds, are sightseeing, wandering down Broadway, Ernest Tubb tourist street maps in hand. Seeing a young woman in trouble and being good hockey players, the Sedins go all Starsky and Hutch, chasing down the villains. They catch the lead robber, grabbing back the purse. A fight breaks out, but the Sedins, though outnumbered, outwit their checks by weaving in and out of traffic, slinging the purse back and forth with artful no-look passes. Lambert gets back her purse and invites the twins back to the studio. The Sedins beg off. They've got a game tomorrow night. But you can't say no to some southern girls. Soon they are in the studio, singing along. There is a party. Miranda takes a shine to her new Swedish friends. And as she herself sings on "Takin' Pills," "Got a Tennessee Mountain point of view / Why have one when you can have two?"

Consequences: Henrik and Daniel leave five hours later, after devouring way too much chocolate fudge pie. The Vancouver Canucks win the Stanley Cup in the summers of 2011 and 2012.

NEW JERSEY DEVILS

Loose Pucks

RECORD: Now New Jersey hockey fans can make their own album with the That's Me Sports New Jersey Devils Personalized CD. Sadly, the offer does not to apply to local artists with existing recording deals. Sorry, Bruce, Bon Jovi, and Lauryn Hill. Adios Yo La Tengo. At Devils home games, the team plays "Ole, Ole, Ole" by the Bouncing Souls, a group from New Brunswick, New Jersey. Inspirational verse: *"We drink beer and wear Adidas everywhere."*

RECORDS:

MOST HAT TRICKS, CAREER: Patrik Elias, 8

MOST POINTS, ONE SEASON: Patrik Elias, 96, 2000-01

MOST ASSISTS, ONE SEASON: Scott Stevens, 60, 1993-94

BEST PLUS/MINUS, CAREER: Scott Stevens, +282

MOST SHUTOUTS, CAREER: Marty Brodeur, 119 (NHL record)

MOST POINTS, ONE PLAYOFF GAME: Patrik Sundstrom, 8, April 22, 1988, vs. Washington (NHL record)

50-GOAL CLUB: None. Brian Gionta holds the franchise record, with 48 in 2005-06.

WORKING OVERTIME: It took 10 periods for the Devils and Dallas Stars to play the last two games of the 2000 Stanley Cup finals. Jersey was up three games to one when Stars netminder Eddie Belfour threw a six-period shutout in Jersey. Mike Modano finally ended the game, tipping in a Brett Hull blueline floater. Next game, it was the Devils' turn. In period five, Patrik Elias threw a perfect no-look backhand out from the corner, into the slot and onto Jason Arnott's stick. A split second later it was in the net and Jersey had their second Cup in five seasons. They would win a third Cup in 2003.

DRAFT-SCHMAFT

TOP-TEN PICKS, 1989-2009: 3

PLAYERS DRAFTED WHO PLAYED 300 NHL GAMES: 35

IMPACT PLAYERS: Bill Guerin, 5th, 1989; Marty Brodeur, 20th, 1990; Scott Niedermayer, 3rd, 1991; Patrik Elias, 51st, 1994; Petr Sykora, 18th, 1995; Scott Gomez, 27th, 1998; Brian Gionta, 82nd, 1998; Zach Parise, 17th, 2003; Adam Henrique, 82nd, 2008.

DRAFT-SCHMAFT RANKING: 3rd

LINE CHANGES

THE A LINE: Jason Arnott, Patrik Elias and Petr Sykora (1999-2002)

ZZ POPS: Youngsters Zach Parise and Travis Zajac and old poop Jamie Langenbrunner (2008-09).

"Have another donut, you fat pig." — Devils coach Jim Schoenfeld, during the 1988 playoffs. It was the worst mess in playoff history. Referee Don Koharski called a costly late penalty. Schoenfeld chased him after

Zach Parise signs a Jersey jersey for a glowing fan.

the game. Koharski slipped on the runway when his skate strayed from the carpet. Rising, the ref accused Schoenfeld of pushing him. "You're through. You'll never coach again in this league." The coach responded with, "You're crazy. You fell, you fat pig. Have another donut." Schoenfeld was suspended without a hearing. The Devils got a restraining order, and Schoenfeld coached. The zebras boycotted the game. Commissioner John Ziegler was strangely missing in action. Ten minutes before the game, the league called in substitute on-ice officials who wore what looked like yellow long johns.

"Rangers suck." — Shouted by Devils fans at every home game.

SKATE THAT ONE PAST ME AGAIN: The great Martin Brodeur lost seven overtime playoff games in a row to begin his career.

BRING ON THE ZAMBONI
CELEBRITY FANS: Hall of Fame catcher Yogi Berra, comedian Joe Piscopo, and filmmaker Kevin Smith.

STUMP THE SCHWAB: Everyone knows Marty Brodeur holds the Devils' club record for shutouts with 119 and counting. Who is number two? Answer: Chris Terreri and Johan Hedberg, seven each.

"You're through. You'll never coach again in this league."

Changing SWEATERS

J.P. Parise played on a line with Phil Esposito in the 1972 Summit Series. And, like every Canadian, he hated German referee Josef Kompalla. In game eight of the series — which was tied 3-3-1 — Canada trailed 1-0 on a two-man power-play goal. Parise was given a legitimate penalty for hauling down Aleksandr Maltsev. "Two for interference," Kompalla shouted. "Guy was carrying the puck!" Parise screamed. "You got 10," Kompalla replied. The referee had now given Canada 47 minutes in penalties compared with six to Russia in just over three periods. "You're going to die right here," Parise said, taking dead aim at Kompalla's head, checking a home-run swing at the last moment. Parise was thrown out, but had made his point. Russia received more penalties than Canada after that. And Canada won what was originally called "The Friendship Series."

Players change teams in hockey. Sometimes they change countries, too. Parise retired to Minnesota, where he was hockey director at Shattuck-Saint Mary's.[1] That's where his son Zach went to school en route to becoming the star and captain of the New

1 Other Shattuck-St. Mary's alumni include Jonathan Toews, Sidney Crosby, Jack Johnson, and, oh yes, Marlon Brando.

FAN-tastic

(Top) The original Jersey devil, as imagined in the Philadelphia Evening Bulletin from January 1909. (Bottom left) Marty Brodeur figurine. (Bottom right) Devils assistant coach Meadowlands Satan on his way to work.

Jersey Devils. In the 2010 Olympics, Zach scored a last-second, game-tying goal *against* Canada. J.P. Parise's other son plays in Kompalla country. Jordan Parise is goalie for the Augsburger Panther, who play in a 7,000-seat, roofed, but wall-less, rink.

Who knows where Zach Parise will finish his career? New Jersey and America's hockey hero is a great offensive force — deadly around the net. Zach is also eligible to become a free agent in 2012, so maybe he'll be playing on another team when you read this. Wherever happens, some team or fan base will be upset. His father, J.P., will understand. Getting upset and getting over it, like changing sweaters occasionally, is all a part of hockey. When "Jeep" was told by a reporter that Josef Kompalla had made the International Hockey Hall of Fame in 2003, the elder Parise was quick to say, "God bless him. He was a nice guy."

Devils May Care More About Women

New Jersey filmmaker and hockey fan Kevin Smith once called for a punishing boycott of Ranger supporters for their alleged mistreatment of women. The director of the upcoming hockey movie, *Hit Somebody*, wrote in a hockey blog:

"Many a Rangers fan will dismissively refer to the Devils as "the Debbies," even going so far as calling Marty Brodeur "Martha." This casual misogyny should concern every lady who loves a Blueshirt-lover — as what's really being said is this: in an effort to diminish a team they despise, some Rangers' fans' idea of an insult is to call the Devils women. It's as if the worst slander they can imagine is equating the black and red with the distaff. Ladies, I don't know about you, but I (and every Devils fan) find that notion repugnant beyond words. . . and worthy of reprisal. Might I suggest withholding sex? In an effort to curb this rampant hate-speech, I'd say you could threaten your men with no coitus 'til the Rangers take home another Stanley Cup, but we don't want a "Children of Men" thing going on in Manhattan; no nookie 'til next season should suffice. And should the nookie-strike prove too taxing and you find yourself pining for the touch of men — real men, who respect women — pop on over to Jersey. There are a bunch of guys just a few miles away who won't be plastered to their televisions for the next week and I'll be more than happy to show a playoff-widow a great time."

Lou's Fancy RED SPORTS CAR?

We thought we knew the New Jersey Devils. Figured we knew old-school GM Lou Lamoriello.

The Devils have never had a 50-goal scorer — no 100-point scorers, either. The club has retired three numbers: 3, 4, and 27. They belong to defensemen Ken Daneyko, Scott Stevens, and Scott Niedermayer. Next up is likely number 30, which belongs to Martin Brodeur, a goalie.

New Jersey invented the neutral zone trap — hockey as five o'clock traffic. Certainly the tactic worked best on the road, where players didn't worry about entertaining fans. Let the home team grow frustrated, make mistakes. The Devils could outwait God. In winning the Stanley Cup in 1995 and 2000, 10 of New Jersey's 16 wins came in the other team's building.

Ask any of the championship Devils to identify their best game and they'll mention May 8, 2000, in the Eastern Conference semifinals against a talented, desperate Toronto Maple Leaf team. In bumping the league's fourth-best offense from the playoffs, the Devils allowed six shots on Brodeur — and just one in the final period.

"It was a perfect game," Patrick Elias sighed after the 3-0 win.

That was the epitome of what was once New Jersey Devils hockey: check, check, check. Playing the Devils was like trying to escape your reflection in a mirror.

The master planner of the franchise was Lou Lamoriello, the son of Italian immigrants. The Lamoriellos had a restaurant in Providence, Rhode Island, that was popular in the 1950s with the Reds, the city's AHL hockey team. Goalie Johnny Bower lived in a spare room at Lou's home.

Growing up, sports were Lou's life — baseball in summer, hockey after that, with homework and church

Ilya Kovalchuk does the receiving line after scoring on the Rangers.

HALL OF CAPE COD FAME 2009

LOU LAMORIELLO

Spent six summers on Cape Cod diamonds as a player and manager. The Providence College athlete played at Harwich (1961-62), Orleans (1963) and Bourne (1964), where he also became manager at age 21. Managed Sagamore to 1965 CCBL title and managed Yarmouth in 1967. Has served as president/GM of the NHL's New Jersey Devils since 1987 and inducted into the Hockey Hall of Fame in 2009.

in between. Lou captained the baseball and hockey teams at Providence College, and was a good enough catcher to be offered a double-A contract with the San Francisco Giants. The hockey Reds offered him a job at right wing, but Lou's heroes were Red Auerbach and Vince Lombardi — coaches. As a kid, he traveled with the Reds to Springfield to watch the immortal Eddie Shore conduct practice.

He stayed at Providence, coaching, eventually becoming athletic director.

With Lamoriello at the helm, Providence was a sports management factory. Baseball manager Bobby Valentine, basketball coaches Rick Pitino and Jeff Van Gundy, and hockey's Ron Wilson and Brian Burke all played or coached under Lou.

"Ron Wilson followed Lou around," Leaf GM Burke once snorted, adding, "If [Lou stopped] short, Ronnie would have broken his nose on his butt." Burke is just getting back at his recent coach for the time Wilson snuck into his dorm and changed the time on his alarm clock. The lumbering defenseman missed practice, earning him a week of 4 a.m. "bag skates" during Christmas holidays. Skating until he could taste copper, one on one with Lou in a dark, cold arena.

Lamoriello's discipline and attention to detail are legendary. His players had to wear a suit and tie everywhere, even to morning practice. Once, Lou drove by the dorm and saw a light on after 10 p.m. He phoned the culprit, lowering the boom. How could he tell who it was from the light?

He'd memorized the players' rooms.

Lamoriello was educated by the Order of St. Dominic — monastic priests devoted to solitude. At Providence, he took secrecy to the extreme. Recruiting Pitino, he met with the Boston University coach three times — always at three in the morning.

And he was unyielding. Never gave the other guy a quarter-inch. Once, Lou was ordered to find room

"The league also fined Lamoriello and the Devils $3 million. Just for messing with them."

for a visiting team's band. This was before the big Brown Bears–Providence Friars game. Providence didn't have a band. And coach Lamoriello didn't want to take away tickets from Friars fans. So he stuck the 35 band members in seats scattered throughout the arena. Blow on that, Brown Bears!

That encapsulates Lou Lamoriello: all business, always thinking, trying to get the edge for the next game. Was there anything else to life? A reporter, seeing a framed photo of coach Lombardi in his New Jersey Devils office, but no family photos, once asked Lou why he wouldn't respond to personal questions, why there were no personal effects in his room.

"Because that's the way it is," he replied.

In the '90s, the Devils players liked to call their team "The Firm," after the dark, mysterious law partnership in the John Grisham novel. A few years earlier, Lou had outwaited the Communist Party, spiriting Viachselav Fetisov in from the Soviet Union. "We all have a saying in the office," a Devils employee told *Sports Illustrated*. "Lou knows who killed JFK. He just isn't saying."

But here's where the story of Lou Lamoriello's New Jersey Devils gets complicated — stops making sense, one might argue. In the spring of 2010, Lou traded prospects for Atlanta star Ilya Kovalchuk, a flashy, fabulous scorer. No biggie there — a decade earlier, Lou had traded to get Alexander Mogilny, another gifted Russian, from Vancouver. The Devils won a Stanley Cup that summer.

Kovalchuk, everyone figured, was a rental. But after the Devils bowed out in the 2010 playoffs, the GM who never gave into player contract demands, who had employees account for long-distance calls and hated seeing lights being left on after work, signed 27-year-old Kovalchuk to a 17-year, $102 million contract.

It was the biggest deal in NHL history — the smelliest, too, some said. No way would Kovalchuk still be playing for the Devils at the end of the deal. Cripes, he'd be 44. A *Buffalo News* commentator, Mike Harrington, called the Kovalchuk signing "eye-popping,

stunning, absurd, insane." The NHL blocked the deal, arguing it was a way around the salary cap. Later, the league permitted a 15-year, $100 million contract that still called for Ilya to be paid a cool half-million in 2026-27.

The league also fined Lamoriello and the Devils $3 million. Just for messing with them.

What could Lou have been thinking of? Was signing sexy Ilya the sign of a mid-life crisis — the GM equivalent of a thwarted suburban dad splurging on a fancy red sports car?

It sure looked bad at first. Kovalchuk began his first post-contract season trying too hard, racing around like a dog chasing its tail. Then Zach Parise got hurt and Marty Brodeur turned out to be human. In a memorable game against Buffalo, down a goal in a shootout, Koval-chuk skated in on Ryan Miller, the Devils' last chance to tie the game and keep the shootout going.

And he mishandled his shot, somehow squirting the puck behind him.

The dysfunctional Devils went 10-29-2 first half of 2010-11. Critics were saying that Lou had lost his touch, and maybe his mind, with the Kovalchuk deal. "Kovalchoke" — that was the sign being waved around enemy buildings.

But wait, the Devils and Kovalchuk came on and went an astonishing 23-3-2 in the second half — missing the playoffs, but still . . .

In 2011-12, Kovalchuk was one of the best reasons to watch hockey, a virtuoso every night, leading the Devils to another hopeful playoff run. Lou, analysts are now saying, didn't lose his mind; he had just figured out the new NHL. With no hitting, no interference, and no more five o'clock traffic, the days of Ken Daneyko were over. Teams needed at least one or two speedballs with offensive flair to break down defenses.

Who better than Ilya? Not only that, but most of the highly paid star's contract is deferred. New Jersey paid Kovalchuk $6.6 million in 2011-12. That's the 16th-highest salary in the league. It's also pretty much what Wade Redden ($6.5 million)

is being paid by the Rangers to play for the Connecticut Whale. And less than Jay Bouwmeester, Dany Heatley, or any one of Washington's underperforming SOBs — Semin, Ovechkin, or Backstrom.

Who would you rather have on your team?

Kovalchuk's contract may cause headaches farther on down the rink. But Lou will look after those troubles when they arise. He'll only be 85 when Kovalchuk's contract comes due in 2027.

(Above) Devils versus Hawks; (bottom) Ilya in action.

NEW YORK ISLANDERS

Loose Pucks

RECORD: The grandson of a Long Island Insurance magnate, Loudon Wainwright III was introduced to hockey by his Canadian first wife, Kate McGarrigle. They lived in Boston at the turn of the 1960s, where Loudon became a Bruins fan. Returning to Greenwich Village to play folk music, the baying underdog in Loudon led him to the Islanders — New York's other team. His best hockey lick, from "Dump the Dog": "*Baseball's fine / Football's rougher / Basketballers all are tall / But I like hockey, hockey's tougher / You must play without a ball.*"

RECORDS:

MOST HAT TRICKS, CAREER: Mike Bossy, 39

MOST GAME-WINNING GOALS, CAREER: Mike Bossy, 82

BEST PLUS/MINUS, CAREER: Bryan Trottier, +470

MOST CONSECUTIVE 50-GOAL SEASONS: Mike Bossy, nine, 1977–78 to 1985–86 (NHL record)

MOST SHUTOUTS, CAREER: Chico Resch, 25

50-GOAL CLUB: Mike Bossy, 69, 1978–79; Bossy, 68, 1980–81; Bossy, 64, 1981–82; Bossy, 61, 1985–86; Bossy, 60, 1982–83; Bossy, 58, 1984–85; Pierre Turgeon, 58, 1992–93; Pat LaFontaine, 54, 1989–90; Bossy, 53, 1977–78; Bossy, 51, 1979–80; Bossy, 51, 1983–84; Bryan Trottier, 50, 1981–82

WORKING OVERTIME: Pat LaFontaine, on a blind, whirl-around slap shot, scored in quadruple overtime on April 19, 1987, allowing the New York Islanders to defeat the Washington Capitals 3–2. It was the seventh game of the series. LaFontaine's goal came on the 132nd shot of the seven-hour marathon.

DRAFT-SCHMAFT

TOP-10 PICKS, 1989–2009: 18

PLAYERS DRAFTED WHO PLAYED 300 NHL GAMES: 32

IMPACT PLAYERS: Zigmund Palffy, 26th, 1991; Darius Kasparaitis, 5th, 1992; Todd Bertuzzi, 23rd, 1993; Bryan McCabe, 40th, 1993; Wade Redden, 2nd, 1993; Zdeno Chara, 56th, 1996; Roberto Luongo, 4th, 1997; Rick DiPietro, 1st, 2000; John Tavares, 1st, 2009

DRAFT-SCHMAFT RANKING: 14th

LINE CHANGES

THE TRIO GRANDE LINE: Clark Gillies, Bryan Trottier, and Mike Bossy. The best line of their era (late 1970s through mid-'80s) led Islanders to four straight Stanley Cups (1980–83).

"I would have scored 500 goals if Bryan Trottier was right-handed." — A joking Clark Gillies, who played on Trottier's left wing.

"Hockey is the only job I know where you get paid to have a nap on the day of the game." — Chico Resch

SKATE THAT ONE PAST ME AGAIN: The Colorado Rockies' Randy Pierce kissed a puck after scoring a

John Tavares around the net. See how big a scorer's eyes get when he's in close.

goal against the powerful Islanders team of 1979 and was given a two-minute penalty. No not for tripping on a hallucinogen — for delay of game.

BRING ON THE ZAMBONI
CELEBRITY FANS: Kevin Connolly (who played Eric on the HBO series _Entourage_); three-time _Sports Illustrated_ cover girl and _Family Guy_ love interest Cheryl Tiegs, who does promo work for the Islanders — her children's favorite team; and Loudon Wainwright III.

STUMP THE SCHWAB: Three forwards have scored five Islander goals in a row. Name them. Answer: Bryan Trottier did it in one game, against Philadelphia on February 13, 1982. John Tavares accumulated five in a row in four games during December 2009. Polish eye chart Mariusz Czerkawski performed the same feat over three games in 1998.

> "Hockey is the only job I know where you get paid to have a nap on the day of the game."

Long Island T

John Tavares threw out the first pitch at a New York Mets game shortly after being claimed first overall by the Islanders in the 2009 draft.

He's the working-class grandson of immigrants — Poles Boleslaw and Josephine Kowal, and Manuel and Dorotea Tavares from Portugal. His father, Joe, threw his gear into a garbage bag to play hockey growing up in Oshawa, Ontario. There was athletic ability in the family. Uncle John turned to football and lacrosse, earning an invitation to the British Columbia Lions' training camp before deciding on North America's oldest sport. Good move: he's still playing at age 43 for the Buffalo Bandits and holds virtually every National Lacrosse League scoring record. The younger John Tavares played lacrosse, too, and credits his spin-away moves in the slot to the sport. Maybe he would've followed his namesake uncle into pro lacrosse, except that as a kid he became friends with an Oakville, Ontario, neighbor with a backyard rink — _a real rink, with cooling pipes and a Zamboni_. Sam Gagner had just such a dream playpen, courtesy of his dad, Dave Gagner, twice a 40-goal scorer in the NHL. Sam and John played hockey outdoors from first frost through spring. Sam now skates for the Edmonton Oilers.[1] Tavares eventually

[1] In 2012, the neighbors and best friends were chosen NHL player of the month in back-to-back months: Tavares in January, Gagner in February.

FAN-tastic

John Tavares as a junior in Oshawa with the author's son, Harry Cole. Alas, as is so often the case, young Mr. Cole's shoes are untied.

became the best junior in Canadian hockey, earning the nickname The Next One, as in the next Crosby/ Lemieux/Gretzky. Islander fans would settle for his being the next Bryan Trottier, another left-shooting center who led the Isles to four Stanley Cups in a row in the early '80s. If he's anything like his uncle, the other John Tavares, he'll get lots of chances. Hockey's John Tavares will be 43 in 2024.

An Island LOST AT SEA

No NHL franchise was happier to see the 2000s disappear than the New York Islanders. The decade commenced with GM and former coach, Mike Milbury losing the team's fortune in an epic, year-long gambling binge. Oh, it was frightful to behold, like one of those scenes in a movie where a reckless thrill-seeker comes undone at a Vegas gaming table.

Before the 2000 draft, Milbury sent goalie Roberto Luongo and Ollie Jokinen, future stars, to the Panthers for Mark Parrish and Oleg Kvasha — Florida swampland. Then, with first pick in the draft, he bypassed Dany Heatley and Marian Gaborik, the best prospects according to scouts, for Boston College freshman goalie Rick DiPietro.

"In the end, if we're wrong, we've made an incredible mistake," an elated Milbury told reporters, still riding a gambler's high. "My job is clearly on the line. If we're not a better team immediately — off with my head."

They weren't. And months later, "Mad Mike" as he called himself, did appear to lose his mind. Desperate to *win now*, Milbury swapped a lanky defenseman still finding himself and the team's first pick in 2001 (number 2 overall) for moody, intermittently useful Alexei Yashin, who was immediately sewn up for 10 years and $87.5 million.

Too few seasons later, Yashin was an untradeable fourth-line center. While the extension-ladder defenseman and future prospect — *sigh* — turned into Zdeno Chara and Jason Spezza. Throwing good money after bad, Islanders owner Charles Wang signed DiPietro to a 15-year, $67.5 contract. He almost immediately got hurt.

Though evidently intelligent — Milbury remains good company on TV, telling it like it is on *Hockey Night in Canada*, TSN, NBC, and NESN — virtually everything Mad Mike did on behalf of the Islanders ended badly. Another trade had him sending future all-stars Todd Bertuzzi and Bryan McCabe to Vancouver for a fading Trevor Linden.

Milbury's coaching record was 56 wins, 111 losses, and 24 ties. His teams never made the playoffs. And as GM, he fired the team's best coach. Pierre Laviolette took the Islanders to the playoffs in 2002 and 2003, was let go, and then took the Carolina Hurricanes all the way to a Stanley Cup win two seasons later.

The Isles haven't made the playoffs since. Milbury was eventually fired, but remained in the organization for a while, one of his jobs being Project Hope — "spread[ing] the joys of hockey to youths in China by providing equipment, coaching clinics and building rinks," according to Islanders promotional bumf. A high-minded, quixotic venture that reminds us of the old Chinese proverb: "Do not climb a tree to look for a fish."

Milbury's successor, Neil Smith, the respected architect of the New York Rangers 1994 Stanley Cup-winning team, lasted 40 days. He was replaced by Garth Snow, the team's backup goalie. Months later, the hockey gods issued an editorial comment: a pipe burst in the Islanders' workout room, showering the team's locker room with fetid sewage.

Workers in gas masks and hoses appeared to suck up the mess. Yes, it could now be said that the Islanders literally stunk out loud.

Still, remaining fans cared. The Nassau Coliseum once knew glory. In the early '80s, prior to Wang and Mad Mike, before bunko artist John Spano owned the team in the '90s, these Islanders ruled the NHL. Denis Potvin was the best defenseman in the world not named Bobby Orr; Bryan Trottier, Mike Bossy, Clark Gillies comprised hockey's premier forward line.

And what a supporting cast! Butch Goring, obtained from Los Angeles when the Leafs wanted too much for Darryl Sittler[2], was a superb forechecker and reliable goal scorer. Not that it mattered, but he was also hockey's worst dresser. Once, Butch wore the same turtleneck several days in a row. Teammates saw him mishandle an airport hot dog — a mustardy wiener escaped down his chest. *What would he wear now?*

"In the end, if we're wrong, we've made an incredible mistake."

2 The Leafs wanted Clark Gillies in exchange for Sittler. So Islander GM Bill Torrey opted to deal with L.A. for his second choice, Goring.

Islanders owner Charles Wang and former GM Mike Milbury

"The team was in perfect balance."

That's why fans remember. And grieve. In 2003, the team lost 5-0 to the hated crosstown Rangers. In response, Islander season-ticket holder Larry Weinberger took out a full-page, $28,000 ad in *Newsday*:

Hey, NY Islanders, where were you the night we played the Rangers? We, your loyal fans showed up! We braved freezing weather and came out looking for a great game. We came out to support you. Where was the energy, the excitement, the electricity, the intensity? Come on now. . . we deserve a better effort. It's a tough road ahead. Your fans are behind you. . . play with passion!!! Let's Go Islanders!

No probs. Butch turned the turtleneck around and lasted out the road trip.

The Islanders' third line — Bob Nystrom, Wayne Merrick, and John Tonelli — was better than many teams' first unit. Bob Bourne, a superb skater, centered the second line. There were two Sutters around for checking — Duane (Dog) and Brent (Pup).

The team was in perfect balance. Goalie Billy Smith had the manners of a serial killer. Upset with a shot in practice, Billy once took off after Mike Bossy, his samurai stick high in the air, and had to be tackled by Nystrom. Skating out to a game in the 1981 finals, the goalie brought his Koho down on the arm of a fan offering encouragement. Turned out she was the wife of the Islanders' team doctor.

Then again, GM Bill Torrey always wore a bow tie. And elegant defenseman Stefan Persson managed 50 assists most seasons without drawing a misconduct.

In taking four consecutive Stanley Cups before bowing out to the Edmonton Oilers, New York won 19 consecutive Stanley Cup playoff series from 1980–84, a sporting record that will likely never be topped.

Yes, let's go. And the Isles have amassed an intriguing talent pool in the last few seasons. Here's hoping that John Tavares, Matt Moulson, Ryan Strome, veteran Mark Streit, and young Nino Niederreiter — three Toronto kids and a pair of Swiss skaters — can take Long Island's team back to glory.

And hey, wouldn't it be something if, instead of Switzerland and the Greater Toronto Area, salvation came from the Far East? If a scout from Charles Wang and Mike Milbury's Project Hope miraculously found a great hockey fish in a tree. A big goalie — Yao Ming on skates — would be nice. Rick DiPietro's contract will be up in 2021.

Former Islander goalie Wade Dubielewicz's
mask paid tribute to championship Islanders.
(Left) Battling Billy Smith and Bob Nystrom.
(Right) Denis Potvin and Bryan Trottier.

NEW YORK RANGERS

Loose Pucks

RECORD: "Hockey Sock Rock" by Phil Esposito and the Ranger Rockers (Ron Duguay, Dave Maloney, Pat Hickey, and John Davidson, a 1979 song with a video shot in a '50s diner, featuring J.D. playing a ketchup-bottle sax solo. Esposito, always a Genoa salami, carries the song off with aplomb, and lyrics integrate hockey with '50s Philly doo-wop: "*You're my favorite chick / My number one draft pick.*"

RECORDS

MOST HAT TRICKS, CAREER: Bill Cook, 11

FASTEST HAT TRICK, FROM START OF CAREER: Derek Stepan, in his first NHL game, October 9, 2010

MOST GOALS, CAREER: Rod Gilbert, 406; Jean Ratelle, 336; Adam Graves, 280

MOST SHORTHANDED GOALS, CAREER: Mark Messier, 23

MOST SHUTOUTS, CAREER: Eddie Giacomin, 49; Henrik Lundqvist, 43

50-GOAL CLUB: Jaromir Jagr, 54, 2005–06; Adam Graves, 52, 1993–94; Vic Hadfield, 50, 1971–72

WORKING OVERTIME: Stephane Matteau snuck one past Martin Brodeur in double overtime of game seven on May 27, 1994, over the hated Devils, propelling New York into the Stanley Cup finals and a date with destiny. Howie Rose's call on the biggest goal in Ranger history: "Matteau! Matteau! Matteau!"

DRAFT-SCHMAFT

TOP-10 PICKS, 1989–2009: 6

PLAYERS DRAFTED WHO PLAYED 300 NHL GAMES: 27

IMPACT PLAYERS: Aaron Miller, 80th, 1989; Doug Weight, 97th, 1990; Sergei Zubov, 164th, 1990; Sergei Nemchinov, 105th, 1990; Alexei Kovalev, 116th, 1991; Mattias Norstrom, 56th, 1992; Marc Savard, 25th, 1995; Henrik Lundqvist, 205th, 2000; Brandon Dubinsky, 60th, 2004; Ryan Callahan, 127th, 2004; Marc Staal, 12th, 2005

DRAFT-SCHMAFT RANKING: 7th

LINE CHANGES

THE BATTERY LINE: Brandon Dubinsky, Artem Anisimov, and Ryan Callahan. Named because their initials match up with battery sizes (D, AA, and C), 2010–present.

THE MAFIA LINE: Don Maloney, Phil Esposito, and Don Murdoch — a Godfather (Esposito) and two Dons, late 1970s.

THE GAG LINE: Vic Hadfield, Jean Ratelle, and Rod Gilbert — scored a goal a game, 1964–75.

Glove story: Henrik Lundqvist snares an Islander blast.

"We only have one person to blame, and that's each other." — Barry Beck

"If hockey fights were fixed, I'd be in more of them." — Rod Gilbert

"I'm just glad it wasn't machete night." — Bob Froese after Rangers fans threw mugs on the ice during mug night

SKATE THAT ONE PAST ME AGAIN: A Ranger talent evaluator gave Mario Lemieux a bad scouting report.

BRING ON THE ZAMBONI

CELEBRITY FANS: Actor Tim Robbins, tennis player John McEnroe, and Henry Kissinger, though they seldom sit together.

STUMP THE SCHWAB: Which New York Ranger enjoyed the longest reign as team captain? Answer: Bob Nevin (1964–71).

"If hockey fights were fixed, I'd be in more of them."

KING of the BLUES

Henrik Lundqvist and twin brother, Joel, were kids trying out for a hockey team in the tiny Swedish ski village of Are, when the coach asked who wanted to be the goalie. Henrik found his hand waving in the air. Brother Joel put it there. The younger-by-40-minutes twin knew what he was doing. King Henrik ascended to throne of Swedish hockey by netting his country a gold medal in 2006, erasing the memory of Tommy Salo's infamous 2002 Olympic flub, when the goalie let a fluttering shot from center ice somehow circle his neck and roll into the net for a game-winning Swiss goal. An amateur musician, Lundqvist arrived in New York with an acoustic guitar and a harmonica in 2005. The only guitar-harp player to make a bigger impression on Manhattan is Bob Dylan. Henrik has been named Ranger MVP five straight seasons, recording a league-high 11 shutouts in the 2010–11 campaign. He's also been named one of the world's most beautiful men (*People* magazine, 2006) and made a best-dressed list (*Page Six* magazine, 2008). Still, he has never repaid his twin his royal favor. Big brother Henrik has yet to allow Joel, a forward for the Dallas Stars, a goal or assist.

FAN-tastic

Miracles on 33rd Street: (Middle left) A New York Ranger fan (or possibly a bank robber taunting authorities) near the Rangers' rink. (Middle right) A New York Duck hunter looking to bag a Selanne or Getzlaf. (Bottom) A distracted woman stepped in front of a Tampa Bay Lightning bus near Madison Square Garden, on 33rd and Eighth. A Ranger fan/hero wearing a Brandon Dubinsky sweater comforted the victim, keeping her still, until EMS arrived.

Hockey's Retirement HOME

New York sports joke: Fans of the Knicks, Mets, and Rangers are sitting together in a bar one night. The Mets fan cries, "Dear God, when are the Mets going to win a World Series again?" And a voice comes booming from on high: "Not in your lifetime." Hearing this, the Knicks fan calls out, "Dear God, when is *my* team going to win an NBA championship?" And God answers, "Not in your children's lifetime." Finally, the Rangers fan nervously enquires, "Dear God, ah . . . when are the Rangers going to win the Stanley Cup again?" There is a pause, the sound of paper being shuffled, and then God finally speaks: "Not in my lifetime."[1]

Money, money changes everything / We think we know what we're doin' / That don't mean a thing . . .
— Queens, New York, hockey mom, Cyndi Lauper

The New York Rangers are worth $411 million, according to *Forbes* magazine. The team has the highest hockey ticket prices in America and sell out every game. What's more, the Rangers are one of the jewels in the MSG TV network, worth an estimated $1.6 billion.

All that Ranger gold hasn't translated into a silver Stanley Cup, alas. The team has won one championship in the last 70 years — in the glorious, red-white-and-blue hockey summer of 1994. It hasn't been for a shortage of star players, mind you. According to the 1998 *Hockey News* list of the greatest hockey players of the 20th century, eight of the top 20 and 16 of the 50 best NHLers all skated for the Rangers: Wayne Gretzky (1st), Doug Harvey (6th), Terry Sawchuk (9th), Guy Lafleur (11th), Mark Messier (12th), Jacques Plante (13th), Howie Morenz (15th), Phil Esposito (18th), Jaromir Jagr (37th), Marcel Dionne (38th), Boom Boom Geoffrion (42nd), Tim Horton (43rd), Bill Cook (44th), Max Bentley (48th), Brad Park (49th), and Jari Kurri (50th).

Of those 16, every one except Jagr — who's not yet eligible — is a Hall of Famer. Collectively, they account for some 35 50-goal seasons, a whopping 22 Hart Trophies as league MVP, seven best-defenseman awards, and nine Vezina Trophies for top goalie.

1 The author heard this joke from a waiter at Carmine's, in the old Fulton Fish Market in New York, probably in 1992.

Here's the rub: none of those 38 trophies came when the players in question were Rangers. And only Jagr, in 2005–06, scored 50 goals for New York.

It gets worse. Forwards Morenz, Geoffrion, Dionne, Bentley, Lafleur, and Kurri all arrived on the wrong side of 30, with only the Little Beaver, Dionne, denting the 20-goal mark (31 in 1987–88).

The Rangers have developed a reputation as NHL poachers. "We hope to build the kind of hockey team that the New York Rangers want to buy," Bobby Smith, former GM of the Phoenix Coyotes, once said.

The spending-spree tactic worked exactly once, in 1994, when general manager Neil Smith famously brought in a sextet of purebred champion Edmonton Oilers — Mark Messier, Kevin Lowe, Adam Graves, Craig MacTavish, Esa Tikkanen, and Glenn Anderson — along with Chicago Blackhawks star Steve Larmer to win the Cup.

Since then: nada. For the last 27 years, it's been more of the same: buy high — like, *really* high — and finish low in the standings. Aging big-buck stars are brought in. Namely, Pat Verbeek, Luc Robitaille, Gretzky, Kurri, Theoren Fleury, Eric Lindros, Pavel Bure, Pat LaFontaine, Martin Straka, Bobby Holik, Sandis Ozolinsh, Vladimir Malakhov, Alexei Kovalev, Martin Rucinsky, Jagr — pause to take a breath — Brendan Shanahan, Markus Naslund, Wade Redden, Scott Gomez, Chris Drury . . .

Ka-ching, ka-ching, ka-ching. . .

And the team keeps finishing out of the Stanley Cup hunt. Though they were the highest-paid club in hockey at the turn of the millennium, the Rangers finished out of the playoffs seven years in a row prior to the salary cap (instituted in 2005). Since then, they've fared better, making the postseason all but once (2009–10). But still, they've never ventured past the second round of the playoffs. Not even with one of the league's best goalies, Henrik Lundqvist.

Lundqvist was 26 and in his prime in 2009, and the Rangers had amassed a pool of young, diligent, two-way players, including character guy Ryan Callahan, Alaskan husky Brandon Dubinsky, and Marc Staal on defense. Dan Girardi, Artem Anisimov, Derek Stepan, Brendan Prust, and Michael Del Zotto were intriguing prospects. They were getting close. But there were pieces missing. Big pieces: a fleet, goal-scoring winger and (that rarest of all talents) a creative, number-one center who you want on the ice when you're down a single goal in the final minute of the game.

It's hard to trade for such players. You either have to take your lumps, finish low in the standings, and hope to grow your own through the draft. Or wait in line with other rich, yet needy franchises and overpay for a veteran free agent.

Guess which direction the Rangers went?

They couldn't help themselves, really. They had the money. And this is New York, the media capital of the world. Manhattan is a drink that needs a big straw to stir it, to paraphrase Reggie Jackson's famous metaphor. In 2009, Minnesota's Marian Gaborik, age 27, was up for grabs — lightning fast with soft hands. Injury-prone, maybe, but what the hey. . . there are eight big hospitals in New York. Lots of experts with stethoscopes running around.

Two off-seasons later, the big free-agent prize was Brad Richards — a little older, at 31, but he could make Gaborik, not to mention the power play, better — *right away!* He'd also won a Conn Smythe Trophy after helping Tampa Bay to a Stanley Cup in 2004.

So the Rangers signed them both. They'd also nailed down Lundqvist to a big contract. Going into the 2012–13 season they will have their three big guys, proven veterans who will be turning 33 (Richards) and 31 (Gaborik and Lundqvist) during the season. All at a cost of $26 million.

Are they ready to win the Cup? Well, the question we have to ask ourselves is how good 33- and 31-year-old hockey players are. Leave us look then, shall we?

Brad Richards in a sober mood.

Since the dawn of the NHL, the average age of top-10 scorers has been:

1917–20: 26.3 YRS OLD
1921–30: 26.7
1931–40: 26.3
1941–50: 27.0
1951–60: 26.4
1961–70: 28.6
1971–80: 24.0
1981–90: 24.5
1991–00: 26.5
2001–10: 24.3

Doing a little more ciphering, we arrive at the conclusion that, for close to 100 years, the average age of an NHL top-10 scorer is somewhere between 26 and 27. Okay, so New York missed that boat for 2012–13. But what Ranger fans really want to know is how the aforementioned top-10ers performed a little farther down the rink of life.

So let's look at how they negotiated the dangerous hairpin turn of hockey at age 30. Since Wayne Gretzky turned pro in the fall of 1979, 50 forwards have landed among the top 10 scorers somewhere between the ages of 26 and 27. Here is their scoring journey as the sand passed through their hourglass.

1979-80
BLAINE STOUGHTON (HARTFORD WHALERS, NEW YORK RANGERS):

YEAR	TEAM	G	A	PTS	GP
79–80	Har.	56	44	100	80
80–81	Har.	43	30	73	71
81–82	Har.	52	39	91	80
82–83	Har.	45	31	76	72
83–84	Har./NYR	23	14	37	37
84–85	NYR	5	2	7	14
85–86	MINORS				

BLAIR "B.J." McDONALD (EDMONTON OILERS, VANCOUVER CANUCKS)

YEAR	TEAM	G	A	PTS	GP
79–80	Edm.	46	48	94	80
80–81	Edm./Van.	24	33	67	63
81–82	Van.	15	18	33	59
82–83	Van.	3	4	7	17
83–84	MINORS				
84–85	RETIRED				

1980-81
CHARLIE SIMMER (LOS ANGELES KINGS, BOSTON BRUINS)

YEAR	TEAM	G	A	PTS	GP
80–81	LA	56	45	101	65
81–82	LA	56	49	105	50
82–83	LA	29	51	80	80
83–84	LA	44	48	92	79
84–85	LA-Bos.	33	30	63	63
85–86	Bos.	36	24	60	55
86–87	Bos.	29	40	69	80

MIKE ROGERS (HARTFORD WHALERS, NEW YORK RANGERS, EDMONTON OILERS)

YEAR	TEAM	G	A	PTS	GP
80–81	Har.	40	65	105	80
81–82	NYR	38	65	103	80
82–83	NYR	29	47	76	71
83–84	NYR	23	38	61	78
84–85	NYR	26	38	64	78
85–86	NYR-Edm.	2	3	5	17
86–87	RETIRED				

1981-82
DENIS MARUK (WASHINGTON CAPITALS, MINNESOTA NORTH STARS)

YEAR	TEAM	G	A	PTS	GP
81–82	Was.	60	76	130	80
82–83	Was.	31	50	81	80
83–84	Min.	17	43	60	71
84–85	Min.	19	41	60	71
85–86	Min.	21	37	58	70
86–87	Min.	16	30	46	67
87–88	Min.	7	11	18	22

DAVE TAYLOR (LOS ANGELES KINGS)

YEAR	TEAM	G	A	PTS	GP
81–82	LA	39	67	106	78
82–83	LA	21	37	58	58
83–84	LA	20	49	69	63
84–85	LA	41	51	92	79
85–86	LA	33	38	71	76
86–87	LA	18	44	62	67
87–88	LA	26	41	67	68

1982-83
Peter Stastny (Quebec Nordiques)

Year	Team	G	A	Pts	GP
82-83	Que.	47	77	124	75
83-84	Que.	46	73	119	80
84-85	Que.	32	68	100	75
85-86	Que.	41	81	122	76
86-87	Que.	24	53	77	64
87-88	Que.	46	65	111	76
88-89	Que.	35	50	85	72

Kent "Mr. Magic" Nilsson (Calgary Flames, Minnesota North Stars, Edmonton Oilers)

Year	Team	G	A	Pts	GP
82-83	Calg.	46	58	104	80
83-84	Calg.	31	49	80	67
84-85	Calg.	37	62	99	77
85-86	Min.	16	44	60	61
86-87	Min./Edm.	18	45	63	61
87-88	Mr. Magic disappeared to Italy to play for Bolzano-Bozen Foxes				
88-89	Italy				

1983-84
Mike Bossy (New York Islanders)

Year	Team	G	A	Pts	GP
83-84	NYI	51	67	118	67
84-85	NYI	58	59	117	76
85-86	NYI	61	62	123	80
86-87	NYI	38	37	75	63
87-88	Retired due to back injury				

Bryan Trottier (New York Islanders)

Year	Team	G	A	Pts	GP
83-84	NYI	40	71	111	68
84-85	NYI	28	31	59	68
85-86	NYI	37	59	96	78
86-87	NYI	23	64	87	80
87-88	NYI	30	52	82	77
88-89	NYI	17	28	45	73
89-90	NYI	13	11	24	59

Bernie Federko (St. Louis Blues, Detroit Red Wings)

Year	Team	G	A	Pts	GP
83-84	St.L.	41	66	107	79
84-85	St.L.	30	73	103	76
85-86	St.L.	34	68	102	80
86-87	St.L.	20	52	72	64
87-88	St.L.	20	69	89	72
88-89	St.L.	22	45	67	66
89-90	Det.	17	40	57	73

1985-86
Mats "Le Petit Viking" Naslund (Montreal Canadiens)

Year	Team	G	A	Pts	GP
85-86	Mon.	43	67	110	80
86-87	Mon.	25	55	80	79
87-88	Mon.	24	59	83	78
88-89	Mon.	33	51	84	77
89-90	Mon.	21	20	41	72
90-91	Played in Switzerland				
91-92	Switzerland				

1986-87
Jari Kurri (Edmonton Oilers, Los Angeles Kings)

Year	Team	G	A	Pts	GP
86-87	Edm.	54	54	108	79
87-88	Edm.	43	53	96	80
88-89	Edm.	44	58	102	76
89-90	Edm.	33	60	93	78
90-91	Played in Italy				
91-92	LA	23	37	60	73
92-93	LA	27	60	87	82

(Played in 1995-96 for New York Rangers)

Dino Ciccarelli (Minnesota North Stars, Washington Capitals, Detroit Red Wings)

Year	Team	G	A	Pts	GP
86-87	Min.	52	51	103	80
87-88	Min.	41	45	86	67
88-89	Min./Was.	44	30	74	76
89-90	Was.	41	38	79	80
90-91	Was.	21	18	39	54
91-92	Was.	38	38	76	78
92-93	Det.	41	66	107	82

MICHEL GOULET (Quebec Nordiques, Chicago Blackhawks)

Year	Team	G	A	Pts	GP
86–87	Que.	49	47	96	75
87–88	Que.	48	58	106	80
88–89	Que.	26	38	64	69
89–90	Que./Chi.	20	30	50	65
90–91	Chi.	27	38	65	74
91–92	Chi.	22	41	63	75
92–93	Chi.	23	21	44	63

1987–88
WAYNE GRETZKY (Edmonton Oilers, Los Angeles Kings)

Year	Team	G	A	Pts	GP
87–88	Edm.	40	109	149	64
88–89	LA	54	114	168	78
89–90	LA	40	102	142	73
90–91	LA	41	122	163	78
91–92	LA	31	90	121	74
92–93	LA	16	49	65	45
93–94	LA	38	92	130	81

(Finished his career with New York Rangers, 1996–99)

MARK MESSIER (Edmonton Oilers, New York Rangers)

Year	Team	G	A	Pts	GP
87–88	Edm.	37	74	111	77
88–89	Edm.	33	61	94	72
89–90	Edm.	45	84	129	79
90–91	Edm.	12	52	64	53
91–92	NYR	35	72	107	79
92–93	NYR	25	66	91	75
93–94	NYR	26	58	82	76

HAKAN LOOB (Calgary Flames)

Year	Team	G	A	Pts	GP
87–88	Calg.	50	56	106	80
88–89	Calg.	27	58	85	79
89–90	Played in Sweden				

DENIS SAVARD (Chicago Blackhawks, Montreal Canadiens, Tampa Bay Lightning)

Year	Team	G	A	Pts	GP
87–88	Chi.	44	87	131	80
88–89	Chi.	23	59	82	58
89–90	Chi.	23	57	80	60
90–91	Mon.	28	31	59	70
91–92	Mon.	28	42	70	77
92–93	Mon.	16	34	50	63
93–94	TB	18	28	46	74

1988–89
BERNIE NICHOLLS (Los Angeles Kings, New York Rangers, Edmonton Oilers, New Jersey Devils, Chicago Blackhawks)

Year	Team	G	A	Pts	GP
88–89	LA	70	80	150	79
89–90	LA/NYR	39	73	112	79
90–91	NYR	25	43	73	71
91–92	NYR/Edm.	20	29	49	51
92–93	Edm./NJ	13	47	60	69
93–94	NJ	19	27	46	61
94–95	Chi.	22	29	51	48

1989–90
ADAM OATES (St. Louis Blues, Boston Bruins)

Year	Team	G	A	Pts	GP
89–90	St.L.	23	79	102	80
90–91	St.L.	25	90	115	61
91–92	St.L./Bos.	20	89	109	80
92–93	Bos.	45	87	142	84
93–94	Bos.	32	80	112	77
94–95	Bos.	12	43	55	63
95–96	Bos.	25	67	92	70

1990–91
BRETT HULL (St. Louis Blues)

Year	Team	G	A	Pts	GP
90–91	St.L.	86	45	131	78
91–92	St.L.	70	39	109	73
92–93	St.L.	54	47	101	80
93–94	St.L.	57	40	97	81
94–95	St.L.	29	21	50	48
95–96	St.L.	43	40	83	70
96–97	St.L.	42	40	82	77

1991–92
MARIO LEMIEUX (Pittsburgh Penguins)

Year	Team	G	A	Pts	GP
91–92	Pit.	44	87	131	64
92–93	Pit.	69	91	160	60
93–94	Pit.	17	20	37	22
94–95	Pit.	69	92	161	70
95–96	Pit.	50	72	122	76
96–97	Retired				

KEVIN STEVENS (PITTSBURGH PENGUINS, BOSTON BRUINS, LOS ANGELES KINGS, NEW YORK RANGERS)

YEAR	TEAM	G	A	PTS	GP
91–92	PIT.	54	69	123	80
92–93	PIT.	55	56	111	80
93–94	PIT.	41	47	98	83
94–95	PIT.	15	12	27	27
95–96	BOS./LA	13	23	36	61
96–97	LA	14	20	34	69
97–98	NYR	14	27	41	80

STEVE YZERMAN (DETROIT RED WINGS)

YEAR	TEAM	G	A	PTS	GP
91–92	DET.	45	58	103	79
92–93	DET.	58	79	137	84
93–94	DET.	24	58	82	58
94–95	DET.	12	26	38	47
95–96	DET.	36	59	95	80
96–97	DET.	22	63	85	81
97–98	DET.	24	45	69	75

1992–93
PAT LAFONTAINE (BUFFALO SABRES, NEW YORK RANGERS)

YEAR	TEAM	G	A	PTS	GP
92–93	BUF.	53	95	148	84
93–94	BUF.	5	13	18	16
94–95	BUF.	12	15	27	22
95–96	BUF.	40	51	91	76
96–97	BUF.	2	6	8	13
97–98	NYR	23	39	62	67
98–99	RETIRED BECAUSE OF CONCUSSIONS				

LUC ROBITAILLE (LOS ANGELES KINGS, PITTSBURGH PENGUINS, NEW YORK RANGERS)

YEAR	TEAM	G	A	PTS	GP
92–93	LA	63	62	125	84
93–94	LA	44	62	106	83
94–95	PIT.	23	19	42	46
95–96	NYR	23	46	69	77
96–97	NYR	24	24	48	69
97–98	LA	16	24	40	57
98–99	LA	39	35	74	82

1994–95
THEO FLEURY (CALGARY FLAMES, COLORADO AVALANCHE, NEW YORK RANGERS)

YEAR	TEAM	G	A	PTS	GP
94–95	CALG.	29	29	59	47
95–96	CALG.	46	50	96	80
96–97	CALG.	29	38	67	81
97–98	CALG.	27	51	78	82
98–99	CALG./COLO.	10	14	24	15
99–00	NYR	15	49	64	80
00–01	NYR	30	44	74	62

1995–96
JOE SAKIC (COLORADO AVALANCHE)

YEAR	TEAM	G	A	PTS	GP
95–96	COLO.	51	69	120	82
96–97	COLO.	22	52	74	65
97–98	COLO.	27	36	63	64
98–99	COLO.	41	55	96	73
99–00	COLO.	28	53	81	60
00–01	COLO.	54	64	118	82
01–02	COLO.	26	53	79	82

ALEXANDER MOGILNY (VANCOUVER CANUCKS, NEW JERSEY DEVILS, TORONTO MAPLE LEAFS)

YEAR	TEAM	G	A	PTS	GP
95–96	VAN.	55	52	107	79
96–97	VAN.	31	42	73	76
97–98	VAN.	18	27	45	51
98–99	VAN.	14	31	45	59
99–00	VAN./NJ	24	20	44	59
00–01	NJ	43	40	83	75
01–02	TOR.	24	33	57	66

SERGEI FEDOROV (DETROIT RED WINGS)

YEAR	TEAM	G	A	PTS	GP
95–96	DET.	39	67	107	78
96–97	DET.	30	33	63	74
97–98	DET.	6	11	17	21
98–99	DET.	26	37	63	77
99–00	DET.	27	35	62	68
00–01	DET.	32	37	69	75
01–02	DET.	31	37	68	81

1996-97
Teemu "The Finnish Flash" Selanne (Mighty Ducks of Anaheim, San Jose Sharks)

Year	Team	G	A	Pts	GP
96–97	Ana.	51	58	109	78
97–98	Ana.	52	34	86	73
98–99	Ana.	47	60	107	75
99–00	Ana.	33	52	85	74
00–01	Ana./SJ	33	39	72	73
01–02	SJ	29	25	54	82
02–03	SJ	28	36	64	82

John LeClair (Philadelphia Flyers)

Year	Team	G	A	Pts	GP
96–97	Phi.	50	47	97	82
97–98	Phi.	51	36	98	82
98–99	Phi.	43	47	90	76
99–00	Phi.	40	37	77	82
00–01	Phi.	7	5	12	16
01–02	Phi.	25	26	51	82
02–03	Phi.	18	10	28	35

Zigmund Palffy (New York Islanders, Los Angeles Kings)

Year	Team	G	A	Pts	GP
96–97	NYI	48	42	90	80
97–98	NYI	45	42	87	82
98–99	NYI	22	28	50	50
99–00	LA	27	39	66	64
00–01	LA	38	51	89	73
01–02	LA	32	27	59	63
02–03	LA	37	48	85	76

Brendan Shanahan (Hartford Whalers, Detroit Red Wings)

Year	Team	G	A	Pts	GP
96–97	Har./Det.	47	41	88	81
97–98	Det.	28	29	57	75
98–99	Det.	31	27	58	81
99–00	Det.	41	37	78	78
00–01	Det.	31	45	76	81
01–02	Det.	37	38	75	80
02–03	Det.	30	38	68	78

(Played 2006–08 for New York Rangers)

1997-98
Pavel Bure (Vancouver Canucks, Florida Panthers, New York Rangers)

Year	Team	G	A	Pts	GP
97–98	Van.	51	39	90	82
98–99	Flo.	13	3	14	11
99–00	Flo.	58	36	94	74
00–01	Flo.	59	33	92	82
01–02	Flo./NYR	34	35	69	68
02–03	NYR	19	11	30	36
03–04	Waived after failing pre-season physical.				

Retired November 2005.

1998-99
Jaromir Jagr (Pittsburgh Penguins, Washington Capitals, New York Rangers)

Year	Team	G	A	Pts	GP
98–99	Pit.	44	83	127	81
99–00	Pit.	42	54	96	63
00–01	Pit.	52	69	121	81
01–02	Was.	31	48	79	69
02–03	Was.	36	41	77	75
03–04	Was./NYR	31	43	76	78
04–05	Locked out				

Martin Straka (Pittsburgh Penguins)

Year	Team	G	A	Pts	GP
98–99	Pit.	35	48	83	80
99–00	Pit.	20	39	59	71
00–01	Pit.	27	68	95	82
01–02	Pit.	5	4	9	13
02–03	Pit.	18	28	46	60
03–04	Pit./LA	10	16	26	54
04–05	Locked out				

Signed with New York Rangers August 2005

1999-00
Owen Nolan (San Jose Sharks, Toronto Maple Leafs)

Year	Team	G	A	Pts	GP
99–00	SJ	44	40	84	78
00–01	SJ	24	25	49	57
01–02	SJ	23	43	69	75
02–03	SJ/Tor.	29	25	54	75
03–04	Tor.	19	29	48	65
04–05	Did not play — injured				
05–06	Did not play — injured				

PAUL KARIYA (Anaheim Mighty Devils, Colorado Avalanche, Nashville Predators)

Year	Team	G	A	Pts	GP
99–00	Ana.	42	44	86	74
00–01	Ana.	33	34	67	66
01–02	Ana.	32	25	56	82
02–03	Ana.	25	56	81	82
03–04	Colo.	11	25	36	51
04–05	Locked out				
05–06	Nash.	31	54	85	82

2000-01
ALEX KOVALEV (Pittsburgh Penguins, New York Rangers, Montreal Canadiens)

Year	Team	G	A	Pts	GP
00–01	Pit.	44	51	95	79
01–02	Pit.	32	33	76	67
02–03	Pit./NYR	40	40	80	77
03–04	NYR/Mon.	14	31	45	74
04–05	Locked out				
05–06	Mon.	23	42	65	69
06–07	Mon.	18	29	47	73

PETER FORSBERG (Colorado Avalanche, Philadelphia Flyers, Nashville Predators)

Year	Team	G	A	Pts	GP
00–01	Colo.	27	62	89	76
01–02	Did not play— injured				
02–03	Colo.	27	77	106	75
03–04	Colo.	18	37	55	39
04–05	Locked out				
05–06	Phi.	19	56	75	60
06–07	Phi./Nash.	13	42	55	57

2001-02
TODD BERTUZZI (Vancouver Canucks, Florida Panthers, Detroit Red Wings, Anaheim Ducks)

Year	Team	G	A	Pts	GP
01–02	Van.	36	49	85	72
02–03	Van.	46	51	96	82
03–04	Van.	17	43	60	69
04–05	Locked out				
05–06	Van.	25	46	71	82
06–07	Flo./Det.	3	8	11	15
07–08	Ana.	14	26	40	68

PAVOL DEMITRA (St. Louis Blues, Los Angeles Kings, Minnesota Wild)

Year	Team	G	A	Pts	GP
01–02	St.L.	35	42	77	82
02–03	St.L.	36	57	93	78
03–04	St.L.	23	35	58	68
04–05	Locked out				
05–06	LA	25	37	62	58
06–07	Min.	25	39	64	71
07–08	Min.	15	39	54	68

2002-03
MILAN HEJDUK (Colorado Avalanche)

Year	Team	G	A	Pts	GP
02–03	Colo.	50	48	98	82
03–04	Colo.	35	40	75	82
04–05	Locked out				
05–06	Colo.	24	34	58	74
06–07	Colo.	35	35	70	74
07–08	Colo.	29	25	54	77
08–09	Colo.	27	32	59	82

2005-06
JOE THORNTON (San Jose Sharks)

Year	Team	G	A	Pts	GP
05–06	Bos./SJ	29	96	125	81
06–07	SJ	22	92	114	82
07–08	SJ	29	67	96	82
08–09	SJ	25	61	86	82
09–10	SJ	20	69	89	79
10–11	SJ	21	49	70	80

2006-07
VINCENT LECAVALIER (Tampa Bay Lightning)

Year	Team	G	A	Pts	GP
06–07	TB	52	56	108	82
07–08	TB	40	52	92	81
08–09	TB	29	38	67	77
09–10	TB	24	46	66	82
10–11	TB	25	29	54	65

MARIAN HOSSA (Atlanta Thrashers, Pittsburgh Penguins, Detroit Red Wings, Chicago Blackhawks)

Year	Team	G	A	Pts	GP
06-07	ATL.	43	57	100	82
07-08	ATL./PIT.	29	37	66	72
08-09	DET.	40	31	71	74
09-10	CHI.	24	27	51	57
10-11	CHI.	25	32	57	65

HENRIK ZETTERBERG (Detroit Red Wings)

Year	Team	G	A	Pts	GP
07-08	DET.	43	49	92	75
08-09	DET.	31	42	73	77
09-10	DET.	23	47	70	74
10-11	DET.	24	56	80	80

2009-10
MARIAN GABORIK (New York Rangers)

Year	Team	G	A	Pts	GP
09-10	NYR	40	42	82	76
10-11	NYR	22	26	48	62

Whew, talk about age 30 being a dangerous turn. As you can see from the chart below, the biggest dip in a star player's production comes when he's rounding 30. Players in the 28–29 age bracket score at a 1.07 point-per-game clip; two seasons later, at 30 or 31, they're under 1.0 and playing nine fewer games, missing about three more weeks of the season.

Years Old	Points	Games	PPG
26–27	106.5	76.8	1.4
27–28	86.3	69.3	1.2
28–29	77.2	71.8	1.07
29–30	72.6	68.5	1.06
30–31	60.3	62	0.97
31–32	54.1	56.1	0.94
32–33	49.7	53.6	0.92

WHAT DO ALL THOSE NUMBERS MEAN?

Going into 2012-13, we might expect Brad Richards, at age 32 (he turns 33 in May) to play 54 games, scoring 50 or so points. That's not enough, you say? He's too good, too consistent, too much of a pro? Hey, we could have said all those things and more about New York Islanders center Bryan Trottier, one of the top five or so players of his generation, and he managed just 24 points in 59 games when he was that age.

As for the injury-prone winger Gaborik, who made the top 10 for the first time right on schedule, at age 27, for the New York Rangers, in 2009-10, he'll be 30-turning-31 in 2012. The chart says Ranger fans can expect him to contribute 60 or so points in 62 games. Let's not dwell on the fact that Trottier's best winger, Mike Bossy, retired with a bad back at age 30.

You never know. Life after 30 is a downhill slide for most players, even stars. Top-10 scorers average close to 107 points in their best season and 54 just four years later — almost half. And there are lots of sudden cliffs going downhill — concussions, tiring legs, crumbling hands.

When Mark Messier was with the Rangers, he once told a reporter, "Biologically, I'm 10. Chronologically, I'm 33. In hockey years, I'm 66."

A rounding-30 age chart of NHL top-10 scorers looks a lot like a post-2008 Dow Jones chart, with productivity going steadily downhill:

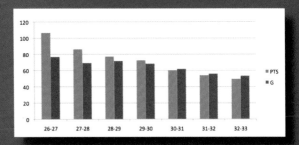

The same stars' points-per-game ratios, as we can see, also slide, even as they play fewer and fewer games:

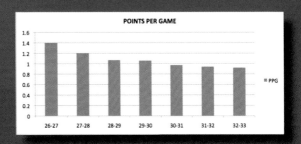

There is no question that players like Gaborik and Richards, both good hockey players, make the Rangers better. For a while, anyway. Maybe that's the problem. A steady infusion of game, hard-eyed veterans, Howard Hawksian pros like Richards and Brendan Shanahan, make a team respectable — almost there. The Rangers' story is one of almost making the

playoffs, almost getting into the second round. But recruiting new 31-year-old stars every couple of seasons, being perpetually "almost there," means you're never there.

That you're forever chasing your hat down a windy street.

Sometimes it's better to let a team die a natural death, like Pittsburgh and Chicago did last decade, and reap the benefits of lucrative draft hauls. That way, you get Howie Morenz, Doug Harvey, Guy Lafleur, Marcel Dionne, and Wayne Gretzky when they're 19, with their best years ahead of them.

The three players who figure to lead the Rangers to the Promised Land in 2012-13 — Lundqvist, Richards and Gaborik — will all be over 30. And only one team in the history of hockey has ever won the Stanley Cup that way.

That would be the NHL's great Over-the-Hill Gang, the 2001–02 Detroit Red Wings, whose top eight scorers — Brendan Shanahan (32), Sergei Fedorov (31), Brett Hull (37), Nik Lidstrom (31), Luc Robitaille (35), Steve Yzerman (36), and Igor Larionov (40), along with goalie Dominik Hasek (37), were all over the Great Age Divide.

And they were all Hall of Famers, playing before the salary cap era.

Good luck, Rangers! But for the team to win in '12–13, the young guys are going to have to step way, way up. Lead on, captain Ryan Callahan (who will be 25). Mush, Anchorage's Brandon Dubinski (26).

Puck-pourri: (Top) Brad Richards accepts congrats from teammates. (Above) "Eddie-Eddie" Giacomin mask. (Near left) A Ranger stands guard over Stephen Colbert ice cream. Which reminds us: former Ranger great Mike Richter has an ice cream flavor of his own at the New York Last Licks Ice Cream chain — Ricky Road. (Far left) Brandon Dubinsky tosses a puck into the crowd.

OTTAWA SENATORS

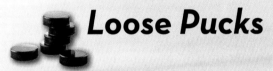

Loose *Pucks*

RECORD: Recorded in 1992, the Ottawa Senators' theme song sounds like the old *Hockey Night in Canada* theme, updated with a burping bass line and Tower of Power horns. It's an instrumental except for one line: "Let's Go Sens." The Senators began playing Stompin' Tom Connors' "Hockey Song" in 1997. Before long, almost every other rink in North America had added it to their playlists.

RECORDS

MOST HAT TRICKS, CAREER: Daniel Alfredsson, 8

MOST GOALS IN A SEASON: Dany Heatley, 50, 2005–06, 2006–07

BEST PLUS/MINUS, CAREER: Wade Redden, + 159

MOST POINTS IN A SEASON, DEFENSEMAN: Erik Karlsson, 66, 2011–12

MOST SHUTOUTS, CAREER: Patrick Lalime, 30

50-GOAL CLUB: Dany Heatley, 50, 2006–07; Heatley, 50, 2005–06

WORKING OVERTIME: The 1927 Ottawa Senators played a playoff game that took two days for anyone to score. What happened was that in the first game of the Cup finals, Ottawa battled Boston to a scoreless tie. Ice in the Boston Arena wasn't good enough to continue, so the teams played again two days later, with Ottawa winning 3–1. The next match, in Ottawa, was another two-game overtime affair; Ottawa finally took the Stanley Cup with another second-game 3–1 win.

DRAFT-SCHMAFT

TOP-10 PICKS, 1992–2009: 8

PLAYERS DRAFTED WHO PLAYED 300 NHL GAMES: 27

IMPACT PLAYERS: Alexei Yashin, 2nd, 1992; Pavol Demitra, 227th, 1993; Daniel Alfredsson, 133rd, 1994; Bryan Berard, 1st, 1995; Chris Phillips, 1st, 1996; Marian Hossa, 12th, 1997; Mike Fisher, 44th, 1998; Martin Havlat, 26th, 1999; Jason Spezza, 2nd, 2001; Erik Karlsson, 15th, 2008

DRAFT-SCHMAFT RANKING: 4th

LINE CHANGES

THE PIZZA LINE: Dany Heatley, Jason Spezza, and Daniel Alfredsson, 2005–10. A local pizzeria gave out free slices whenever the Sens scored five goals. Heatley, Spezza, and Alfredsson kept fans rolling in pizza dough for half a decade.

"The crooks had good taste." — Sens assistant coach E.J. McGuire, after the Senators' video room was burgled halfway through the team's last-place rookie season of 1992–93. The crooks stole six VCRs,

Daniel Alfredsson lets a slap shot fly.

a large-screen TV, and a satellite receiver, but left every one of the team's game tapes. Ottawa had 10 wins, 70 losses, and four ties that year.

"Mother Teresa would have a bad reputation in Ottawa. You can't go down the street and so much as sneeze without something going wrong." — Islander GM Mike Milbury upon getting trouble magnet Alexei Yashin from the Senators for Zdeno Chara and the draft pick used to select Jason Spezza. The trade would help turn the Senators into a perennial Stanley Cup contender. And Milbury into a pretty good TV analyst.

SKATE THAT ONE PAST ME AGAIN: One Sens fan, 99-year-old Russell Williams, attended the 1927 game that saw Ottawa win its 10th Stanley Cup, and then, 80 years later, showed up at the team's win over Anaheim in game three of the 2007 Cup final.

BRING ON THE ZAMBONI
CELEBRITY FANS: Actor Matthew Perry and comedian Tom Green.

STUMP THE SCHWAB: What is Daniel Alfredsson's dog's name? Answer: Bono. Alfie is a big U2 fan. The Scotia-bank Centre plays U2's "Beautiful Day" whenever the winger scores.

BORN and RAISED in Ottawa

Lord Stanley of Preston, Canada's sixth governor general (1883–93), saw his first hockey game in 1889. Striding with his entourage into Montreal's Victoria Rink, he acknowledged a thin, wavering rendition of "God Save the Queen" from a brass band laboring in the cold. What's this, then? He plunked himself down, perhaps availing himself of the five-cent hot-potato hand warmers sold outside arenas, and proceeded to fall for the sport of hockey hook, line, and pocket watch. No wonder: for a man of politics, a pursuit slower than cricket and less civilized than boxing, how thrilling was it to be alongside genuinely happy citizens watching athletes perform feats of geometric daring on brightly lit ice! Like countless future Canadians, Lord Stanley celebrated his enthusiasm for hockey by building a backyard rink, ordering construction of an ice surface at Rideau Hall. His sons and daughter played hockey there. Lord Stanley even

(. . .continued from page 143)

drove his lads, Algernon (sounds like a net-hanger!) and Arthur, to out-of-town games. Not that much of a sacrifice perhaps, given that they were traveling on a private train. On March 12, 1892, the governor general gave lasting shape to his love of hockey, dispatching an aide to a stuffy Rideau Club dinner to give the following speech:

I have for some time been thinking that it would be a good thing if there were a challenge cup which could be held from year to year by the leading hockey club in Canada.... Considering the interest that hockey matches now elicit and the importance of having the games played under generally recognized rules, I am willing to give a cup that shall be held annually by the winning side.

Later that year, aides picked up the silver trophy, at a cost of 10 guineas ($1,400 today) from a Regent Street silversmith in London. Before long, the Stanley Cup would become, after the transcontinental railroad, Canada's second national dream. More often than not, the Stanley Cup remained in Ottawa in the early 20th century. From 1903 through 1927, the Ottawa Senators won the trophy 10 times.

FAN-tastic

(Top) A Daniel Alfredsson fan celebrates his hero's goal. (Middle) Hot over the collar: Senator fans on their way to sweep a series. (Bottom left) Ottawa game faces.

The EMIGRANTS

The first Swedish migration to Canada began in the 1890s and consisted mainly of farmers escaping European famines by settling in western provinces and northern Ontario. Today, a third of a million Swedes live in Canada. You have the towns of Stockholm, Saskatchewan; Thorsby, Alberta; and Upsala, Ontario. Swedish-Canadian hockey players include Eric Lindros (London, Ontario), Glenn Anderson (Vancouver), and Bob Nystrom (born in Stockholm, but raised in Hinton, Alberta).

And if the careers of Lindros, Anderson, and Nystrom don't demolish the specious chicken-Swedes cliché, how about this: *Darth Vader* is a Swedish-Canadian! Or at least he was when Vancouver's Hayden Christenson played him in *Attack of the Clones* and *Revenge of the Sith*.

Many Minnesota NHLers are also sons of Sweden — all of your Brotens (Aaron, Paul, and Neal), Paul Holmgren, Dustin Byfuglien, and Erik Johnson. The list goes on.

But back to Canada, the last Swedish migration began in 1995, when Daniel Alfredsson flew in from Stockholm, landing in Ottawa, who were dead last in the NHL and sinking. A local reporter, Ken Warren, gave him a lift into town and asked what he knew about his new team.

"[Just] something I read in Sweden," Alfredsson shrugged. "The article said, 'With Alexei Yashin, the Senators are a terrible team. Without him, they are even worse.'"

That was about right. And who could have guessed that here was the player who would turn the franchise around? That the not-so-young rookie (22), a sixth-round 1994 draft flyer, would be rookie of the year six months later? Furthermore, that he would eventually captain and take the team to the Stanley Cup finals? And would make such a good impression on his first and only NHL team, in fact, that 17 years later Sweden is now Ottawa's preferred shopping center for hockey talent.

Today, Erik Karlsson, the NHL's highest-scoring defenseman, is poised to replace "Alfie" as the face of the Senators. And Ottawa's top three prospects — centers Mika Zibanejad and Jakob Silverberg, along with goalie Robin Lehner — are all Swedish.

The Senators certainly weren't counting on Alfredsson to lead them to the promised land. At age 20, he scored but a single goal playing center for what was then a second-division pro team, the Frolunda Indians. He was still an Indian, earning $6,000 and working construction in the off-season, when the still-agentless player worked out his first NHL contract over the phone.

Alfredsson soon discovered the Senators didn't expect him to make the team his first season. Flipping through the Sens' media guide, the rookie looked in vain for his entry, finding his name way at the back, a small listing on the "In the System" page.

Clearly, the Senators didn't know Alfredsson. Probably, the player himself didn't know how good he could be. For Daniel Alfredsson's greatest skill has always been perseverance, fighting through adversity. He needed a challenge to become a great player. Being told he couldn't make the team was just the incentive he needed.

"[Daniel's] stubbornness comes from his mother," suggests his father, Hasse Alfredsson. Daniel's mom, Margarita, battled multiple sclerosis without complaint through the family's early years, going through life in a wheelchair. "When you have an illness like that, you never give up," Hasse says. "You never back away and you have to stay positive. I really think it did influence Daniel quite a bit."

"I don't think it was really until later that I realized how tough she had it," Daniel has said of his mother. "She didn't want to show it too much to her kids, but I'm sure it had an effect on us."

The Alfredssons grew up more than just competitive. Father Hasse had to prohibit sons Daniel

> # "A gifted skater and brilliant passer, Karlsson resembles a young Paul Coffey."

and Henrik from playing tennis. Though they idolized national hero Bjorn Borg, the brothers had the temperament of Borg's nemesis, Jimmy Connors. One of the boys would break or steal the other's racket upon losing.

"Dad would ask what happened," Henrik recalled. "We would say stuff like 'I stepped on it by accident' or whatever. After a while, Dad got tired of the excuses and said, 'No more tennis rackets.'"

Given his temperament, it's perhaps not surprising that Alfredsson improved dramatically upon arriving in the NHL. The competitor who hoped to be a cop if the NHL didn't work out was invigorated by North American hockey, which is more physical than its European counterpart. (Brother Henrik today works for the Ottawa police force.) Besides, Daniel was never a speed merchant. He could always get around, but not like fellow countrymen Markus Naslund or Peter Forsberg, who employed booster rockets to make a final swoop past defenders.

A shorter ice surface got Daniel to the net quicker. North American composite sticks made his shot faster. Increased practice time, more games — challenges that sometime overwhelm European players — were for Alfredsson welcome building blocks.

He developed his own arsenal of skills — a quick pivot and first step that helped him gain space in the offensive zone. Over time, Alfredsson became clairvoyant in the way of all good scorers. Could read plays a fraction of a second before they happened. Hours of work resulted in a hard, deadly accurate shot.

The late bloomer had his best years when he was in his early to mid-30s. Playing beside Jason Spezza and Dany Heatley, he scored 112 goals and added 167

Ottawa's latest golden boy from Sweden, Erik Karlsson.

assists from 2005–06 to 2007–08. He also helped Sweden to a gold medal in the 2006 Olympics.

Still, he kept going and going. Success and exemplary work habits gave him the fortitude to deal with slumps, injuries, and mistakes. Being hated by Toronto, vilified for running choirboy Darcy Tucker (*not!*) one year in the playoffs, didn't bother him. Not in the least. He understood Toronto fans had playoff rabies.

There were good moments — the Olympic gold medal, beating Toronto with a goal seconds after thumping Tucker, going to the Cup finals in 2007. There were bad times — game-seven playoff losses to the Leafs, having Buffalo penalty killer Jason Pominville waltz around him and score to bump the Sens from the postseason in 2006.

Always he persevered, came back — kept on ticking. And at age 39, there was Alfie, swanning about his hometown rink at the 2012 NHL All-Star game — the grateful citizens of Ottawa having stuffed the ballot boxes to get him in the game. In the second period of that exhibition match, he flew through the other team for a goal, and then a few moments later teamed with the Sedins for a second goal on a furious, pinball-fast — ping-ping-ping — three-way passing play.

After both goals, there were three generations of Alfredssons there to cheer: father Hasse, brother Henrik, and and three of Alfie's young children, Hugo, Loui, and Fenix. A fourth generation was there, too. Erik Karlsson, who lived with the Alfredssons his rookie year, was on the ice for both his mentor's goals.

A gifted skater and brilliant passer, Karlsson resembles a young Paul Coffey — a comparison that is, mostly, high praise. Watching him learn how to play NHL defense on the job has been a thrilling, sometimes exasperating affair for Senators fans. For 22-year-old Erik is still one of those players who can keep both teams in a game, setting up goals with astonishing plays one shift, and committing ghastly mistakes the next.

In the 2011–12 season, Karlsson showed signs that he may emerge as a perennial Norris candidate. Being around Daniel Alfredsson can only help. He showed at Alfie's home in Kanata for Christmas Eve 2012 — when Swedes traditionally celebrate the holiday. Andre Petersson, one of the Senators' Binghamton farmhands, was there as well. So was Daniel's brother and his parents, Hasse and Margarita.

They spent much of Christmas Eve eating. Swedes invented the smorgasbord, which at Christmas is a three-course indulgence starting with bread dipped in ham broth, moving on to seafood — from pickled herring to eel and lox — eaten with boiled eggs washed down with snaps. And that's just for starters. Next, you move on to Christmas hams, sausage, and cheese, after which the warm dishes are paraded out: Swedish meatballs, smoked pork, and potato sausages and lutfisk — dried cod served with white sauce.

And on Christmas day, the Alfredssons served a traditional big turkey dinner.

If Erik Karlsson was smart, he ate everything that Uncle Alfie did.

And there are more Swedes coming to Ottawa. Selected sixth overall by the Senators in the 2011 draft, Mika Zibanejad might be in Ottawa in 2012–13. Goalie Robin Lehner is considered Ottawa's goalie of the future. In 2011, he led Binghamton to the AHL championship, earning MVP honors. Very soon,[2] he will be battling incumbent Craig Anderson for the number one goalie position. Whoever wins, the Senators will have a Swedish goalie in net. Anderson is Swedish-American, you see. When he arrived in the NHL with the Blackhawks, the name on the back of his jersey was Andersson.

---

2 Lehner proved his worth upon being called up in February 2012, shutting out the Bruins 1–0 in Boston. Erik Karlsson scored the lone goal.

PHILADELPHIA FLYERS

Loose Pucks

RECORD: The Flyers played Kate Smith's recording of "God Bless America" before a game in 1969 and won. The tradition continued. Prior to game six of the 1974 finals, Kate appeared to perform the song in person at the Spectrum. The Bruins figured they'd jinx the Flyers. Bobby Orr and Phil Esposito shook her hand at the end of her performance. It didn't matter: Flyers won 1-0. A statue of Kate stands near the Wells Fargo Center.

RECORDS

MOST HAT TRICKS, CAREER: Tim Kerr, 17

MOST POINTS, ONE SEASON: Mark Recchi, 123, 1992-93

MOST GOALS BY A MOOSE, CAREER: Moose Dupont, 59

BEST PLUS/MINUS, CAREER: Bobby Clarke +506

MOST SHUTOUTS, CAREER: Bernie Parent, 50

50-GOAL CLUB: Reggie Leach, 61, 1975-76; Tim Kerr, 58, 1985-86; Kerr, 58, 1986-87; Kerr, 54, 1983-84; Kerr, 54, 1984-85; Mark Recchi, 53, 1992-93; John LeClair, 51, 1995-96; LeClair, 51, 1997-98; Rick MacLeish, 50, 1972-73; Bill Barber, 50, 1975-76; Leach, 50, 1979-80; LeClair, 50, 1996-97

WORKING OVERTIME: On May 5, 2000, big, tall, talented Keith Primeau ended a career playoff goal-scoring slump with a beautiful goal in the fifth over-time against Pittsburgh, hurtling down the right side, turning defender Darius Kasparaitis inside, and wristing a perfect shot over Ron Tugnutt's shoulder.

DRAFT-SCHMAFT

TOP-TEN PICKS, 1989-2009: 4

PLAYERS DRAFTED WHO PLAYED 300 NHL GAMES: 22

IMPACT PLAYERS: Mike Ricci, 4th, 1990; Mikael Renberg, 40th, 1990; Peter Forsberg, 6th, 1991; Simon Gagne, 22nd, 1998; Patrick Sharp, 95th, 2001; Jeff Carter, 11th, 2003; Mike Richards, 24th, 2003.

DRAFT-SCHMAFT RANKING: 16th

LINE CHANGES

THE LEGION OF DOOM: Eric Lindros, John LeClair, and Mikael Renberg, late '90s

THE HAIRLINE: Scott Hartnell, Jeff Carter, and Joffrey Lupul — so named because of Hartnell's uncontrollable Brillo Pad hairdo. The Flyers even had a wig giveaway night during the 2008-09 season.

"There are no heroic tales without heroic tails." — Former Flyer coach Fred Shero

"People usually get what's coming to them — unless it's been mailed." — Shero

"Win today and we walk together forever." — Shero

All's well at Wells Fargo Center: Flyers and their fans celebrate another win.

SKATE THAT ONE PAST ME AGAIN: Flyer goalie Ilya Bryzgalov was once benched for a few games. When asked how he felt about returning to action, he replied, "Three hundred Spartans! We go to the Hot Gate, we march, brothers, fathers, we march. Give them nothing, but take from them everything – King Leonidas."

BRING ON THE ZAMBONI
CELEBRITY FANS: David Boreanaz, star of TV's *Angel* and *Bones* and friend of former Flyer Mike Richards. After the trade, Boreanaz tweeted, "Never shld of gotten rid of Mike Richards. Bad Move. Gonna hurt."

STUMP THE SCHWAB: What was former defenseman Larry Goodenough's nickname? Hint: it wasn't compliment. Answer: Izzy.

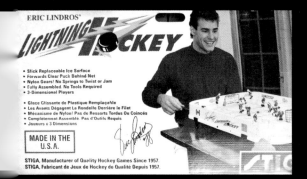

young Eric Lindros had his own table hockey game.

The DOOMED Legionnaire

At 18, he made Team Canada, helping his country win the 1991 Canada Cup with three goals and as many KOs, eliminating Ulf Samuelsson (Sweden), Martin Rucinsky (Czechoslovakia), and Eric Weinrich (U.S.) with pulverizing checks. Eric Lindros wouldn't play with Quebec, who owned his NHL rights. No endorsement potential, his agent father said. Even if it were true, it was a stupid thing to say. So Eric was traded to roughneck Philadelphia. That figured to be the best place for a 6´4″, 240-pound scorer who played as if every night was the Eve of Destruction. He found his way to the Legion of Doom line, with John LeClair and Mikael Renberg. There was an MVP trophy, at age 22. But you don't last long by playing like a middle linebacker in the NHL. Not over 100 games or so a season. Lindros's Philadelphia vital statistics tell how number 88 played the game: 11 hat tricks, six concussions, four 40-goal seasons, three bar altercations, one Stanley Cup final (a loss to Detroit, in 1997), and a collapsed lung (1999). Why was he so hard on others? Why so hard on himself? Rebellion was in his blood — great-grandfather Axel left Sweden at age 17 after being locked out in a

FAN-tastic

Orange you glad you're a Flyer fan? (Top) Spilling from the Wells Fargo Center after a win. (Middle left) Luke Skywalker outside the Philly arena (presumably, he turns into his father, Darth Vader, once inside). (Middle centre) Agents orange. (Middle right) Ghoul friends. (Bottom) Hammer head: German World War II helmet celebrating former Flyer Dave "The Hammer" Schultz.

union dispute. That's right, Sweden. Renberg wasn't the only Nord on the Legion of Doom. Maybe, growing up in the 1970s and '80s in Canada, Eric heard too much crap about chicken Swedes. Certainly, his father, Carl Lindros, who played junior for St. Catharines, resented his hockey experience. "They had two tests for me: fight Ken Hodge and fight Peter Mahovlich," he told a reporter. Maybe going to Philadelphia, land of the Broad Street Bullies, Smokin' Joe Frazier and Rocky Balboa, was a bad career move. Maybe Eric Lindros should've gone to Quebec City, home of Jean Beliveau and Guy Lafleur.

Who Will SAVE the Day?

Goaltending once seemed easy for the Flyers. They grabbed Bernie Parent and Doug Favell in the 1967 expansion draft and were set for a decade. After that, Philly were content to shop for bargain goalies. Pete Peeters (1977) and Ron Hextall (1982) were late-round gambles. Pelle Lindbergh (1979) went 35th overall.

Didn't matter — bing! bing! bing! — they all came up Halloween-orange cherries; every goalie, like Parent, a future Vezina Trophy winner.[1]

And there was something almost predestined about all this. Hadn't Parent and Favell won a Memorial Cup for the Flyers of Niagara Falls in 1965? Teenage Lindbergh, far away in Stockholm, saw a highlight film of Parent winning the Cup in 1974 and announced to friends he was going to be a Philadelphia netminder. A crazy thought — no Swedish goalie had ever made it in the NHL.

Pelle even adopted Parent's white Darth Vader mask. A decade later, sure enough, he was in Philly, with Parent his tutor and spiritual advisor.

For his part, Hextall played like a Frankenstein goalie assembled from old Broad Street Bullies — a little bit of Moose (Dupont) and a whole lot of Hound Dog (Kelly). In the late '80s, he scared the hell out of hockey, wielding his stick like a scythe.

The Flyers were one of the NHL's three or four top teams in the 1970s and '80s, making it to the Cup

1 Pete Peeters was great with Philadelphia, but won his Vezina with Boston, in 1983

finals six times. Only Montreal, with eight, had more appearances. In 1979–80, with Peeters and Phil Myre in net, the Flyers went undefeated for three months — 35 games in a row, an NHL record.

What with all their menacing forwards, from Hammer (Schultz) and Hound Dog to The Rat (Ken Linseman) and later the Legion of Doom, Flyers developed a deserved reputation for fierce play. But it was their penalty-killing goalies that allowed them to play an aggressive style. And Flyers knew it. Sometimes in practice, the Broad Street Bullies pulled Parent around on a rocker, like an ancient emperor or king being ferried about in a sedan chair.

The team felt the same about Lindbergh. The Flyers once had a secret-Santa tradition of exchanging Christmas gag gifts. In 1984, defenseman Miroslav Dvorak drew Pelle and gave him a statue depicting an Asian worker carrying two bowls tied to a stick.

In one bowl, he wrote "Defenders" and in the other, "Forwards."

Alas, the Flyers' luck with goalies came with a curse. The heroes in question left too soon and always with unfinished business. Parent succumbed to eye and back injuries. Hextall, who played hockey like kidnappers were holding his wife ransom, grew erratic. Both were pretty well finished before 30. Then there was Lindbergh, a small, bouncy Swede, everyone's friend, immensely popular with teammates. Parent loved Lindbergh like a son. Saw himself in the 26-year-old.

The goalies shared more than a white mask. Both had unflinching focus, the ability to strip away time and the worry of winning and losing, and somehow follow the darting, disappearing puck.

One time, late in a game that the Flyers were leading, Dave Poulin skated to Lindbergh. The Flyers were killing a penalty — what's new? — and Poulin wanted to discuss how to kill the remaining seconds. The goalie nodded, but looked far away. After the game, another Flyer win, Lindbergh approached his teammate in the dressing room.

"Don't tell me anything about time," he said, smiling now, but serious. "I don't look at the clock. I don't think about the clock. I just play. When the whistle blows, I get off the ice."

Lindbergh didn't play on Saturday, November 9, 1986. The Flyers beat Boston, 5–3 at home, with Bob Froese in nets. Pelle didn't even feel like going to the post-game party celebrating Philly's 10-game winning

The late Pelle Lindbergh in action against the Penguins.

His last move that season was replicating the shower scene in *Psycho*, startling the Canadiens' Chris Chelios with a banshee attack in the corner, flailing away. The resulting suspension was for a dozen games, but really, the penalty was far worse — 12 years and counting. For that's how long Philadelphia has been without great, shutdown, Vezina-caliber netminding.

Once the Flyers' greatest strength, goaltending is now the team's perpetually wounded Achilles' heel. Goalies come and go, often in the same game. In the team's two-series playoff run in 2011, the Flyers made seven in-game goalie changes, jumping back and forth from Sergei Bobrovsky to Brian Boucher to Michael Leighton — easily an NHL record. Another telling statistic: the Flyers were the only team in the NHL in 2010-11 not to record a shutout in the regular season or playoffs.

You can't say the Flyers haven't had a good goalie since Ron Hextall checked into the Bates Motel. Brian Boucher and Roman Cechmanek had nice runs. Hextall returned in 1995-96, turning in an impressively trim 2.17 goals-against average.

Still, the Flyers have never had "Da Man." Too many Philadelphia goaltending seasons have been like Donald Trump's *The Apprentice*, with humiliated job applicants being slapped around and let go. Three times in the last decade, the team needed five netminders to get through a season — in 2003-04 (Robert Esche, Jeff Hackett, Sean Burke, Antero Niittymaki, and Neil Little), 2006-07 (Niittymaki, Esche, Martin Biron, Michael Leighton, and Martin Houle), and 2009-10 (Leighton, Ray Emery, Brian Boucher, Jeremy Duchesne, and Johan Backlund).

Worse, the Flyers have sometimes been right there, on the verge of swinging a big deal to land a savior, but hesitated, turned squeamish, and pulled

streak. His mom and fiancée were visiting; he went home to tuck them away. Still, the goalie figured he should be with the guys. Be a good teammate and everything. Besides, with his $100,000 customized Porsche, he'd be there and back in no time.

At one o'clock on Sunday morning, Pelle flew from his townhouse to a bar near the Flyers' practice rink in Voorhees, New Jersey. He was in too much of a hurry to get home a few hours later, his reflexes dulled by alcohol, and smashed his prized cherry red car against a five-foot stone wall on a twisting road near Somerdale.

Pelle would be named by fans to the 1987 all-star game in Hartford months later. The honor was posthumous, though. By then he had been buried in a Stockholm cemetery, a few rows from Greta Garbo. His grave is hard to miss, except when it snows. There is an orange Flyer logo atop the tombstone.

Hextall took over the next season, taking the Flyers to the Stanley Cup finals, nearly upsetting Gretzky's Oilers. Number 99 called him "the greatest goalie I've ever faced." In the playoffs two seasons later, however, the always-close-to-the-edge Hextall came fatally unglued, playing well on occasion, scoring a goal on an empty net, but letting in nine goals on 17 shots another game and chasing officials and opposition forwards around the ice.

out, paying for their mistakes with premature playoff departures.

How can a team with Bobby Clarke on its masthead be timid? Perhaps because Clarke was there in the glory years and saw young goalies come out of nowhere to save the day. For the longest time, clothes made the man with the Flyers. Goalies put on the team's bright orange jerseys and turned superhero.

How can a team with Bobby Clarke on its masthead be timid?"

Clarke probably half-believed that whatever goalie he picked would work out. Once upon a time, they always did.

Here is a list of available, there-for-the-taking number-one goalies that *might* have saved the day for Philadelphia.

Coming off a disappointing first-round playoff upset in 1998, the Flyers had intriguing free-agent goalie options: Curtis Joseph and Mike Richter were the prizes, though it was unlikely the Rangers would let the hero of '94 go. John Vanbiesbrouck was the stopgap aging-veteran alternative.

Joseph, a hungry, seasoned, playoff-tested goalie still in his prime, announced an interest in Philadelphia. But Clarke startled the hockey world, signing Vanbiesbrouck early in the off-season — getting him cheap, it's true. Less than half what Curtis Joseph would eventually command in Toronto ($6 million a year).

Sure enough, in the playoffs, the Flyers and Toronto Maple Leafs met. The Beezer threw a shutout in game one, and Flyers were all over the Leafs in game two, in Toronto, leading 1–0 with two minutes left. But then the Prudent Fiscal Alternative suddenly lost his allure — and the game, letting the Leafs

back in the series on a weak backhand by Steve "Stumpy" Thomas. Seconds later, Sundin scored on another iffy backhand.

Joseph, the guy who wanted to play in Philly, shut the Flyers out in game six to seal the deal. And he was great for five more years. Vanbiesbrouck lost his job to Brian Boucher the following season.

Now our story turns cruel.

Philly was about to send Jeff Carter and Robert Esche to the Florida Panthers in the 2006 off-season for Roberto Luongo. But then, at the last second, the Flyers' feet began to freeze. Carter was taken off the table. The Panthers instead traded Luongo to Vancouver, where he was superb, coming second to Marty Brodeur in the Vezina sweepstakes.

The Flyers won only one of their first eight games that fall. GM Clarke fell on his stick, retiring to become senior vice-president. Esche played five games, finishing the season in the press box.

In the summer of 2010, having lived through a crazy, improbable season that saw the team employ five goalies, then make the playoffs on a shootout the last game of the season, then roar back in the playoffs from trailing Boston by three games to win game seven (they were down in that game, too, remember — 3–0 again). . . after all that, and losing to Chicago in the finals in a after giving up 24 goals in six games, the Flyers were once again offered a future Vezina Trophy winner.

Right there on the table. Just say yes. The Boston Bruins wanted to trade Tim Thomas, who would be the best goalie in the world the following year, to Philadelphia for Jeff Carter.

And the Flyers turned them down.

PHOENIX COYOTES

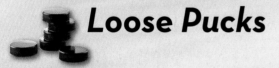

Loose Pucks

RECORD: Coyotes play Joe Satriani's Hendrix-y "Crowd Chant" after home goals. The 2006 song originally sampled sound effects from *Star Trek* and was called "Party on the Enterprise." Presumably, fans would play it after Captain Kirk scored with a blonde or greenhead. But the guitarist couldn't secure permission from *Star Trek*'s people. Out went Spock and Kirk. And the song has become an NHL arena staple.

RECORDS:

MOST HAT TRICKS, CAREER: DALE HAWERCHUK, 12 (with Winnipeg Jets)

MOST GAME-WINNING GOALS, CAREER: Shane Doan, 59 (with Winnipeg and Phoenix)

MOST ASSISTS, ONE SEASON: Phil Housley, 79, 1992–93 (Winnipeg)

MOST PENALTY MINUTES, ONE SEASON: Tie Domi, 347, 1993–94 (Winnipeg)

BEST PLUS/MINUS, CAREER: Keith Carney, +46; Teppo Numminen, +42

50-GOAL CLUB: Teemu Selanne, 76, 1992–93 (Winnipeg); Dale Hawerchuk, 53, 1984–85 (Winnipeg); Keith Tkachuk, 52, 1996–97 (Phoenix); Tkachuk, 50, 1995–96 (Winnipeg)

WORKING OVERTIME: In 1987, Winnipeg Jets radio station CKY ran a playoff promotion, handing out white Stetsons. *Dumb idea — who wants to sit behind a guy in a Stetson?* The station ran out of hats, so it encouraged fans to dress in white. The Winnipeg White Out was born. The Winnipeg franchise transferred to Phoenix in 1996, where the White Out continues.

DRAFT-SCHMAFT
TOP-10 PICKS, 1989–2009: 8

PLAYERS DRAFTED WHO PLAYED IN 300 NHL GAMES: 23

IMPACT PLAYERS: Keith Tkachuk, 19th, 1990; Alexei Zhamnov, 77th, 1990; Nikolai "The Bulin Wall" Khabibulin, 204th, 1992; Shane Doan, 7th, 1995 (**ALL** the aforementioned were drafted by Winnipeg); Daniel Briere, 24th, 1996; Keith Yandle, 105th, 2005

DRAFT-SCHMAFT RANKING: 21st

LINE CHANGES
The Olympic Line: Olympians Teemu Selanne (Finland), Alexei Zhamnov (Russia), and Keith Tkachuk (USA), 1992–96

The OMG Line: Oleg Saprykin, Mike Zigomanis, and George Laraque, 2006–07

"It's a miracle our wives ever had babies." — Igor Larionov on Russian coach Viktor Tikhonov's internment of Red Army players in a no-TV, no-booze, and definitely no-girls barracks outside Moscow. Viktor

Standing still for once: Teemu Selanne figurine

had kids, however. Son Vasily coached in the San Jose Sharks' farm system. Grandson Viktor Tikhonov, the Coyotes' first-round pick in 2008, is still trying to crack the Phoenix lineup.

SKATE THAT ONE PAST ME AGAIN: In 1979, Winnipeg Jets coach Tom McVie benched part owner/player Bobby Hull for showing up late. The incident marked the only time in sports that the guy with a whistle trumped the guy with the wallet.

BRING ON THE ZAMBONI

CELEBRITY FANS: Alice Cooper is a season ticket holder.

STUMP THE SCHWAB: Winnipeg Jets rookie of the year Teemu Selanne (1992–93) and his wife, Sirpa, formerly Miss Finland, have three kids with double E in their name. And they are? C'mon, you got the "ee" hint; do we have to spell them out for you? We do? Okay, here goes: Eemil, Eetu, and Leevi.

"How are we today, Mr. Salami?"

Tommy LIGHTNING

Mr. Nice Guy, Teemu Selanne, has spent the last 15 winters in California smiling every time a hotel clerk beamed, "How are we today, Mr. Salami?" That's not where his career began, however. Teemu (Tay-moo) was a sensation with the Winnipeg Jets in his rookie year of 1992–93, firing 76 goals. Only Gretzky, Lemieux, and Brett Hull scored more in a season. He was the Finnish Flash, in such a hurry to learn that he let go of his interpreter. "Only way I was going to learn the language was talking," he said. That he was a fast learner shouldn't surprise: Selanne's mother taught kindergarten. Teemu helped out at 15, filling empty hours. When the teenager joined the army (patrol point man), he was up at 6, on duty until 3, playing hockey at night. After joining the Finnish elite league, he got a day job teaching kindergarten. The boundless energy served him well as a North American pro. Fast to the net, active in children's charity, with a fleet of race cars (he owns an Enzo Ferrari, which has been clocked at 330 km/h, or more than 200 mph). And the hockey player who enters FIA races as Teukka Salama ("Tommy Lightning") gets great mileage, too. In 2005–06 and '06–07, at ages 35 and 36, Teemu became the oldest NHLer to record back-to-back 40-goal seasons. In 2010–11, he was a top-10 scorer at age 40.

FAN-tastic

The 40-Year-Old VERSION

In NHL history there have been 59 skaters, either forwards or defense, who have played past the age of 40. More than half (31) have shown up since the year 2000. What gives? A number of things. Players are in better shape. And in today's NHL salary-cap world, GMs appreciate proven commodities — good-example types who do their job with maximum enthusiasm and never leave a mess to clean up afterward. Guys like 40-year-old Ray Whitney, a player who has been around NHL dressing rooms more than a quarter-century.

Yeah, the math is right. When Ray was growing up in Edmonton, his policeman dad was the Oilers' practice goalie, and Ray became the team's stick boy during the Oilers' championship years.[1] Although kinda small — he'd grow up to be 5'10", 170 pounds, the same size as a geography teacher — Ray always had big eyes. He figured out the game early.

He never spent the $100 bill Wayne Gretzky gave him as a tip in 1985. ("All I did was cut his sticks and put baby powder on them," he's said.) Never forgot how, one night, coach Glen Sather called captain Mark Messier out, tearing a strip off him of him for not working hard enough. "He came out next period and dominated," Whitney remembers. "Everyone on a team sometimes needs coaching."

Ray is such a team guy that, once a year, he'll pick up and do one load of towels "to remember where I came from. . . I want to make Sparky [the Oilers' equipment man, Lyle Kulchisky] proud."

"Every team Ray's gone to, the trainers all say he's one of the best guys in the dressing room because he knows what they do.

He used to be one of them," Kulchisky proudly reports.

The post-lockout zero-tolerance rules for obstruction allowed swift, hard-working veteran forwards like Whitney to stay in The Show a little longer. The first Stanley Cup after the lockout was proof of that. The

1 The other stick boy on the team was future Oiler star Ryan Smyth, then 11.

Ray Whitney scored a career-high 77 points the season he turned 40.

Carolina Hurricanes won, with a team full of veterans — Whitney, Rod Brind'Amour, Doug Weight, Glen Wesley, and Mark Recchi were all over 35. Recchi later won another Cup, with Boston in 2011, at age 43.

Both Recchi and Whitney conform to the prototype of the game, aging NHL veteran forward. They're smart, complementary players who fit into any environment. And they bring a terrific work ethic to the game that can only be beneficial to younger players.

After winning his Stanley Cup for Carolina in 2006, Whitney skipped the rubber-chicken banquet circuit. The forward underwent two weeks of physical therapy at the University of Alberta, attending to aching limbs, and then attended a conditioning camp. "Ordinarily, I start on the bike three or four days after the season ends. I go five, six days a week all summer," he said. And he's back on the ice in August.

All of which perhaps helps explain why the 40-Year-Old Version of Whitney is so good. He was Phoenix's leading scorer in 2011–12. In 2010–11, he finished number two, with 58 points.

"He's a rare player," Coyotes GM Dan Maloney has said. "A guy who became better after he turned 30. . . . His instinct and feel for the game with possession are second to none."

The 40/40 CLUB

Nope, this isn't baseball's 40-home-run-and-stolen-base club, or a list detailing hip-hop mogul Jay-Z's nightclub chain of the same name. This is the group of NHL players who have recorded 40 points in a season when they were at least 40.

Player	Age*	G	A	Pts	Season
Gordie Howe	41	44	59	103	1968–69
John Bucyk	41	36	47	83	1975–76
Gordie Howe	40	39	43	82	1967–68
John Bucyk	40	29	52	81	1974–75
Teemu Selanne	40	31	49	80	2010–11
Ray Whitney	40	24	53	77	2011–12
Gordie Howe	42	31	40	71	1969–70
Alex Delvecchio	40	18	53	71	1972–73
Mark Messier	40	24	43	67	2000–01
Teemu Selanne	41	26	40	66	2011–12
Mark Recchi	40	23	38	61	2008–09
Nicklas Lidstrom	41	16	46	62	2010–11
Dave Keon	40	10	52	62	1979–80
Ray Bourque	40	7	52	59	2000–01
Ron Francis	40	22	35	57	2002–03
Gordie Howe	43	23	29	52	1970–71
Nicklas Lidstrom	40	9	40	49	2009–10
Mark Recchi	42	14	34	48	2010–11
Dave Keon	41	13	34	47	1980–81
Adam Oates	40	9	36	45	2002–03
John Bucyk	42	20	23	43	1976–77
Mark Messier	43	18	25	43	2003–04
Mark Recchi	41	18	25	43	2009–10
Igor Larionov	41	11	32	43	2001–02
Igor Larionov	42	10	33	43	2002–03
Dean Prentice	40	26	16	42	1972–73
Gary Roberts	41	20	22	42	2006–07
Gordie Howe	52	15	26	41	1979–80
Mark Messier	42	18	22	40	2002–03
Gary Roberts	40	14	26	40	2005–06
Ron Francis	41	13	27	40	2003–04
Jaromir Jagr	40	19	35	54	2011–12
Igor Larionov	40	9	31	40	2000–01

*at end of season

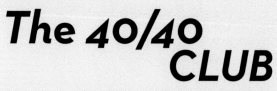

PITTSBURGH PENGUINS

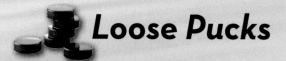

Loose Pucks

RECORD: Folk-rocker Jimmy T wrote a great playoff song, "The Penguins Are Going to Win the Stanley Cup," with couplets like these scattered everywhere: *"Maxime Talbot's not afraid of a fight / And even though he never wins it's all right . . . Sykora's got a better shot than John Wayne / And I don't ever want to see another high ankle sprain . . . Between Malkin and Crosby I can't tell who's first / But they're the two best players in the universe . . . Ryan Malone will score lots of goals for us / Gary Roberts' leg ain't broken / He's in jail for beating up Chuck Norris."*

RECORDS

MOST HAT TRICKS, CAREER: Mario Lemieux, 40; Kevin Stevens, 10; Rick Kehoe, 8

LONGEST GOAL-SCORING STREAK: Mario Lemieux, 12 games, October 6–November 1, 1992 (NHL record)

MOST GOALS SCORED IN ONE PERIOD: Mario Lemieux, 4, vs. Montreal, January 26, 1997 (NHL record)

MOST SHORTHANDED GOALS IN A SEASON: Mario Lemieux, 13, 1988-89 (NHL record)

BEST PLUS/MINUS, CAREER: Jaromir Jagr, +207; Mario Lemieux, +115; Larry Murphy, +102

50-GOAL CLUB: Mario Lemieux, 85, 1988-89; Lemieux, 70, 1987-88; Lemieux, 69, 1992-93; Lemieux, 69, 1995-96; Jaromir Jagr, 62, 1995-96; Rick Kehoe, 55, 1980-81; Kevin Stevens, 55, 1992-93; Lemieux, 54, 1986-87; Stevens, 54, 1991-92; Pierre Larouche, 53, 1975-76; Jean Pronovost, 52, 1975-76; Jaromir Jagr, 52, 2000-01; Mike Bullard, 51, 1983-84; Sidney Crosby, 51, 2009-10; Lemieux, 50, 1996-67

WORKING OVERTIME: Petr Sykora scored in the third overtime of game five of the 2008 finals in Detroit to keep the series alive. The Wings won the next game, though, to take the Stanley Cup.

DRAFT-SCHMAFT

TOP-10 PICKS, 1992-2009: 5

PLAYERS DRAFTED WHO PLAYED 300 NHL GAMES: 31

IMPACT PLAYERS: JAROMIR JAGR, 5TH, 1990; Markus Naslund, 16th, 1991; Marc-Andre Fleury, 1st, 2003; Evgeni Malkin, 2nd, 2004; Sidney Crosby, 1st, 2005; Kris Letang, 65th, 2005; Jordan Staal, 2nd, 2006

DRAFT-SCHMAFT RANKING: 9th

LINE CHANGES

THE SKY LINE: Mario Lemieux (6´4˝), Jaromir Jagr (6´3˝), and Kevin Stevens (6´3˝), 1990s

"Every day is a great day for hockey." — Bob Johnson

"I don't order fries with my club sandwich." — Mario Lemieux's response when asked what he did to stay in shape during the summer

Hart Trophy candidate Evgeni Malkin was hot spit for the Penguins in 2011-12.

"When we've got the puck, they can't score."
— Paul Coffey

BRING ON THE ZAMBONI

CELEBRITY FANS: *Batman* actor Michael Keaton. Actress Hilary Duff married former Penguin Mike Comrie. She once told an interviewer, "I like to sit in the audience — you know, I don't sit up in a box or anything — and people started to know that I'm sitting there, and they'll be like 'Mike sucks!' Or try to rile me up. And I'm like, 'Hey, watch it! I'll come up there, you know.'"

STUMP THE SCHWAB: Ah, this is too easy. On December 19, 1970, this Penguin scored a hat trick against the Detroit Red Wings. Both the goal scorer and goalie would become Stanley Cup–winning GMs. Name 'em. Answer: Glen Sather and Jim Rutherford.

Recipe for SUCCESS

In the middle of the 2011-12 season, Pittsburgh's big three centers — Sidney Crosby, Evgeni Malkin, and Jordan Staal — were down to one. The Kid was dogged by a concussion. Staal had a wobbly knee. Coach Dan Bylsma had no choice but to overplay his remaining star, Malkin, who responded to 25-minute games with the best hockey of his life, barging through traffic, reaching around trouble, dominating the slot. Returning from a torn-up knee, who would have guessed Gino could ever improve on his 2009 playoff performance, that magic spring where, fueled by his visiting mom's borscht, he took the Penguins to the Stanley Cup, winning both the NHL scoring race and the Conn Smythe Trophy. Still, there he was, carrying more than a full load. (Sixty minutes are supposed to be divided among four centers, remember?) Malkin's unit, with James Neal and Chris Kunitz, was suddenly the NHL's best line. How did that happen? What was Natalia Malkin's red borscht recipe again?

Here it is, from the *Toronto Sun*:

NATALIA MALKIN'S RED BORSCHT RECIPE

INGREDIENTS:

1 lb any kind of meat (except penguin), cubed
3 medium baking potatoes, peeled and cubed
1/2 medium head of cabbage, cored and shredded
8-oz can of diced tomatoes, drained
1 tbsp of vegetable oil
3 medium beets, peeled and shredded
3 carrots, peeled and shredded
1 tsp white sugar
3 cloves of garlic, minced
6-oz can of tomato paste
3/4 cup of water
Salt and pepper to taste
1/2 cup of sour cream for topping
Chopped parsley for garnish

DIRECTIONS:

Fill a large pot halfway with water (about 2 quarts), add the meat and bring to a boil, reduce the heat and cover the pot. Add the potatoes and bring to a boil. Add the cabbage and the can of diced tomatoes and cook until tender, about 15 minutes. Heat the oil in a skillet over medium heat. Add the beets, and cook until tender. Add the carrots, the white sugar and the raw garlic. Stir in the tomato paste and water until well blended. Add skillet contents to the soup and bring to a boil, cover and turn off the heat. Let stand for 15 to 20 minutes. Taste, and season with salt, pepper and additional sugar, if desired. Ladle into serving bowls, and garnish with sour cream and fresh parsley.

FAN-tastic

(Top) Crosby kids: Sid and Gino fans in Pittsburgh. (Left) An 11-year-old with a playoff beard. (Below) Rick Tocchet and Jaromir Jagr glasses. (Bottom) Some Penguin fan gets shirty with Pennsylvania hockey neighbors.

Dempster's
presents
1-on-1
with
Sidney Crosby

TOCCHET 22

JAGR 68

SOMEDAY MY SON YOU WILL
MAKE A GIRL VERY HAPPY
FOR A SHORT PERIOD OF TIME.
THEN SHE WILL LEAVE YOU
FOR MEN TEN TIMES BETTER
THAN YOU CAN EVER HOPE TO B
THESE MEN ARE CALLED
PENGUINS FANS

FLYERS

Graduation
YEAR

It was the best sales brochure for our game imaginable. That, and a reminder that nothing beats a good hockey playoff series. Except maybe four good ones in a row!

The 2008–09 Pittsburgh club came with a Disney movie storyline: the Penguins were a bird saved from extinction by a former star who didn't want to see His Team leave town — or, it's true, watch His Deferred Salary swirl down the drain.

So Mario Lemieux, who once came back from cancer treatment to win a scoring title, accumulating 160 points around a two-month hospital stay,[1] brought the Penguins back to life, buying and taking over the bankrupt franchise in 1999. Four years later, a teenage rescue squad began arriving: Marc-Andre Fleury, Evgeni Malkin, Sidney Crosby, Kris Letang, and Jordan Staal.

The Penguins frightened Detroit in the 2008 finals, but still looked years away from a Cup. The young stars could tie their own skates, but didn't yet know how to untie their tongues. Malkin needed Sergei Gonchar to speak English. Maxime Talbot was Fleury's French–English translator.

Grad year in pro sports is always the hardest. And the Penguins didn't appear ready for their final exams. The team was out of the playoffs most of the year. Coach Michel Therrien was fired, replaced by Dan Bylsma in mid-February. The unilingual Fleury was up and down.

The Pens made the postseason, but in the first round of the 2009 playoffs, cross-state rival Philadelphia seemed more committed and were about to vanquish Pittsburgh in their own building. In the third period of game two, the Flyers had a 2–1 lead and an open net. John Carter fired quickly, but Fleury, stranded on the wrong side of the net, somehow made a pinball-flipper leg save. Malkin tied it minutes later and the Pens' late-season rent-a-vet, Bill Guerin, won the game in overtime.

There were bigger, more slippery holes to climb from. But this was an ingenious team, one equipped with talent, character, and ingenuity. Entering game six against Philly, Pittsburgh was ahead in games, 3–2, but

1 Mario came back from cancer in the 1992-93 season.

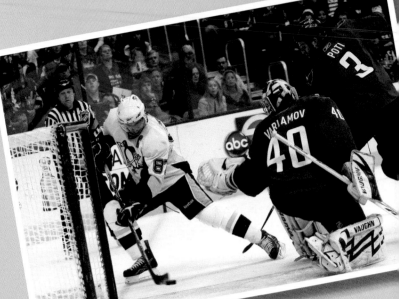

(Top) Sid the Kid scores on Washington in the 2009 playoffs. (Left) Maxime Talbot demonstrates the old angry-librarian move.

in real trouble, having just lost 3–0 in their own rink. Now they were again down 3–0, having managed eight shots on Philly's net. You could hear the Flyers' fans celebrating, gloating even. A withering "Crosby sucks" chant broke out every time number 87 touched the puck.

Then Maxime Talbot foolishly — or so it seemed — picked a fight with Philadelphia heavyweight Dan Carcillo. Maxime went down in stages, like a well-hammered nail. But he jumped right up again, placing a finger to his lips, shushing 20,000 hooting Flyer fans.

The old angry librarian move. Hoo boy — balls? *Balls.*

Seconds later, the Pens scored. Then they scored again and again (Crosby), and again and again (Crosby). The last Crosby goal sailed into an empty net. With that, the Philly playoff balloon popped, hissing away. "CROSBY SUCKS, Crosby sss. . ." the crowd complained, but every successive shout was less defiant,

Basic NHL math: 8 doesn't go into 87.

until the only sounds were happy Penguins and shuffling feet. Afterward, Crosby suggested Talbot's daft courage got the team going. "We were pumped after that," he said. In the *Pittsburgh Post-Gazette*, Ron Cook agreed, arguing Talbot's "one-sided loss" did the Flyers in.

"It was the right time" is how Talbot would explain his decision to become a human sacrifice, corking the erupting Philly volcano. "The crowd was right into it, and I wanted to do something that would help them lose momentum. I think I got one punch in," he smiled.

"Maybe I shouldn't have, I don't know," Carcillo said of the fight.

"It was nice to get that last one and hear a bit of silence," Crosby chirped.

On to Washington!

Of course, great hockey stars had met before in the playoffs. At the turn of the millennium, Detroit's Stevie Yzerman and the Fab Five[2] vs. Colorado's Joe Sakic and Peter Forsberg was an annual playoff treat. Gretzky's Edmonton superstars against Calgary's almost-as-super stars made for superb entertainment in the '80s.

2 The Russian Fab Five included Viacheslav Fetisov, Vladimir Konstantinov, Vyacheslav Kozlov, Sergei Fedorov, and Igor Larionov.

But not since Rocket Richard and Gordie Howe collided in the '50s did the league have its two name attractions on playoff display, bumping egos. They did now. Pittsburgh against Washington meant Crosby vs. Ovechkin, Canada vs. Russia, The Kid against The Cossack.

And these guys didn't like each other.

"Like it or lump it, that's what he does," Crosby said of Ovechkin's frantic, post-goal celebrations. "Some people like it, some people don't. Personally, I don't like it."

"What can I say about him?" Ovechkin said. "He's a good player, but he talks too much."

In game two, both name attractions contributed hat tricks, with Ovie assembling the more impressive highlight reel, punctuating every goal by vaulting into the glass.

Washington had a two-game lead going into Pittsburgh. Game three went into overtime. The Caps win, that's it, you gotta figure — they'd have been up three-zip. But Kris Letang won the game with a long shot off Washington defender Shaone Morrisonn. The series went back and forth, deliciously tense. Ovechkin tied game five late, only to have Malkin score in extra play, another shot deflected into Washington's net by a too-helpful defenseman (Tom Poti). Give the Caps credit, though: there they were in game six, in Pittsburgh, stealing past death's door. Crosby scored to tie the game with time running out, but Washington prevailed in overtime.

Ovechkin was once again a warship and a show-boat. He collected three assists and four hits this game. And when Washington scored the winning overtime goal, he skated off the ice with a finger to his lips — принять, что вы пингвинпо! (Take that, you Penguin.)

Game seven, back in Washington, started with more high drama: an Ovechkin breakaway. This series was like a movie trailer — nothing but colliding high-lights. Alex the Great made a superb move, deking Fleury, but the goalie reached back with his glove hand and calmly snatched away a sure goal.

A few minutes later, Crosby scored, but chose not to celebrate, contrasting himself to you-know-who. Eight seconds later, Pittsburgh tallied again. The young Washington goalie, Semyon Varlamov, played well this series. Twice he'd been done in by friendly fire. Now he began to unravel. It was 5–0 late in the second when Ovechkin stole the puck and fired in a

wraparound goal. There was no bouncing off glass for this one, though — Ovie knew his team was done. In the third, Crosby stole the puck at his blue line and did what Alexander the Great hadn't — score on a breakaway.

See how it's done?

The series had been the dramatic confrontation the NHL had hoped for — the hockey equivalent of Bird and Magic, Tiger vs. Phil. It was incredible how the stars dominated. Crosby had 12 points on eight goals and four assists. Ovechkin was one better, eight goals and five helpers. But the Penguins and Crosby were moving on. In the dressing rooms after the game, both superstars went Old School — *if you win, say little; if you lose, say less.*

"If I score first goal, maybe a different game," Ovechkin observed.

"He's a great hockey player," is all Crosby would say of his famous adversary.

Next up were the Carolina Hurricanes. The 2006 Stanley Cup winners had already upset both Boston and New Jersey, going the maximum 14 games. The 'Canes were on a roll — after a so-so regular season, finding their championship form in the playoffs. There was an intriguing rivalry here, too: Eric against Jordan Staal. And a question: Would the incredibly strong and determined Rod "The Bod" Brind'Amour, the very eye of the Hurricane, be able to knock Crosby off his game? He would, a bit. But the Penguins had three fabulous young centers — Crosby, Staal, and . . . what was the other guy's name?

In the '50s, the correct answer to the question, "Who's better: Richard or Howe?" was often Jean Beliveau. In the same way, Evgeni Malkin was sometimes superior to Crosby and Ovechkin. The sophomore center was certainly bigger and stronger — over 6′3″ with powerful, hanging arms. Sometimes, Gino looked like a big kid frustrating younger children in shinny, pushing everyone aside.

And though English was still largely a mystery, Malkin would take a front seat to no one. Though younger, Crosby arrived in Pittsburgh a year before Gino. And Sid liked to be the last player out of the dressing room and onto the rink. So did Malkin. There was a standoff early on, both centers standing there at the boards, waiting for the other to go first.

"I was a pro before you," Sidney said, gesturing. You go.

Malkin shook his head, grumbling about Metallurg Magnitogorsk, the team he played for two seasons in a grey mining town near the Ural Mountains. Crosby waited and waited, and then hopped on the ice. After that, it was always Sid followed by Gino.

Malkin had his beautiful blonde girlfriend in the crowd for these playoffs. And his parents, Vladimir and Natalia, were in from Magnitogorsk. Mom cooked up a storm before every home game. Evgeni gave his touring cheering section lots to celebrate: five goals and three assists in a four-game sweep.

But make no mistake, the first three games were life-and-death. The opening match ended with the Hurricanes swarming the net while trailing by one. Carolina was up midway through the second game, but then Malkin, fortified on mom's borscht, pulled off his first career hat trick. On the last goal, he won a faceoff, curled around the net, and executed a great post-up move, changing direction midway through a wraparound and backhanding the puck past a befuddled Cam Ward.

The 'Canes scored first in game three, at home, but Malkin retaliated with two more goals, both great individual efforts. *The Force was still with him — stewed beets stay with a man, for sure.* Eighty-seven tipped another one in. And with that, the Hurricanes were reduced to a minor storm. They played hard, but Gino and the Penguins were too much.

Few teams win a Stanley Cup final their first try. Players don't appreciate just how steep the last step in the playoff staircase can be. The season before, Detroit beat Pittsburgh four games to two, but you always knew the Wings were going to win. The shots taken by both teams told the story: Detroit 222, Pittsburgh, 143.

Pittsburgh's top players were still ridiculously young — Malkin 22, Crosby 21, Staal 20, Marc-Andre Fleury 24 — but they appeared to know what they were up against this time. Detroit won the first two games in their home building by identical 3–1 scores. But the games were close — Pens competed, outshooting Detroit both contests.

Pittsburgh held serve at home, winning the next two. The key interlude was a stretch in the fourth game where, with Pittsburgh down 2–1 and killing a double penalty, the Pens managed both to keep their composure and the puck out of the net. Down a single man, Jordan Staal swept around a defenseman and used his long reach to guide a puck past Chris Osgood.

The Mellon Arena exploded, sending a jolt through both clubs. Suddenly, it was like a heavyweight fight where bloodied combatants channel a roaring crowd and trade haymakers. For the next five minutes, the teams exchanged scoring chances, but only the younger, faster Penguins connected. Malkin set up Crosby to make it 3–2 and then Chris Kunitz, Crosby, and Tyler Kennedy combined on an intricate three-way pass to make it 4–2.

The entertaining shootout ended in a 6–4 Pittsburgh win.

Strong, excitable young teams sometimes follow their feelings in the wrong direction, however. And in the next game in Detroit, the Pens went on an inexplicable crime spree, taking 12 of the game's 15 penalties. Detroit scored three second-period power-play goals. Fleury had an off game and was pulled halfway through. Sidney was yapping, Malkin hooking and cross-checking. Penguins racked up 37 minutes of penalties in the last four minutes, taking out their frustration on the referees.

Wings were up three games to two. Now Pittsburgh would have to beat Detroit two games in a row. Something they hadn't done since Mario was in the lineup.

And guess who was in the dressing room when the Pens stormed in, cursing in a variety of tongues? Mario Lemieux. The players were surprised — Mario never visited the dressing room. But here he was, rallying the troops. After mingling with players, the part-owner retreated with coach Bylsma and staff behind closed doors. "All he said, basically, was, 'We'll be all right,'" Bylsma reported. "He did the same thing with the coaches in Washington, D.C., after we lost the first two games of that series. I clearly remember him saying, 'It's a long two months.'"

Bylsma was buoyed by Lemieux's visit. GM Ray Shero sent Mario a text message thanking him. Seconds later, a return message showed up in Shero's box, from Mario:

We are a family and in this together. We don't need anyone that is only with us WIN or TIE. I really think this is our year. Let's forget about tonight . . . It happens. We will win Tuesday and win the Cup Friday.

Shero showed the text to Bylsma, who asked if he could relay the message to players. Lemieux agreed. The Pens indeed won game six, with third-liners Staal and Kennedy accounting for the goals in a 2–1 win.

The record book says Mario has 76 goals and 96 assists in 107 playoff games. After the '09 finals, maybe we should give him another assist. The series was going back to Detroit for game seven, and Mario knew how badly Detroit would want to win at home. History was calling. Seventeen Wings were 29 years or older. Most had won four Stanley Cups. A fifth would put them in the same league as the '80s Oilers and late-'50s Canadiens — rarefied company indeed. Before game seven, Lemieux asked coach Bylsma if it was okay to send the team another text.

"Of course," the coach said.

And so, that morning every Penguin awoke to find the following message on their cell phones:

This is a chance of a lifetime to realize your childhood dream to win a Stanley Cup. Play without fear and you will be successful! See you at center ice.

Play without fear. That was the key. Forget about empires. You weren't up against the tide of history; you were only playing hockey.

So Mario played his part, acing the role of wise general. And we already know how wonderful superstars Malkin and Crosby were in this series. Sports historians subscribe to the Great Man theory of history. And sure enough, the great emperor Penguins came up big in the spring of 2009. Still, every championship team has a full choir of unsung heroes. Staal kept Henrik Zetterberg off the score sheet. And the previously fallible Hal Gill (just ask Boston or Toronto fans) played with exemplary focus, leading the blueline corps with a +8 rating. Fellow American defenseman Bob Scuderi was similarly effective.

And Maxime Talbot — what could you say about Max? He not only took Philadelphia off their game these playoffs, he kept Marc-Andre Fleury's head on straight. Joking, slapping the goalie around. Advising him what to remember and forget. Talbot was often Fleury's postgame interpreter. One time, Talbot translated a torrent of Fleury's French into a simple, "I made a lot of big saves."

"I never said that!" Fleury quickly said, laughing.

Talbot just smiled. He was keeping the kid happy, bringing him along, tricking him into speaking English even. Talbot will make a good coach someday. Or a terrific spy maybe.

Once, in a preseason exhibition game, Talbot put on Crosby's uniform to mess with a Toronto crowd.

"The second goal, though, was a beauty, a coolly deliberate wrist shot. "

In the seventh game of the 2009 Stanley Cup finals, he became Crosby, scoring the team's only two goals. (Good thing, too: the real Crosby was missing after a second-period hit by Johan Franzen.) Talbot's first goal came on a wild scramble, after which he skated back to center and pumped his fist at Fleury. It was like a catcher in baseball, getting a big home run, then returning to the bench to deal with the pitcher, his primary obligation.

The second goal, though, was a beauty, a coolly deliberate wrist shot. Talbot waltzed in from the blue line on a two-on-one, took aim in the middle of the circle, and picked the top corner just inside the post.

Mario couldn't have done it better.

The agonizing final 10 minutes of the seventh game were played in Pittsburgh's end. Jonathan Ericsson scored from the point on a great one-timer with six to go. The Pens started to run around a little. Fleury was tiring, falling too early on shots. With two-and-a-half to go, Niklas Kronwall ripped one off the crossbar. Next whistle, Fleury turned to the net and gave the crossbar a loving tap.

Thanks. My bad.

You knew the Red Wings had one more push. All those future Hall of Famers were out there — Lidstrom, Zetterberg, Datsyuk. Pittsburgh went into a penalty-killing box, keeping the puck outside. The Wings continued pressing, passing the puck around, looking for that one shot.

Just like in that old coffee commercial, this series was good to the last drop — of the puck. With six seconds left, Zetterberg won a faceoff back to Brian Rafalski, who fired it deep into a forest of bodies in front of the net, just hoping for some Red Wing rebound. Sure enough, the puck landed on Zetterberg's stick. He slapped at the puck. Fleury fell. The puck hit his right outstretched pad. There was a second

rebound. Lidstrom at the left point saw it before anyone else, jumping into the play. He had half an empty net — all the short side, really — but had to shoot quickly. There were 1.6 seconds left.

Still down, Fleury pushed hard on his left skate, propelling himself across the crease. The puck hit him right in his penguin crest, then dribbled away.

Penguin winger Craig Adams jumped on the puck. The hourglass was empty. Pittsburgh had won the Stanley Cup.

A few minutes later, the big silver mug made its way from Penguin to Penguin, all of them grown men suddenly. You had to be to lift the Stanley Cup.

NBC reporter Pierre McGuire grabbed Fleury for an interview. The little goalie easily answered his questions in English.

Crosby and Ovechkin carry their feud to the walls of the PNC Arena in Raleigh.

ST. LOUIS BLUES

Loose Pucks

RECORD: What else? The Blues are named after the first-ever jazz standard, W.C. Handy's "St. Louis Blues," a 1914 song that inspired the foxtrot. The Blues hockey team skate out onto the ice as the organist plays an up-tempo version of what has been called the jazzman's Hamlet.

RECORDS

MOST HAT TRICKS, CAREER: Brett Hull, 27

MOST GOALS, ONE GAME: Red Berenson, 6, November 7, 1968, vs. Philadelphia

BEST PLUS-MINUS, CAREER: Chris Pronger, +140; Al MacInnis, +132

MOST SHUTOUTS, CAREER: Glenn Hall, 16

MOST CONSECUTIVE SHUTOUTS: Greg Millen, 3, December 1, 3, and 6, 1988

50-GOAL CLUB: Brett Hull, 86, 1990-91; Hull, 72, 1989-90; Hull, 70, 1991-92; Hull, 57, 1993-94; Wayne Babych, 54, 1980-81; Hull, 54, 1992-93; Brendan Shanahan, 52, 1993-94; Shanahan, 51, 1992-93

WORKING OVERTIME: Facing playoff elimination against a Calgary team so good that Brett Hull was a healthy scratch, the Blues were down 5-2 with 12 minutes left. Then St. Louis caught fire, and Calgary went down in Flames. Brent Sutter scored on a bad rebound off Mike Vernon, then set up Greg Paslawski for a tip-in. With a minute left, Paslawski stripped defender Jamie Macoun rounding his own net, and whipped the puck past a snoozing Mike Vernon. Doug Wickenheiser scored in OT, capping what is now called the Monday Night Miracle.

DRAFT-SCHMAFT

TOP-10 PICKS, 1989-2009: 3

PLAYERS DRAFTED WHO PLAYED 300 NHL GAMES: 24

IMPACT PLAYERS: David Backes, 62nd, 2006; Erik Johnson, 1st, 2006

DRAFT-SCHMAFT RANKING: 25th

LINE CHANGES

ST. LOUIS'S MOST FAMOUS LINE EVER WAS MORE OF A DUO: Hull & Oates, a riff on the name of the musical group Hall & Oates. Brett Hull scored 228 goals in three seasons (1989-92) on Oates's right side.

THE SLOVAK PACK: Pavol Demitra, Michal Handzus, and Lubos Bartecko, 1999-2000

THE AMERICAN PIE LINE: Keith Tkachuk, Doug Weight, and Bill Guerin, 2000s.

THE KID LINE: David Perron, T.J. Oshie, and Patrik Berglund, 2008-present.

David Backes on his way to the net.

"Nobody can be as perfect as he was when he was here."

Mr. ALMOST Perfect

"I always tell Bobby he was up in the air so long that I had had time to shower and change before he hit the ice." — Blues goaltender Glenn Hall on allowing Bobby Orr's flying Cup-winning goal in 1970.

SKATE THAT ONE PAST ME AGAIN: In 1992, St. Louis GM Ron Caron missed winning a $42 million lottery jackpot by one number — 17. The next day, the Blues' number 17, Danny Felsner, was demoted to Peoria.

BRING ON THE ZAMBONI:
CELEBRITY FANS: *Mad Men* star Jon Hamm.

STUMP THE SCHWAB: Who was the first Blues player to score a hat trick? Answer: Camille Henry, November 3, 1968, against Detroit.

If Hollywood ever wants to remake the 1940s serial *Jack Armstrong, the All-American Boy*, they might consider having David Backes play the square-jawed scientist/superhero. The Prairie-born Blues captain married his kindergarten sweetheart ("We were holding hands while they were reading books to us") and grew up to be an academic All-American, majoring in electrical engineering. The self-proclaimed "Super Nerd" played baseball early on, but wanted something to do in Minnesota when the snow arrived. Hockey came easily, especially when he filled into his 6'3" frame. At Minnesota State–Mankato, Backes was captain of the hockey team, its leading scorer, and a 4.0 student. "Nobody can be as perfect as he was when he was here," coach Troy Jutting said. Arriving in St. Louis in 2006, Backes recorded a point on his first shift. A dependable 30-goal man, David became the 20th captain of the Blues and signed a $22.5 million contract in 2011. He and wife Kelly, who will celebrate their 25th anniversary before turning 30, are pet activists, with three adopted dogs and two cats. But don't let Backes's 4-H Club values fool you; like Jack Armstrong, the strong and silent forward turns into a world-beater when pushed too far. In a 10-day stretch

FAN-tastic

(Top) A Blues fan hits a fashion high note. (Bottom left) Another supporter (and Evgeni Malkin lookalike) is pleased to find a fire-hydrant accessory. (Bottom right) What's wrong with the Hull and Oates picture? Hull should be on the right side. Brett scored 228 goals on centre Oates's starboard side.

(Inset) Expansion hockey's first star,
the Red Baron — Red Berenson

in January 2010, he took on all-Canadian boys Jonathan Toews, Corey Perry, and Rick Nash in fights — going two for three, with only Nash, in an abbreviated tussle, getting the best of him.

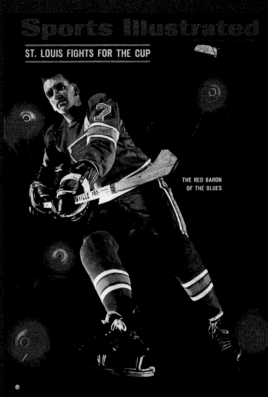

Sports Illustrated
ST. LOUIS FIGHTS FOR THE CUP

THE RED BARON
OF THE BLUES

'68 BLUES

By the spring of 1968, the '60s were traveling at warp speed. An hour before the St. Louis Blues' first-ever playoff game, Martin Luther King was assassinated. Riots ensued — Chicago, Washington, Baltimore, Louisville, and Kansas City burst into flame. That weekend, what *The Globe and Mail* called "the most chaotic, confusing and emotionally draining convention in Canadian political history" played out in Ottawa. Not that Pierre Elliott Trudeau seemed bothered. PET

breezed through the furor — he was seen catching grapes in his mouth one ballot — to become Canada's 15th prime minister.

That Saturday night, Montreal celebrated its native son's victory in grand style, withstanding Bobby Orr's first playoff point to down Boston 5–3. In the next game, the Canadiens embarrassed Boston in their own rink, 5–2. "Habs sock it to Bruins, lead 3–0," sang a Montreal *Gazette* headline, borrowing a catchphrase from the comedy show *Laugh-In*. Boston fell in four. Next up was Chicago — gone in five. Prime Minister Trudeau dropped in for the deciding game wearing green suede shoes, jumping with the crowd when Jacques Lemaire undressed Hawk goalie Denis DeJordy with a game-winning slap shot.

"Tough game," Trudeau told Toe Blake in the Forum dressing room afterward.

"Never get anything good easy," the coach sighed.

Toe, an old worrywart, could fret, but with Bobby Hull, Chicago, and the real NHL teams out of the way, life felt good in Montreal, where *Les Glorieux* were midway through an incredible run of 15 Stanley Cups in 24 years. The Habs were the class of the NHL, a team so deep that two future 50-goal scorers, Mickey Redmond and Danny Grant, seldom removed their skate guards.

The only thing still standing in Montreal's way was the winner of the West Division final between two expansion teams. Not that anyone figured that'd be a problem. Months earlier, the NHL had expanded from six teams to 12. It seemed incredible — foolish, maybe. Since the Brooklyn (née New York) Americans folded in 1941, there had only ever been six teams and five colors — black, white, red, blue, and yellow — in the NHL. That seemed the way it should be, like 10 commandments and two hands.

But these were the hurry-up '60s, the costume party decade. And so, in 1967, the NHL finally got with it — six new clubs in a wild variety of colors. The Philadelphia Flyers wore trick-or-treat Halloween orange. The Oakland Seals, after starting out in nautical blue-and-green garb, would soon sport kelly-green-and-gold

jerseys. . . and white skates. Like figure skaters.

The Los Angeles Kings wore mustard yellow and bruised-eye purple! (Although they called the latter hue "Forum blue.") Could anyone from this pajama-party bunch really beat Montreal? The *Gazette* headline after the Habs beat Chicago in the semifinals said it all:

MONTREAL WINS THE STANLEY CUP . . . OOPS NOT YET

Toe was right, though. Toe was *always right*. You never get anything good easy. Fretting helped Blake prepare, and the expansion team that emerged to challenge Montreal worried him plenty. For the St. Louis Blues were run by a 34-year-old wunderkind who just happened to be a Blake protégé.

Scotty Bowman learned to see everything coming in hockey the hard way. A kid playing for the Montreal Junior Canadiens, he raced in with a breakaway one night against Trois-Rivières. Montreal was up 5–0. Montreal was *always* up 5–0. Frustrated, Reds' Jean-Guy Talbot swung his stick, cracking Scotty's skull like you would a soft-boiled egg.

Bowman's playing days were nearing an end. Before long, he was hanging around the Forum, reporting to Habs consigliere, Sam Pollock. Officially, he was a coach-in-training. Scotty learned the Xs and Os of coaching by watching the great Montreal teams of the '50s. More important were Friday afternoons, when he dropped into Toe's office and listened to the coach map out weekend strategies.

That's when he learned the Ys.

Why Floyd Curry some shifts? Why Donnie Marshall and not Phil Goyette late in periods? Before long, Scotty was Montreal's chief ranch hand, coaching throughout the Canadiens' far-flung farm system in Peterborough, Omaha, and Sherbrooke, always winning, chewing ice instead of gum behind the bench.

As if that helped him think hockey more clearly.

Come expansion, Pollock allowed Bowman to join St. Louis as a favor to Lynn Patrick, the Blues' GM and coach. Like everyone else in the rummage-sale expansion draft, St. Louis thought defensively, choosing

Glenn Hall, a marvelously acrobatic goalie, first. After that, they drafted five straight plowhorse defenders. The Blues' best skater was Jimmy Roberts, a checkaholic who could play forward or defense. St. Louis was designed to challenge the NHL's senior six. To roll with the punches and counterattack when the better team ran out of ideas and energy.

At first, the Blues seldom got to the second part. The team had no offense. And the punching bag was coming apart. Bowman was assisting behind the bench in mid-November, with the Blues up a goal late in the second period. The assistant advised head coach Patrick to switch a forward with a minute left. A Blakean move. Play it safe.

Patrick didn't heed the advice, and the other team scored. St. Louis lost again. Of 16 games, they'd won just four. That evening, Bowman got a call in the middle of the night. "Scotty, you must take over the team," Patrick said. He'd had it. Being GM and coach was too much.

Bowman wasn't sure. Was he walking into a firing squad? The next day, he phoned Pollock.

"Well, Scotty, all I can tell you is that someone is going to coach the team," Montreal's GM said. "What if the team becomes successful and you didn't take the job?" The message was clear: You called for the puck. Shoot.

"Okay, I'll take it," Bowman told Patrick. "Only I want to make some changes."

Pollock was right. Maybe Scotty didn't know it himself yet, but he was ready. Bowman spent off-days driving to Kansas City to scout the Blues' farm team — 480 miles, there and back. Eight hours on the road listening to Al Martino and the Bert Kaempfert Orchestra on the radio. Dinner was maybe a hot dog at the rink. Grueling, but Scotty knew there was help in KC, and his first move a coach was to call up an entire, fast-moving line: Gary Sabourin, Terry Crisp, and Frank St. Marseille.

That wasn't enough, though. Bowman knew that. The Blues needed more speed. And grit. Bowman told owner Sidney Salomon III he wanted to trade Ron Stewart, the team's most accomplished forward, to New York for wild-ass Barclay Plager and Red Berenson, a helmet-wearing college phenom who'd shown he could skate in Montreal.

Salomon looked up Berenson's numbers. He'd scored two goals for the Rangers in 19 games. The season before was worse. "It says here he didn't score at all last year," the owner moaned.

Plager was another question mark. Brother Bob was already in St. Louis; Billy "The Kid" Plager would join them later. The Plagers were something else. Their dad, Gus, settled sibling rivalries with boxing mitts. Out the boys would troop into the backyard, hurling oaths. Gus would throw them the gloves and order them to go to it. While he refereed.

Kirkland Lake neighbors called the old man Squirrel Plager. He was raising a bunch of nuts.

Though skeptical, Salomon agreed to the deal. A week later, Detroit let Jean-Guy Talbot go — Bowman's one-time nemesis. "Grab him," Scotty said.

This was Bowman at his best, seeing what was coming. If God dropped everything, the Blues might make the playoffs. If they made it through the West, they'd meet Montreal. Who better to challenge the *bleu, blanc et rouge* than players Montreal had discarded?

Roberts, Talbot, Berenson, and Noel Picard had all been sent away by Montreal. Bowman talked 36-year-old Dickie Moore, a Hab immortal, out of retirement. The quarterback of the great Habs' power play, Doug Harvey, was standing by as a player/coach in Kansas City.

Seven aggrieved ex-Canadiens who would give an arm and leg to prove Montreal wrong.

With Bowman alone behind the bench, the Blues improved. Unburdened by worry, Berenson blossomed. He and the Kansas City line gave St. Louis speed. The rink no longer seemed uphill. The Plagers turned the front of the net and the corners into forbidden zones. Talbot and Moore helped.

St. Louis was finally good enough to let goalie Glenn Hall shine. As he had when he played for Chicago, Hall had reported late to training camp the previous summer. He was always painting his Alberta

barn well into the pre-season, prompting Blackhawk GM Tommy Ivan to say, "Hall must have the biggest barn in Canada."

Hall was a fascinating goaltending case study — a glib non-conformist who viewed every game as a day at the beach. . . during the Normandy Invasion. Hockey goaltending at the time was the most physically hazardous job in sports. Netminders weren't supposed to wear masks — Hall didn't. And he was hockey's first butterfly-style goalie, crouching to see the puck. Once, an errant skate sliced his face open so bad he could stick his tongue out his cheek.

Goalies at the time wore little padding. A slap shot on the arm meant you couldn't lift it to eat breakfast the next morning. Still, you played. Backup goalies were tourists. Hall once played 502 complete games in a row. Vomiting before every one of them, and sometimes between periods, hockey fans knew.

And at every season's end, he returned to his farm outside Edmonton and screamed into the wind, "Screwwww youuuuuuuu."

Predictably, Hall had taken St. Louis's woes to heart, head, and stomach. In mid-November, he approached Scotty. "I'm sorry, but I've lost my touch. . . I'm packing up," he said. Hearing this, Bowman recalled that Lynn Patrick had once said he regretted how, in Boston, he let Terry Sawchuk quit.

"When your goalie is fair, [tell him] he's good," Patrick said. "When your goalie is good, [tell him] he's great. Never knock your goalie. If he wants to quit, stall. Do anything, but don't let him go home."

Bowman convinced Hall to finish the road trip. That night, Glenn shut out the Oakland Seals, and days later helped St. Louis to a 2–1 win over Toronto. The Blues took off, winning or tying 12 of 16. That St. Louis turned things around was as big a relief to Hall as Bowman. The goalie enjoyed life on the Mississippi. The team had a lounge for wives and family. St. Louis respected its players. Chicago, on the other hand, had once sent Hall a contract addressed to Glen Howell.

And St. Louis paid top dollar. In the expansion draft, the Philadelphia Flyers advised Hall they planned to draft him first, and asked how much he'd want. Hall knew he'd be walking into a shooting gallery.

"Fifty grand," the goalie said.

"Hey, Glenn, I don't make that much money," GM Bud Poile said.

"Bud, you're not a goalie," Hall responded.

The Flyers chose Bernie Parent instead. The Blues took Hall next, making him the highest-paid goalie in NHL history. His new teammates in St. Louis respected and enjoyed playing with him, even if they didn't always understand his sense of humor.

One time, Hall came into the St. Louis dressing room with bad news: wolves had killed half his cattle back home. That's terrible, teammates murmured. Then one remembered Hall had a grain farm. "Hey, how many cattle are there on your ranch?" he asked Glenn.

"Two," he said.

A happy Hall played the hockey of his career for St. Louis in the 1968 playoffs. The city, which already owned the 1967 World Series–winning Cardinals, courtesy of "Bullet" Bob Gibson, now had a winter infatuation: hockey. Every game, organist Norm Kramer played "When the Saints Go Marching In" as the Blues skated out.

All of hockey sang along. Unless you were a Montreal fan, watching the Canadiens dispatch Boston and Chicago by a combined score of 37–18 was as dramatic as following the progress of a tractor through a field. By contrast, every Blues game was the Battle of Thermopylae.

Who'd have guessed it? Expansion teams were saving the NHL playoffs!

In their first postseason game, the Blues came out flat, scoring just once and letting first-place Philadelphia flail away at Hall. Still, the Flyers couldn't squeeze an ounce of rubber past Mr. Goalie. Final score, 1–0 St. Louis. The series saw two double overtimes, which the teams split. There were fights. Shouting matches between coaches — are-so, are-not kind of stuff. The Plagers ran wild.

Better goaltending and more determined play in corners gave St. Louis a seven-game win. It was a

> ## "Just outside the circle, he wound up and put all of his weight into a shot that Hall could only flinch at."

turning point in hockey. Philadelphia owner Ed Snider vowed never to be intimidated again. In time, he'd have a team of Plagers.

The Blues' struggle against Minnesota seemed impossible. Trailing two games to one, St. Louis was down 3–0 to Minnesota in game four, with 10 minutes left, but stormed back to win 4–3 in overtime. Moore turned his odometer back 30,000 hockey miles, scoring a goal and assist. Hall had an off night in game six, giving up five. He was tired. The next day, he told Bowman that if he had to go with backup Seth Martin in game seven, he understood.

Uh-oh. Before practice, Bowman pulled Harvey aside, asking him to have the boys aim for Hall's pads. Confidence was more important than timing with goalies. "Keep your eye on, him, Doug," the coach said.

The St. Louis goalie was terrific in that seventh game. Nevertheless, the Blues were losing 1–0 with seconds left when, with Hall pulled for an extra man, Moore one-timed a pass over Minnesota goalie Cesare Maniago's shoulder to even things.

Mr. Goalie played like a superhero after that. For two overtimes, the 36-year-old down-to-one-cattleman was incredible, rolling and tumbling between the pipes, throwing out a limb where and whenever required. With the exception of Bobbies Hull and Orr, and maybe Montreal's Roadrunner, Yvan Cournoyer, no player in hockey at the time was more fun to watch than Hall when he was on his game.

Minnesota had eight great chances to score in two overtimes; St. Louis, three. The Stars' Wayne Connelly, a goal scorer with snap in his stick, was in alone and whistled one past Hall. He shoots. He . . . No, the goalie reached back, his trapper mitt a blur, to snare the puck as it was about to cross the line.

Then St. Louis got their fourth opportunity. Ron Schock was sent in home free and blew one past Maniago. St. Louis was in the Stanley Cup finals, beginning on May 5, less than two days later.

"Oh when the Saints go marching in, when the saints. . ."

It was a classic, though convoluted storyline: the upstarts against the establishment . . . except the new guys were older than the "old" guys. Harvey (slow as church after a groin pull), Moore, and Talbot had played for Montreal more than a decade earlier. Hall first played with Detroit in 1952-53. Al Arbour had won a Cup with the Wings in '54. Seven Blues were older than their coach.

The Canadiens, meanwhile, boasted a good nucleus of youngsters — Rogie Vachon, Serge Savard, Cournoyer, Lemaire, Grant, and Redmond, all under 25. If the 1968 Stanley Cup final wasn't exactly a battle for the ages, it was certainly a battle *of* the ages.

And the Canadiens were rested, having played nine games in a month. What with all the overtime, the Blues had played the equivalent of 16 games in 27 days. The question had to be asked: If Montreal beat Chicago 9-2 one game in the semifinals, how would they fare against an old, tired St. Louis team?

"Oh when the Saints go marching in. . ."

The first period began in classic, heavyweight-title-bout style — the teams tentative, feeling each other out. Then a surprise: Barclay Plager ventured beyond Montreal's blue line and slapped a hard shot through a screen past Gump Worsley.

Their lip bloodied, Montreal responded like a champion. Seconds later, Henri Richard skated through the Blues, tucking the puck under the crossbar. The Habs continued attacking, skating hard. Lord, they could move. That season, the Canadiens didn't

have a single top-10 scorer, yet they led the NHL in goals. Everyone could fly and finish plays.

Not this day, however. There were always two Blues sticks in the way, and after the forechecking turnstiles, there was the acrobatic, Hall bouncing around his crease, slapping away pucks. Midway through the second, the Canadiens lost their patience; Savard tried to do too much and was stripped of the puck at center. Moore made him pay. St. Louis was ahead, 2–1.

And attacking again. Montreal seemed disoriented. Larry Keenan slipped one past Worsley — clang, off the post. It goes in, St. Louis wins. No way could Montreal have scored three or more on Hall — not today. But the puck chimed off the post, wide.

The Habs settled down. Cournoyer, on a nice pass from John Ferguson, tied the game. St. Louis wouldn't quit, though. The teams matched each other chance for chance. Montreal collected 38 shots, St. Louis 36. Rotund, gum-and-defenseman-chewing Worsley was as good as Hall.

Early in overtime, Gump saw St. Marseille out of the corner of his eye on a two-on-one and slid out to block what looked like the winning goal. A few shifts later, Lemaire flew down the ice. Just outside the circle, he wound up and put all of his weight into a shot that Hall could only flinch at.

Montreal won, 3–2.

Afterward, Bowman said his boys should have won — if only that puck off the post had caromed right, not left. Blake praised Worsley, then Hall, and conceded he was worried about all those Montreal ghosts playing for St. Louis. One reporter complemented Berenson on his game. "Well, if I can't get up for a game against Montreal," he said, and then stopped.

Worsley, toweling off, entertained reporters with his assessment of the Blues — 15 words, eight of them the same: "They check, check, check, check. They play for the breaks and check, check, check, check," said the always colorful goalie sportswriter Dick Beddoes once described as a pound of butter left out of the fridge overnight.

On the day off, talk turned again to politics, especially in Montreal, where some worried (and others hoped) that the largest general strike ever, the May 1968 protest that was now paralyzing France, might spread to its former colony. Eleven million workers and students took to the streets in Paris and other French cities. Politics was in the air everywhere. Bobby Hull told reporters after losing to Montreal in the semifinals that he was thinking about running as a Liberal in the upcoming 1968 Canadian election.

Meanwhile, on the rink, Montreal put their house in order. In the next two games, they outshot St. Louis 46–15, playing alert, disciplined hockey. Every few minutes, they'd put on power-play pressure, storming the net. Still, they could never secure a comfortable lead.

The Blues were harder to shake than a summer cold. Bowman rotated six defensemen with three, sometimes four lines, with every forward unit playing defensive-minded hockey. Finally, there was Hall, resolute and determined, the Iron Butterfly in nets.

It was scoreless forever in game two, before Claude Provost, killing a penalty, hurried down the ice in his peculiar, sitting-down skating style, setting up Savard, who bulled past Roberts for the game's only goal. Game three in Montreal was a wonderful spectacle. As in the first game, the two teams slugged it out. Every time Montreal got ahead, St. Louis startled the Forum with a sudden, lethal counterattack.

Down to 2–1, the Red Baron flew down the left side, unleashing a slap shot that eluded Worsley's glove. Behind another goal minutes later, Berenson stripped J.C. Tremblay of the puck, then danced the puck past Worsley who, letting out a curse, retrieved and fired the puck into the stands.

That's when something extraordinary happened: growing applause and cheers. A smile spread across the collective face of the Forum. They wanted overtime, to see more of Hall and all the old Montreal ghosts. Not just Berenson, who was really just an early-'60s apparition, but Harvey and Moore — great Canadiens enjoying an Indian summer in the rink they helped make famous.

Habs fans were cheering the other team — an expansion club playing over their heads and so bringing honor to the game.

No surprise, the Canadiens scored in overtime, with Dick Duff, who could always be counted on for one good solo per game, racing down the ice and setting up Bobby Rousseau. They won game four, too, another one-goal game, 3–2 this time.

Yes, Canadiens won the Stanley Cup — again. But this, the 1968 Cup, remained true to the hallucinatory era in which it was played. For there were tears in the winners' quarters, and crazy laughter in the losers' dressing room.

The great Toe Blake announced he was retiring. He blamed his nerves. Too much worrying. The Canadiens were understandably subdued. Down the corridor, when Glenn Hall returned from the shower, he found that a Plager had cut the sack out of his underwear. "Which one of you [expletives] did this?" he asked, giggling.

Afterward, he was philosophical with reporters. "We were close, close is good," he said, before allowing himself a final joke. "Too bad we weren't playing horseshoes."

SAN JOSE SHARKS

Loose Pucks

RECORD: The team famously skates out of a giant, fog-belching shark at the beginning of games. The theme from *Jaws* is played when the Sharks are on the power play. And when San Jose scores, fans hear Gary Glitter's "Rock and Roll, Part 2," done on a jazzy organ, complete with foghorn bleats and a drumroll.

RECORDS

MOST HAT TRICKS, CAREER: Jonathan Cheechoo, 9; Patrick Marleau, 4

MOST GORDIE HOWE HAT TRICKS, CAREER: Ryane Clowe, 2

MOST GOALS, ONE GAME: Owen Nolan, 4, December 19, 1995, vs. Anaheim

MOST PENALTY MINUTES, ONE SEASON: "Missing" Link Gaetz, 326, 1991–92

MOST POINTS, ONE SEASON: Joe Thornton, 114, 2006–07

BEST PLUS/MINUS, CAREER: Joe Thornton, +127; Marc-Edouard Vlasic, +62

50-GOAL CLUB: Jonathan Cheechoo, 56, 2005–06

WORKING OVERTIME: Brent Burns's wife, Susan, looks after two toddlers when Brent is away. There is also the defenseman's time-consuming hobby to care for. Burns once overcame a fear of snakes by buying a couple. Now he has 150, including lots of pythons (which feed on frozen rats that must be thawed in the sink). Brent also has exotic birds, dogs, and fish, including a real shark. All of that is back in a carefully constructed home outside St. Paul, Minnesota.

DRAFT-SCHMAFT

TOP-10 PICKS, 1991–2009: 10

PLAYERS DRAFTED WHO PLAYED IN 300 NHL GAMES: 32

IMPACT PLAYERS: Ray Whitney, 23rd, 1991; Sandis Ozolinsh, 30th, 1991; Evgeni Nabokov, 219th, 1994; Miikka Kiprusoff, 116th, 1995; Patrick Marleau, 2nd, 1997; Jonathan Cheechoo, 29th, 1998; Christian Ehrhoff, 106th, 2001; Joe Pavelski, 205th, 2003; Devin Setoguchi, 8th, 2005

DRAFT-SCHMAFT RANKING: 13th

LINE CHANGES

An online poll to provide a nickname for the line of Jumbo Joe Thornton, Dany Heatley, and Patrick Marleau resulted in "Jumbo Heated Patty." The same unit played together in the 2010 Olympics for Canada, and so were also called the Olympic Line.

SKATE THAT ONE PAST ME AGAIN: See Working Overtime.

*Former Rocket Richard Trophy winner
Jonathan Cheechoo.*

BRING ON THE ZAMBONI

STUMP THE SCHWAB: Evgeni Nabokov is the only Shark goalie to score a goal, lobbing a rink-long shot net into Vancouver's empty net in 2002. Which San Jose goalie hit the post against Montreal in 1996? Answer: Chris Terreri. Bonus question: Who scored on the rebound? Answer: Ville Peltonen.

Five Seasons in CALIFORNIA

In 2011–12, he played for the Peoria Rivermen — the 12th city the 31-year-old pro has played in since leaving Moose Factory to play hockey at age 14. Before that: Timmins, Kapuskasing, Kitchener, and Belleville, Ontario; Lexington, Kentucky; Cleveland, Ohio; a stop in northern California; Jonkoping, Sweden; Ottawa; Binghamton, New York; and Worcester, Massachusetts. The life of a pro is a blur of travel and cities, of injuries pulling you from sleep in the night and motel wake-up calls surprising you too soon after that. Certainly, though, when Jonathan Cheechoo retires many cities from now, he will remember one stop in the whirlwind. For six seasons in California, he was an NHL star — won the Rocket Richard Trophy, scoring 56 goals in 2006–07. How? Cheech didn't play organized hockey until he left home — a one-store Cree settlement established

around a Hudson Bay Company fort in 1673. Working hard, moving your legs forever, and hockey were part of Cheech's heritage, however. Grandfather George, a trapper, made his 30-mile trek on snowshoes. Jonathan's dad organized a family team (the Moose Factory Brawlers) that won three Ontario Native Hockey titles. Marvin Cheechoo built a backyard rink for his son. In summer, there was a shed to shoot against and, eventually, through. The community understood Jonathan's passion. At age eight, he suffered frostbite playing outdoors for six hours in minus-50°C temperatures. "I had to crawl around for a week," he said. Cheech's obsession became Moose Factory's dream. Neighbors raised $15,000 to send him to a Toronto skating school. He would endure bodychecks and racism — one scouting report said, "He should make it if he stays off the firewater." A concussion cost him an AHL season. Finally in 2003, he made the Sharks. That off-season, he devoted himself to training — power skating, sprints, weights — and scored 28 goals. The NHL lockout of 2004–05 took a year from his career. But in 2005, he won an in-season audition on Joe Thornton's line. This was his chance. Cheech played all-out every shift, scoring 49 goals in 57 games. He was third in NHL goal scoring going into the final weeks of the season, and then went on an eight-goal tear, blowing past Ilya Kovalchuk and Alexander Ovechkin. He scored 37, with a broken thumb, the following season. After that, injuries and 20 hard hockey winters eventually took their toll. He drifted

FAN-tastic

(Left and middle) Preschool shark pups. (Top) More finny stuff.

from the Ottawa Senators to the minors. Still, the best scorer in all of hockey in 2006–07 was Moose Factory's Jonathan Cheechoo. It will say so forever in the NHL record book.

Joe Thornton scores against Detroit.

Why NOBODY Likes Jumbo Joe...

...EXCEPT in SAN JOSE

Before San Jose traded for Joe Thornton in the fall of 2005, the last-place team had lost 10 in a row. With the XL-sized playmaking center in the lineup, the Sharks went into a feeding frenzy, making the playoffs. Joe won the league's scoring race and MVP trophy.

Linemate Jonathan Cheechoo piled up 56 goals. Joe was even better the next year, accumulating a career-high 114 points. Going into 2011–12, no NHL player had more points in the previous seven seasons — 684, almost 100 more than his nearest competitor (Ilya Kovalchuk, with 591).

Jumbo Joe hasn't lifted a Stanley Cup, but the 6′4″, 230-pound center has won a World Junior Championship in 1997 and an Olympic gold medal in 2010. *Yeah, but he wasn't the best Canadian on either team,* you can hear one of his critics saying. Okay: in 2004, Joe led Canada to the World Cup, finishing third in tournament scoring. He also set up the winning goal in the championship game, chipping a delicate backhand from behind the net to a wide-open Shane Doan, who snuck the puck behind Miikka Kiprusoff.

Yeah, but...

The next year, 2005, Joe was World Champion-

ship MVP in Austria, scoring 16 points in nine games, leading Canada to a silver medal.

Okay, okay, but he's never any good in the Stanley Cup playoffs, where you separate the men from the boys.

What's this "real man" stuff? Thornton completed 379 games in a row at one point in his seven-year reign as league's top scorer. Played through injuries and —

Shut up! In the NHL playoffs. . .

Thornton is second in San Jose playoff scoring history, with 64 points in 74 games. The franchise leader is Patrick Marleau, with 24 more points (88) in 50 additional games. And Joe has often played very well — Calgary fans will confirm that. He threw them out of the 2008 postseason with a last-second goal. Ask Los Angeles supporters. He beat their team with an overtime marker in 2011. He collected a career-high 17 playoff points in '11, playing through a separated shoulder. He was a Conn Smythe candidate before Vancouver, a better team with Thornton obviously hurt, finally bumped San Jose from the playoffs in the semis.

Still, there is almost no love for Joe outside San Jose. How come? Why all the "Ah, he's a choker" diatribes in Internet chat rooms? How many times have you heard a hockey media expert nail San Jose's star center with something like, "If Joe Thornton is going to live down his reputation as a player who doesn't come up big in big games. . .'"

As if his status as an underperformer is a given. Here, in descending order, are the top 10 reasons why Jumbo Joe Thornton is underappreciated.

1. DEPARTING IS SUCH SWEET SORROW. One of the best movies about Boston is *The Departed*, a crime story where no one gets out alive. That's true about Boston sports stars, too. When the marriage ends, hold on to your lawyer. After Terry Francona was fired in 2011, the Red Sox front office leaked stories about their former skipper having issues with painkillers. Bobby Orr left Boston unhappily — *Bobby Orr!* Carlton Fisk, Roger Clemens, Mo Vaughn, and Nomar Garciaparra

had wicked miserable departures. (Boston writers also like to kick around the ashes of cremation victims. In a 1960 *Sport* magazine piece, "Why We Pick on Ted Williams," Harold Kaese wrote, "In Boston, a man does not qualify as a baseball writer until he has psychoanalyzed Ted Williams.")

Boston traded Joe Thornton in 2005 for three players, Marco Sturm, Wayne Primeau, and Brad Stuart — a terrible deal. Bruin fans continue to boo Joe, as if it's his fault. (It doesn't help that the Sharks are 4-0 in Boston since the trade.)

2. BAD LOCATION. If San Jose were in the NHL's Eastern Conference, Joe would have been in a few Stanley Cup finals by now. Since 2005, Western Conference teams have enjoyed a winning record in interconference play every season, topping out at .574 in 2009-10.

3. THE MACY'S PARADE SYNDROME. It's inevitable: big guys are referred to as floaters. XL stars have long, gliding strides and look like they're in cruise control. Not so for smaller players, with their furious, egg-beater skating styles. Mario was called a floater. Chicago fans figured Phil Esposito for a lazy bum. Same with the Big M, Frank Mahovlich. Montreal occasionally fans booed *Le Gros Bill*, Jean Beliveau. In Pittsburgh, when Sidney Crosby goes into a slump, he's "trying too hard." Whereas big Evgeni Malkin's dry patches are evidence of a flawed character. He's lazy.

4. THE RICHARD NIXON SYNDROME. It's an old story: the U.S. national media work out of New York. Toronto is Canada's Big Megaphone. *Read all about it, as long as it's in the East.* Boston is still crowing about getting Robert Parish and Kevin McHale from Golden State for Joe Barry Carroll in 1980. Stealing Esposito and Cam Neely from Chicago and Vancouver — those are great stories, too. But when deals don't work out for a "national" team, they remain bad news. And so we have Mike O'Connell maligning Joe after the Boston won the 2011 Stanley Cup. The Bruins' former GM popped up on CBS Radio Boston, saying the team wouldn't have won with Joe. He lacked character.

There were unspecified off-ice issues. Like another Californian, Richard Nixon, Joe is the victim of an Eastern media bias.

5. NOT ENOUGH GET THE NEW MATH. There is still a stigma about players not winning a Stanley Cup — the idea being you can't be great without one. But players shouldn't be judged like in the old days, when there were six or 12 teams. As recently as 1992, there were only 22 NHL teams. Now we have 30, a salary cap, and four punishing rounds of playoffs. Lots of great players have never won the Big Trophy. Since 2000, seven NHLers have gone into the Hall of Fame without a ring. Doesn't mean they don't belong. And if a Bruins fan, dissing Joe, tells you otherwise, remind him that Cam Neely is one of the seven.

6. WORKING-CLASS RESENTMENT. American football networks promote glamour, hiring photogenic quarterbacks and receivers — pretty boys Troy Aikman, Dan Marino, Steve Young, Cris Collinsworth, and Ahmad Rashad. In hockey, the ex-athletes who get TV-analyst gigs are more often goalies and plugger/plumber fourth-line types. Going into 2010-11, ESPN's commentators were mullet holdout Barry Melrose, a rugged, cheerful fifth defenseman, and Barry Melrose, a chippy wrestling villain. The loudest voice on the *The NHL on NBC* is Mike Millbury, educated at Colgate, but a bullying tyrant on the air. *Hockey Night in Canada* has working-class hero Don Cherry, a career minor-leaguer (proud of it, and why not!). Sportsnet employs enough muscle to start a collection agency — Nick Kypreos, Louie DeBrusk, and Brad May. For hard jobs, they could call on Leaf and Sabre color men Bob McGill and Rob Ray. Yes, we're skipping over those who don't fit the profile — Jeremy Roenick, Ray Ferraro, and Eddie Olczyzk. Also, some former journeymen — Kypreos, for instance — do a good job on air. There is nothing wrong with hockey wearing a blue collar. Still, the hockey TV media, which is populated by lots of scrappy, bandaged Davids, aren't likely to be sympathetic to a $7 million Goliath like Joe Thornton.

7. HE'S LED TOO CHARMED A LIFE. In Boston, Joe had a $2.75 million downtown penthouse. He's bought a new home in Los Gatos-Saratoga. Has a farmhouse in St. Thomas, Ontario. His last two contracts have been worth $41 million. What happened during the 2005 lockout? No job, bills piling up, Joe played in Switzerland for HC Davos, on a line with Rick Nash and Niklas Hagman. The team won everything, including the Spengler Cup. Joe met his beautiful blonde wife, enjoyed the nightlife — Bar Rotliechtli, Cava Grischa, and the Cabana Club. Joe liked Davos so much he bought a third residence, where he spends a month every year. It would seem that the only hard part of Joe's life is pronouncing his wife, Tabea Pfendsack's surname.

8. IT'S THE BEARD. Come playoff time, Joe's five o'clock shadow appears just after breakfast. Nixon had the same problem. First week of the playoffs, he looks like the first bad guy to die in a Bruce Willis movie.

9. IT'S THE SHARK THING. It's human nature to cheer against anything with serrated teeth.

10. THE ELEPHANT IN THE ROOM. Reputations are like nicknames. Once you've got one, you've got it. It's Joe Thornton's fate to be underappreciated. Unless he wins the Stanley Cup.

"Reputations are like nicknames. Once you've got one, you've got it."

TAMPA BAY LIGHTNING

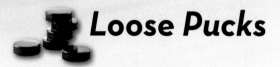 ## *Loose Pucks*

RECORD: The Lightning's goal song is a mega-techno remix of the '90s club hit "Fluxland." "*Wha-oh-oh, oh-oh, oh-oh. . .!*"

RECORDS:

MOST HAT TRICKS, CAREER: Vincent Lecavalier, 6; Martin St. Louis, 6; Steven Stamkos, 5

MOST HAT TRICKS, ONE SEASON: Wendel Clark, 3, 1998–99

MOST POINTS, ONE SEASON: Vincent Lecavalier, 108, 2006–07

BEST PLUS/MINUS, CAREER: Martin St. Louis, +35[1]

BIGGEST PLAYOFF CROWD: 28,183 for a playoff game against the Philadelphia Flyers on April 23, 1996 (NHL record)

50-GOAL CLUB: Steven Stamkos, 60, 2011–12; Vincent Lecavalier, 52, 2006–07; Stamkos, 51, 2009–10

WORKING OVERTIME: Martin St. Louis scored three overtime goals in the Lightning's triumphant 2004 Stanley Cup playoff march — none bigger than his crucial sixth-game, second-overtime rebound tally over Calgary's Miikka Kiprusoff in the finals.

1 As of March 19, 2012

DRAFT-SCHMAFT

TOP-10 PICKS, 1992-2009: 9

PLAYERS DRAFTED WHO PLAYED IN 300 NHL GAMES: 11

IMPACT PLAYERS: Roman Hamrlik, 1st, 1992; Pavel Kubina, 179th, 1996; Vincent Lecavalier, 1st, 1998; Brad Richards, 64th, 1998; Steven Stamkos, 1st, 2008; Victor Hedman, 2nd, 2009

DRAFT-SCHMAFT RANKING: 28th

LINE CHANGES

THE MVP LINE: Martin St. Louis, Vincent Lecavalier, and Vaclav Prospal, 2005–06. St. Louis did, in fact, win the Hart Trophy as league MVP in 2006.

"I only have one goal in each stick." — Petr Klima, explaining why he smashed his weapons after scoring goals with them.

SKATE THAT ONE PAST ME AGAIN: When they were 16, Brad Richards and Vincent Lecavalier, stars of the 2004 Stanley Cup–winning Lightning, were bunkmates at boarding school while playing for the Notre Dame Hounds.

BRING ON THE ZAMBONI

CELEBRITY FANS: Wrestler Hulk Hogan

STUMP THE SCHWAB: Former GM Phil Esposito's daughter married which Tampa Bay player? Answer: Alexander Selivanov. "He asked me if he could marry Carrie before he asked her," Espo reported. "I said, 'You want to what?' I thought he was just going to ask me for more ice time."

*Lightning vs. Hurricane: Victor Hedman
in action against Carolina.*

LIGHTNING *Response*

Yeah, it was a fleeting incident in just another game. But it may also have been a crucial moment in modern hockey. Tampa Bay was near the end of a punishing four-game, week-long road trip in December 2011. While warming up, former league MVP Marty St. Louis took a puck in the face from teammate Dominic Moore — breaking his nose, putting him out of the lineup. Tampa sucked it up, outplaying the league-leading Rangers the rest of the way. In New York! The score was 1–1 in the second when Tampa received a power play. Stamkos teed one up. Brett Connolly jumped in front to set a screen, the way you should. Stamkos's blast hit him in the sternum. *Imagine taking a baseball bat to the chest.* The Rangers raced up ice, firing one home as Connolly struggled to the bench. Afterwards, the scorer, Artem Anisimov, whirled, dropped to one knee, and pretended to take a rifle shot at netminder Mathieu Garon. That was it. Tampa had had enough. They'd already shot two of their own men, and lost five in a row. The team was in no mood for ridicule. Captain Lecavalier chased Anisimov. Teammates protected the Ranger forward, the way you should. Stamkos threw a punch through a screen,

knocking Anisimov down. Afterwards, Tampa redoubled their efforts. Garon was a wall. Moore scored in the third to tie it up, and then tallied the only goal of the shootout. Tampa won. So did hockey. A crew from HBO's illuminating series 24/7 happened to be on hand and saw Ranger coach John Torterello's cringing response to Anisimov's kiddy-cowboy pantomime. In the dressing room after the loss, the young Russian forward looked like a dog that had just stained the carpet. "Hey guys, sorry by me," Anisimov said, manning up. The goal and what happened afterwards went viral. Every player, and hundreds of thousands of kids, saw it. All digested or relearned a lesson: Whenever you try to put a little extra on the hot dog in hockey, you end up with mustard in the eye.

Artem Anisimov shoots his own team in the foot.

FAN-tastic

(Top) Marty St. Louis throws a puck to the crowd. (Middle) Victor Hedman opens his pen for autographs. (Bottom) Surely you joust: fans outside the Tampa Bay Times Forum.

The Slot MACHINE

Tampa Bay's former president/GM and current radio color guy Phil Esposito likes to tell the story of how, early in his Boston career, the big center traveled into the corner after the puck and found angry winger Wayne Cashman there, seething.

"What the hell are you doing?" Cashman demanded. "Get in front of the net where you belong."

Get into the slot. Do your job — score. Actually, many good centers are pass-first types. When pivot Joe Thornton won the MVP in 2005–06 for San Jose, he posted 29 goals and 92 assists. Other centers, like Esposito, Joe Sakic, and Eric Staal, keep the other team guessing. What's he gonna do — pass or shoot?

Espo's offensive game achieved a perfect Zen-like harmony with Boston in the early '70s. In 1969–70 he shovelled in 76 goals, most of them fast rebounds or quick, accurate snap shots from front, if memory serves. At the same time, he accumulated 76 assists.

A fluke? Next season he totalled 66 goals and 67 assists. Both years, Esposito drove defenses mad. They were always guessing. . . and usually wrong.

In the last 10 seasons, only two centers have scored 50 goals — Vincent Lecavalier with 52 in 2006–07, and Steven Stamkos with 51 in 2009–10 and 60 in 2011–12.

This is no coincidence. Both played for Tampa Bay and enjoyed the support of the same playmaking winger: the uniquely talented Martin St. Louis, who is built and behaves like an NBA point guard, running the puck down the rink, a sedan moving in and out of diesel traffic, looking around, dawdling, waiting for his center to spin off a check.

Then — *boom-boom* — the pass is on the momentarily open forward's stick and in the net.

Fortunately for St. Louis, he has played with two superb offensive finishers. Lecavalier may not have Espo's hands, but he's bigger, quicker, and more creative with the puck. In 2006–07, Vinnie was 40 percent Esposito and 60 percent Jean Beliveau, the once-fabulous Montreal Canadien luxury liner.

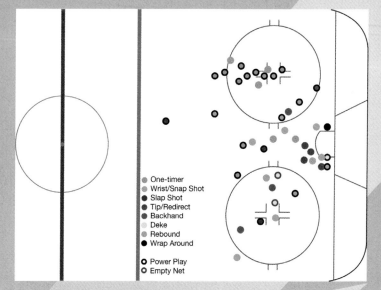

Lightning strikes 47 times: How Steven Stamkos scored 47 goals going into the last stretch of the 2009-10 season. He would total 51, tying Sidney Crosby for the Rocket Richard Trophy; (bottom) Steven Stamkos does his thing.

Stamkos is something else again — a mix of Joe Sakic and Brett Hull. Quick feet and fast hands, accurate shot. We may not have a proper record of how Esposito scored all his goals with Boston in the early '70s, but in 2010, NHL.com provided a helpful graphic summary of how Stamkos and St. Louis worked their magic.

As you can see, Stamkos did his damage with a varied arsenal — 12 one-timers, 12 wrist or snap shots, seven slap shots, and so on. What sets him apart from other forwards, what makes him the NHL's best slot machine, is his quick, unfailingly accurate release. That's how he accumulates the majority of his one-timer and wrist/snap shot goals.

Stamkos has been working on his shot since he was nine. "I was always a good skater back then, but I could never really shoot the puck," he once said. "[My dad, Chris,] took me to a shooting school — it was one on one with an instructor in the Mississauga area. It was just on that synthetic fake ice. He just basically taught me the technique of shooting.

"It's really the same as a golf swing, a tennis shot, the pitcher's mechanics. You don't have to be the biggest and strongest guy to have a good shot."

Stamkos would fire 500 shots or so a session, twice a week. Growing into his teens, applying his quick release to game situations, he came upon an epiphany that has become his goal-scoring mantra. When setting up in the left circle, "go short side."

"It's tough for the goalie because he's sliding over, so that short side is going to be open," Stamkos explains. "It's tough to shoot to the far side on an angle like that. You might hit traffic in front of the net, or you might hit the goalie as he's coming across."

Former coach and all-star forward Rick Tocchet suggests there is more to a great one-timer than a quick release. The best shooters, he said, are masters at accepting a pass and getting their wheelhouse shot mechanics in motion.

"Anyone can take a one-timer, but it has to be a perfect position," Tocchet said. "Brett Hull was the best at that, adjusting to the pass, and could still get the puck on net. That's what makes them special — they adjust in a fraction of a second if the puck changes direction. That's a big part of the arsenal, and Stamkos has that."

At 22 years of age, the best scoring center in the NHL also has close to 175 goals.

What was the name of that Mississauga shooting coach?

TORONTO MAPLE LEAFS

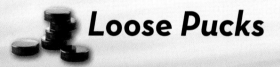

Loose Pucks

RECORD: Lots of choices, ranging from such '60s novelty items as "Clear the Track, Here Comes Shack" and "Honky the Christmas Goose" to the wicked "Love to Hear the Boos," by MC5Hole (The Big Em-inem?), a rip on the Buds, and "Love the Way You Lie." The best ever is the Tragically Hip's hockey haiku "Fifty Mission Cap," a terse, chilling account of Bill Barilko's disappearance after scoring the Cup-winning overtime goal in 1951.

RECORDS:

MOST HAT TRICKS, CAREER: Darryl Sittler, 18

MOST POINTS, ONE GAME: Darryl Sittler, 10, (six goals, four assists), February 7, 1976, vs. Boston (NHL record)

MOST GAME-WINNING GOALS, CAREER: Mats Sundin, 79

MOST SHORT-HANDED GOALS, CAREER: Dave Keon, 25

MOST ASSISTS, CAREER: Borje Salming, 620

BEST PLUS/MINUS, CAREER: Borje Salming, +155; Mats Sundin, +99; Lanny McDonald, +89

50-GOAL CLUB: Rick Vaive, 54, 1981–82; Andreychuk, 54, 1992–93; Andreychuk, 53, 1993–94; Rick Vaive, 52, 1983–84; Vaive, 51, 1982–83; Gary Leeman, 51, 1989–90

DRAFT-SCHMAFT
TOP-10 PICKS, 1989–2009: 6

PLAYERS DRAFTED WHO PLAYED 300 NHL GAMES: 26

IMPACT PLAYERS: Felix Potvin, 31st, 1990; Tomas Kaberle, 204th, 1996

DRAFT-SCHMAFT RANKING: 26th

LINE CHANGES
THE KID LINE: Baby-faced Charlie Conacher, Joe Primeau, and Busher Jackson, 1929–36

THE HOUND LINE: Wendel Clark, Russ Courtnall, and Gary Leeman, all of whom were products of the Notre Dame Hounds, 1985–86

"If you can't beat 'em in the alley, you can't beat 'em on the ice." — Former Leaf owner Conn Smythe

"Would you trade your second-leading scorer for a first-round pick? I wouldn't. Draft, schmaft." — GM Cliff Fletcher

"I will personally challenge anyone who wants to get rid of fighting to a fight." — Current Leaf GM Brian Burke

SKATE THAT ONE PAST ME AGAIN: The rodeo was in Maple Leaf Gardens in late November 1963, and workers didn't clean up in time for the November 30 contest between the Red Wings and Leafs that would forever after be remembered by the Leafs' equipment staff as "The Brown Ice Game."

Brian Burke and the frown that has been his mask in Toronto.

BRING ON THE ZAMBONI

CELEBRITY FANS: Mike Myers and Stephen Harper.

STUMP THE SCHWAB: Which Maple Leaf goalie holds the club record for most lifetime assists? Answer: Mike "Popcorn Kid" Palmateer, with 16.

Red, White, and Then Blue

He grew up known as Red Burke because of his hair. He was the fourth of 10 kids in a boisterous Irish-American family. Dinner started with the saying of grace, and while the potatoes were passed, the kids introduced a new word of the day, using it properly in a sentence. After dinner, there was food for thought — an hour's worth of reading. Between them, the Burke children earned 14 degrees. Brian has two, the second from Harvard's law school. Forget all that, though; it was a lesson his grandmother taught that stuck deepest. "Who started the fight?" she'd ask if a Burke came home with a fat lip. The next, and most important question: "Who ended it?" Red's hair would turn white from combat — he's been a hockey player, agent, NHL disciplinarian, GM of four teams, and bicoastal dad, retuning to Boston to visit his first family every other weekend. Through it all, he remained battle ready.

Running toward Stanley Park while GM of the Vancouver Canucks, he was heckled by construction workers. Burke looked up, snarling, "Someone come down and we'll settle this." His feud with Kevin Lowe, his opposite number in Edmonton, culminated in Burke offering to rent a barn and have the two GMs duke it out. Such theatrics, not to mention the shamrock tattooed on his hip, reveal the grandiloquent Irish romantic who rules Burke's soul. He wooed second wife Jennifer with a box of fortune cookies that read, "You are falling in love with Brian Burke."

The hockey executive's romance of Leaf Nation, alas, remains incomplete. A student of the Civil War, Burke must wonder if he was "too much of the lion and not enough of the fox" — Lee's assessment of one of his generals — in his first year with the Leafs, 2008-09. That off-season, he signed defenders Mike Komisarek and Francois Beauchemin because of their stellar work alongside Andrei Markov and Scott Niedermayer. Those moves amounted to picking the wrong partners from talented dance teams — dreaming of Fred Astaire and acquiring Ginger Rogers. The instant rebuild didn't work. The Leafs gave up three high draft picks to get Phil Kessel, the most curious of all talents — a great goal scorer without a slap shot. Burke has been better at the GM poker table subsequently, stealing Dion Phaneuf from Calgary for ballast and swindling Anaheim by dealing Beauchemin for Joffrey Lupul and Jake Gardiner. In the fall of 2011, Burke's monthly

FAN-tastic

Adventures in Leaf-land: (Top) Mini-skirted cheerleaders (with Eaton's catalogs under their socks?) take to the streets. (Middle right) Other T.O. fans drown their no-playoffs-again sorrows with Stewie at a local tavern. (Middle left) An honorary member of the Hound Line with his favorite chew toy. (Bottom right) A mounted horseman guards Maple Leaf Gardens, presumably from shoppers. The hockey shrine is now (bottom left) a supermarket.

I SAY... WATCH THE GAME HERE AT SEVEN...
LEAFS VS OTTAWA
A WORTHY OPPONET INDEED.
TALLBOY CANS 4.50 DURING GAME ONLY
GO LEAFS GO..
VICTORY IS MINE..!

Bill Barilko's Blou

tinkering seemed to yield results. The team looked to be on its way, playoff bound. Prickly coach Ron Wilson received a Christmas extension. "Burkie's" apparent success was more proof that the Leafs fared best when ruled by a determined Celtic SOB — think Conn Smythe, Punch Imlach, Pat Burns, and Pat Quinn. "If you hire Brian Burke to run your team, there will only be two hands on the steering wheel, and they'll both be mine," Burke tells every employer. In the first week of 2012, that was a comforting notion for a franchise wrecked by decades of boardroom shenanigans — from terrorist bombs (Ballard destroying Maple Leaf Gardens) to Tanenbaums. And then, without warning, in Burke's own words, the 18-wheeler he was driving "went right off a cliff." Leaf losses piled up in January and February of 2012. Goalies got smaller and collars tighter. Wilson was fired. Randy Carlyle, coach of Burke's Anaheim 2007 Stanley Cup–winning team, was brought in. Bad times continued. On a March weekend in which the Leafs lost twice, failing to score a goal, Burkie was feuding with broadcast legend Don Cherry — Grapes's fault, from the sound of things, but perhaps more evidence that straight-shooter Burke had trouble holstering his gun.

Forget about the Cherry quarrel, though. The question Leaf fans must wonder about is a variation on the one Brian Burke's grandmother asked: Who will end the fight to get the Leafs back in the Stanley Cup hunt? Despite the Leafs' disappointing 2011–12 season, there is reason to believe that that guy remains Brian Burke. Character is fate, the Greeks believed. And certainly Burkie carries himself with the bold assurance of a conquering general. There is the 2007 Cup win with Anaheim. And no one can forget how Burke buried his 21-year-old son Brendan with heroic dignity, days before helping take the U.S. to a silver medal in the 2010 Vancouver Olympics. But it was what happened later, when not everyone was looking, that is truly impressive. To honor Brendan's life, to continue giving it meaning, Burke has marched in subsequent Toronto Gay Pride parades and, in a gesture calculated to mend difficult borders, donated a horse to the Toronto police department in his son's memory.

That's the Burke style, to get on with it. Work hard, and then harder still. When your work is finished, find something else to do. This is a family of strivers. And yes, a family that sticks together and finishes fights — one of those great Irish families that cry when they have to and laugh when they can. Brendan, who wanted to be a hockey GM like his old man, came out to elder brother Patrick, a Notre Dame grad who works for the Philadelphia Flyers. They were driving home. "I had a bunch of bags in the car and he said, 'I have something to tell you: I'm gay.'" Patrick remembered. "I said, 'Are you being serious?' . . . He said, 'No, I'm serious.' I said, 'Well, that doesn't change anything, and I love you — now grab those bags and let's go inside.' The whole conversation lasted about 30 seconds long, and when I opened the door I yelled, 'Mom, you owe me 20 bucks — I told you he was gay.'"

Rent-a-GOALIES

PART ONE: CINDERFELLA

The day before American Thanksgiving 2011, the Minnesota Wild were stuck without a goalie and had to look beyond the bench for help.

Regular goalie Niklas Backstrom's wife had gone into labor. He was at the hospital. Backup Josh Harding was set to play, but what if he got hurt? The team phoned its affiliate in Houston to get Matt Hackett sent up on the double.

But it was Thanksgiving. No flights were available.

The Wild looked for their 51-year-old practice goalie, Paul Deutsch, finding him at his shop. It was 3 o'clock, just hours before Minnesota's game with Nashville. The printer, who had only begun playing goal in a beer league at age 37, said yeah, he could be there on time, no problem. *It's not like I'm going*

Jacques Plante in the Montreal nets at Madison Square Garden, days before succumbing to asthma in Toronto. Look at all those suits in the Ranger crowd.

to have to play, right? The Wild faxed him an NHL contract. He signed and faxed it back.

Deutsch was wearing jeans and a hooded sweatshirt. "Bob, what should I wear?" the replacement asked goalie coach Bob Mason. He'd started to tense up. What if Josh, the first-string goalie gets hurt?

"Do I have to present myself in a pro manner?" Deutsch asked his new coach.

"Paulie, get your gear and get your A-S-S to the arena," Mason said.

Deutsch raced home, got his bag, and bumped into his 18-year-old-daughter on his way out the door. "Hey, I'm going to skate for the Wild tonight!" he said.

"Okay, Dad. We're going out to get something to eat." Totally not listening.

In the Wild dressing room, he expected kidding, but the players had their game faces on. There was an embarrassing moment when Deutsch opened his bag and found a roll of toilet paper — some rinks he played in didn't have all the amenities. As for the goalie's Sponge Bob T-shirt, well, he just hoped no one noticed.

Once out on the ice at the Xcel Energy Center, Deutsch tried to get into the rhythm of the warmup, but got caught going the wrong way in a skate-around. Other than that, he was fine. Mason explained his part. Once Harding had enough shots, he'd skate off. That's when Paul jumped in the barrel.

To a view of the TV coverage, Deutsch looked okay. But he couldn't fool a real student of the game. Former Wild coach Jacques Lemaire, watching the pre-game preparations on TV, called GM Mike Ramsey on his cell.

"Is that our Paulie?" Lemaire asked, before indulging in a chuckle and a light French curse.

Minutes later, just before the national anthem, Matt Hackett arrived from Houston. It was midnight for Cinderfella. At least Paul got to keep his uniform — not game-worn, but practice-worn, at least — which he threw minutes later into his bag, next to the just-in-case toilet paper.

Deutsch watched the game, of course. The Wild won 3–2. Afterward, he shook the hands of the players and

"Sure, he was the best kid netminder in Toronto. But back in the 1950s, no young goalie figured he'd make the NHL."

Toronto teenager Len Broderick comes to the rescue of the Canadiens.

said see you around. Wait, not so fast, a few players shouted out.

"You owe 200 bucks for violating the team dress code!" somebody shouted.

Rats, they'd noticed the Sponge Bob T-shirt.

PART TWO: FATHER AND SON NIGHT, OCTOBER 30, 1957

Thirty minutes before he led the Montreal Canadiens to a victory over Toronto at Maple Leaf Gardens, Len Broderick never expected to play in the National Hockey League.

Sure, he was the best kid netminder in Toronto. But back in the 1950s, no young goalie figured he'd make the NHL. Why, it was easier to become premier of a province. There were 10 provinces, after all, and only six NHL teams. Besides, no club kept a backup. The seventh-best goalie in the world played in the minor leagues.

Len wouldn't have been a goalie if not for his dad. Mr. Broderick was a factory worker who got his oldest boy goalie pads for Christmas in 1945. Then he flooded their backyard into a big rink.

Why he did all this is a mystery. Mr. Broderick didn't play hockey. He'd grown up in the United States. But he had a hunch that Len, who was reserved but determined to meet any challenge, might take to goaltending.

He was right. Winter nights, the seven-year-old flopped on imaginary rebounds in the darkened theater of his backyard rink. Eventually, Len wanted real competition. Racing home after school, he changed into his hockey gear, then charged back to the rink at

Annette Street Public School, where he issued a public challenge: "Who wants to take shots on me?"

Turning away thousands of pucks, Len developed fast hands and feet. And he experienced a glow of satisfaction every time he snatched a sure goal from his net. Len liked being a goalie.

One winter, a local jeweler sponsored a kid's hockey team. Len tried out for nets. Not only did he make the team, but a few months later the club upset an all-star Toronto Marlboros Midget team to take the city championship.

Len's dad wasn't sure he wanted his son to try out for the Marlboros, the Maple Leafs' junior team. The Brodericks were religious. And the Marlies played Sunday afternoons. Mr. Broderick finally let his boy play, though, and before long found himself hurrying to Maple Leaf Gardens after church. In fact, it was Len's dad who made sure his son got an even shake with the Leafs organization.

At first, Len played well for both the Marlies and their Junior B affiliate, the Weston Dukes. But he wasn't the top goalie for either club. The Leafs weren't looking for the best goalie, they were looking for the best prospect — someone who might become the best goalie.

Len was depressed. Seeing this, his dad confronted the team's general manager, Stafford Smythe,

whose father, Conn, owned the Maple Leafs. The Smythes were millionaires with bad tempers. That didn't matter to Mr. Broderick. He caught up with Smythe one night under the stands.

"I don't think you're treating my boy, Len, fairly, Mr. Smythe," Lorne Broderick said.

"You don't, do you?" Stafford Smythe barked.

Mr. Broderick looked Smythe in the eye. "No, I don't."

Next time Smythe saw Len at practice, he took him aside and said, "You know, no one has ever talked to me like your father."

Len nodded.

"What do you want, Len?"

"Well, I think the best goalie should play nets."

After that, Len started playing every Junior B game. Better yet, the Junior A coach, Turk Broda — a former Leaf goalie — began teaching him tricks of the trade. Broda knelt behind the net during practice. Afterward, he took Len aside. "Sometimes you can fool a shooter," he said. "I gave a guy something to shoot at. I'd leave one side of the net open, then, just as he lowered his head to shoot, I'd slide over and take the shot away."

Broda drove Len home after practices. One night, after a long silence, Broda told Len he was starting the last game of the season for the Marlies. That was a pretty big assignment. The St. Catharines Black Hawks featured Bobby Hull and Stan Mikita, the two best young shooters in Ontario, not to mention future NHL stars.

Len shut the Hawks out. After the game, Broda told the 17-year-old he was the number one goalie. That turned out to be a smart move. Len helped the Marlies win the Memorial Cup, Canada's junior hockey championship, in 1956.

Still, Len never figured he'd make it as

On frozen pond.

an NHL goalie. Especially during the 1957 Maple Leaf training camp, when a gangling Leaf rookie named Frank Mahovlich beat him with the same move every practice, sweeping in from the side, forcing Len to slide across the crease with him, then ramming the puck between his open legs.

"You get me every time," Len joked to Mahovlich. The Big M just laughed and skated away.

At the time, NHL teams were cheapskates. They only traveled with one goalie. If that goalie got hurt, the home team provided a substitute — often a teenage junior who sat nervously in the stands, waiting. At age 18, Len became the Leafs' substitute goalie.

Normally, he liked to get to the games an hour early, just in case. But the morning before one Wednesday game, his dad told him, "Hey, I'm going to the Leaf–Canadien game tonight. My boss has tickets; maybe we can all go together?"

"Sure thing," Len said.

Len picked his beaming father up after work. Mr. Broderick hadn't been to a Leaf game in years; now here he was, being chauffeured to a Leaf game by his emergency-goalie son. Traffic was bad and Len didn't get to the Gardens until seven-thirty, shortly before faceoff. Inside the crowded arena, he said goodbye to his dad, then hurried to the players' entrance, where he found three men searching the crowd.

"There he is," one shouted. "You're playing, kid — where's your equipment?"

"You're kidding," Len replied, trying to arrange his face into a smile.

The men hurried Len to the Montreal dressing room. Sure enough, there was Canadiens coach Toe Blake, a bear with a thorn in his paw minutes before a big game. He would be especially mad tonight, with goalie Jacques Plante out with an asthma attack.

"Len?" Blake rasped.

The young goalie nodded.

"You're playing tonight, son. Get dressed."

"You're kidding," Len said again.

"We need you," Toe said firmly.

Len thought of his dad, upstairs finding his seat, even as he was kneeling on the dressing room floor, strapping on pads retrieved from the Marlie dressing room. Then a thought occurred to him — the Leafs, his favorite team. *He was going to be playing against the Leafs!* Against his old Marlie teammates Bob Pulford and, uh-oh, the young star everyone was talking about, Frank Mahovlich.

Len was suddenly a Canadien! How could that be? He'd worn a Leaf jersey his entire life. Now here he was, suddenly a Hab! It was like growing up a dog, then looking into a mirror and discovering that you're a cat.

Toe Blake talked to some players in French and others in English. But then even he got confused, chasing an obviously sick French player, Boom Boom Geoffrion, into the washroom and screaming, "I told you not to eat that spaghetti!"

Suddenly, Rocket Richard was beside Len on the dressing room bench. "Don't worry," the Rocket said, smiling. "We'll look after you." Jean Beliveau and Henri Richard — the Pocket Rocket — also came over to wish him well.

Minutes later, the team was up and whooping, "Let's go!" and "*Allons-y!*" Len couldn't say anything. There was no saliva in his mouth.

He was still nervous when the game started. Play seemed speeded up, like a car's windshield wipers in heavy rain. Then a Montreal defender stumbled and Mahovlich, a barging skater with ever-lengthening strides, gobbled up a loose puck and stormed the Montreal net.

Len skated out to meet him. Suddenly, he remembered something Turk Broda said — you can fool a shooter. Len opened his legs, inviting the Big M to try his favorite move.

Sure enough, Mahovlich danced Len across the crease. This time, however, Len clamped his legs shut before the Leaf forward shot. A split-second later, he felt a satisfying thud in his pads. He'd stopped the Big M on a breakaway! The Toronto crowd let out a moan. This is why you were a goalie — to feel yourself in control of a crowd. Len bounced up ready to play hockey.

In the first half of the game, Montreal scored four times, with elusive Henri Richard skating miles and his older brother the Rocket firing home a 50-foot missile that confirmed his nickname.

For two periods, Len shut the Maple Leafs out. Once, after making a sharp save in a goalmouth scramble, Pulford complained, "What are you doing to us, Lennie?"

The teenager never imagined being a Hab could be such fun!

Sitting in the dressing room between the second and third periods, Len sucked on carved orange sections and dreamed about — was it possible? — shutting out his hometown heroes. Could his dad, who he was sure somewhere in the stands high above, chewing on his knuckles, handle that?

Len made a few more good saves early in the third. Then there was a flash of sticks during a goalmouth scramble. Len made one save, but a Leaf scored on the rebound. The shutout was gone. A Canadien defender came by to tap Len on the pads. "Don't worry," he said.

The game ended, with Montreal winning 6–2. Len had stopped 20 of 22 shots. Afterward, in the dressing room, Toe Blake praised the young goaltender in a voice loud enough for everyone to hear.

"What if Mahovlich scores on that breakaway?" Toe asked. "The game might have been completely different. I don't know how to thank you." Blake then turned to Len and said, "If I ever need a goaltender, I'll certainly think of you."

After accepting further congratulations from the Rocket and Geoffrion (who had recovered from his plate of bad pasta enough to net a booming goal), Len floated out of the arena on the crowd noise. Everyone was staring at him. "There's the kid who played for the Canadiens," he heard people whispering. Len didn't think he could feel any better until he saw his father waiting for him at the door, smiling with all his face.

"There's the kid who played for the Canadiens."

VANCOUVER CANUCKS

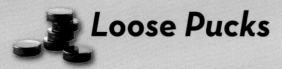

Loose Pucks

RECORD: The Canucks' 2011 playoff drive excited support from local musicians, none cooler than Punjabi-Canadian *bhangra* singer Sony Dhugga, who took pen in hand after Alex Burrows's second-game OT goal on Boston in the Cup finals. Here's an English translation of the Abbotsford native's ode to the Canucks: "*The Canucks have removed the grievances their fans had / They've created an aura of éclat. . . / Have dislodged the net with their forceful play / And taught Boston a lesson / The boys come charging like a bullet / Are broad-chested / They've got hockey sticks in their hands / They are fearless / And go off their opposition like a thunderstorm.*"

RECORDS

MOST HAT TRICKS, CAREER: Tony Tanti, 10; Markus Naslund, 10; Pavel Bure, 9; Stan Smyl, 7

MOST GOALS, ONE SEASON: Pavel Bure, 60, 1992–93 and 1993–94

MOST GAME-WINNING GOALS, CAREER: Daniel Sedin, 60, Markus Naslund, 49

BEST HOT STREAK: Petri Skriko nets two hat tricks and one four-goal game in a five-game stretch, November 1986

BEST PLUS/MINUS, CAREER: Henrik Sedin, +181; Daniel Sedin, +160

BEST TRADE: Pat Quinn swaps lumbering Alek Stojanov to Pittsburgh for the fleet, fabulous Markus Naslund, March 23, 1996

50-GOAL CLUB: Pavel Bure, 60, 1993–94; Bure, 60, 1992–93; Alexander Mogilny, 55, 1995–96; Bure, 51, 1997–98

WORKING OVERTIME: In 1994, the Canucks had a magical overtime ride. Down three games to one in the opening round, they rallied to win three straight in OT, with Pavel Bure ending the series on a sixth-period breakaway. The Canucks had three more memorable extra-session wins on their way to the finals. There might've been a fourth, too: down a goal with two minutes left in game seven against New York, Nathan Lafayette hit the post.

DRAFT-SCHMAFT

TOP-10 PICKS, 1989–2009: 9

PLAYERS DRAFTED WHO PLAYED IN 300 NHL GAMES: 25

IMPACT PLAYERS: Pavel Bure, 113th, 1989; Petr Nedved, 2nd, 1990; Mike Peca, 40th, 1992; Mattias Ohlund, 13th, 1994; Daniel Sedin, 2nd, 2000; Henrik Sedin, 3rd, 2000; Ryan Kesler, 23rd, 2003. And we're betting Cody Hodgson, drafted 8th in 2009, will be one soon.

DRAFT-SCHMAFT RANKING: 15th

Ryan Kesler follows the play against the Phoenix Coyotes.

LINE CHANGES

The West Coast Express: Markus Naslund, Brendan Morrison, and Todd Bertuzzi, 2000–06

THE LIFE LINE: Geoff Courtnall, Cliff Ronning, and Trevor Linden, 1990s

"Last season, we couldn't win at home, and we were losing on the road. My failure was that I couldn't think of anywhere else to play." — Coach Harry Neale, 1979

"We're not going to kiss anyone's butt to play here. We have a beautiful arena, our own plane, and one of the best cities in the world.... He wants out, I'm going to move him." — GM Brian Burke, shortly before trading Pavel Bure in 1999.

SKATE THAT ONE PAST ME AGAIN: In 1988, assistant GM Brian Burke phoned Trevor Linden, asking him to come to Vancouver for a psychological test. "Sorry, sir, I have to help my father with the cattle that day," the 18-year-old said, adding, "It's kind of important. As the cattle come into the pen, I'm the one who throws them down and pins them while they brand and castrate them." Burke thought a moment, then said, "It's okay. You can skip the test."

BRING ON THE ZAMBONI

CELEBRITY FANS: Michael Buble canceled a show to watch game seven of the 2011 Stanley Cup finals. William Shatner showed up at a Cup game wearing a Canuck tattoo. *How I Met Your Mother* star Cobie Smulders is a fan. So is actress Kim Cattrall and actor Michael J. Fox. Basketballer Steve Nash's sister is married to Canuck Manny Malhotra.

STUMP THE SCHWAB: Ten Canucks share the record for most goals in a game, with four. Name them. Answer: Bobby Schmautz (twice), Markus Naslund (twice), Rosaire Paiement, Rick Blight, Petri Skriko, Greg Adams, Tony Tanti, Pavel Bure, Martin Gelinas, and Daniel Sedin.

West Coast Offences

Vancouver is the most hated team in hockey, apparently. Why? Because Alex Burrows once bit the Bruins' Patrice Bergeron's finger, igniting hockey's first cannibalism scare. "If I had known in the late '70s that it was okay to pig out on human flesh, I would have eaten Guy Lafleur," Mike Milbury said. And they're hated because, after Vancouver's Raffi Torres torpedoed Chicago's Brent Seabrook in the 2011 quarter-finals and wasn't suspended when he maybe should have been arrested, GM Mike Gillis whined about officiating, suggesting the referees cost Vancouver three straight games — contests Vancouver lost by a combined score of 16–5. *What, the refs tied Canucks up in*

FAN-tastic

Scenes from the 2011 Stanley Cup march: (Top) Premature drinking from the Stanley Cup. (Middle left) Former star Trevor Linden graces an eagle kite. (Middle center) Sedin lookalikes bare witness to their heroes. (Middle right) Canucks drivers pick up a Bruin hitchhiker. (Bottom) A true blue fan apologizes for the riots that followed the Canucks' Stanley Cup loss to Boston.

ON Behalf of my team and my city, I'm Sorry!

the dressing room? They're hated because sometimes, like ill-behaved children, Canuck executives complain and carry on when they should simply apologize, as when Brian Burke tenaciously defended Todd Bertuzzi after the winger keelhauled Colorado's Steve Moore in 2004. Maybe they're remembered as complainers, and therefore hated, because Vancouver happens to be pretty darned good at complaining. Remember Burke saying, "Sedin isn't Swedish for 'punch me'" one playoff? More recently, coach Alain Vigneault suggested that Chicago enforcer Dave Bolland "has an IQ the size of bird seed and a face only a mother can love." They're hated because, when it became apparent in game seven of the 2011 Stanley Cup finals that Vancouver wasn't going to win, their fans began throwing bottles at giant public TV screens and burning cars, triggering the worst sports riot in Canadian history.

But mostly they're hated because, while no one likes a poor loser, not everybody likes a winner, either — at least not in Canada. When Edmonton, Montreal, and Toronto enjoyed championship runs, they too became disliked as well as admired elsewhere in the Dominion. For the record, here is the overall regular-season record of what might be called The Canadian Division for the decade from 2001-11:

	Team	Wins	Points	Trailing by
1	Vancouver Canucks	408	904	–
2	Ottawa Senators	389	872	32
3	Calgary Flames	361	823	81
4	Montreal Canadiens	362	821	83
5	Toronto Maple Leafs	350	805	99
6	Edmonton Oilers	314	756	148

The
Contrarian

When Ryan Kesler was growing up in Michigan, the Red Wings reigned supreme, while Colorado was Detroit's hated rival. Nevertheless, young Ryan's favorite player was the Avs' Joe Sakic. And he wore a Minnesota North Stars sweater as a going-out fancy-dress shirt.

When Kesler went to college, he chose Ohio State over Michigan. He was a Buckeye, not a Wolverine. In Michigan, where Ohio is college enemy number one, only joining the Taliban would be considered a more treasonous act.

He displayed evidence of an independent spirit when he first put on skates at age four. This was at the Eddie Edgar Arena in Livonia, Michigan. "He went around the rink once and held my hand," his father, Mike Kesler, recalled, "and then he threw my hand to the side and said, 'I don't need your help anymore, Dad.' He skated on his own from that point on."

At 13, Ryan was cut from every AAA team he tried out for and ended up playing on his father's bantam team in Livonia. That couldn't have been easy, holding Dad's hand again. At the first practice, Mike Kesler was explaining a warmup drill to the team, noticed a stirring, and turned to see Ryan making a contorted, mocking face.

"Practice is over for you," the father shouted. Young Ryan left the ice and phoned his mother, upset and complaining.

"Ryan, I'm not picking you up," Mrs. Kesler responded. "You'll have to work things out with your father."

He did, and they did, magnificently. Mike Kesler, a former college player (Colorado), preached defense-first hockey — how to play in all three zones. Teenage Mike grew to be an antagonistic forechecker, a big-bodied nuisance who specialized in keeping the other team's top scorer out of synch.

He was strong, fast, hated losing, and wasn't afraid to get his yapping trap in the other guy's face — the kind of forechecker who could get under the skin of a turtle. When Vancouver took him with their first draft pick in 2003 (23rd overall), he projected to be a shutdown third-line center.

And so he was the opposite (again!) of most middle men, who make the pros on their scoring ability, then hang around because they learn how to backcheck. In his first 101 games with Ohio State, the (AHL) Manitoba Moose, and the Vancouver Canucks, Kesler scored only 16 goals. Having a big deer on his sweater in Winnipeg seemed to rub off. He hit the weights, put on 20 pounds, and scored 30 goals during the 2004–05 NHL lockout season. He and fellow Moose Alex Burrows and Kevin Bieska (the three are best friends) jumped up to the NHL for good in 2006, giving the Canucks much-needed size and spirit.

Sometimes it takes someone else falling in love with you to make your own partner appreciate what they

Ryan Kesler groomed just so for a fashion shoot

eight games for stomping on Kesler's leg.

What drives everyone crazy about the Vancouver center? It's Kesler's combative, fiercely competitive nature. The Vancouver forward plays best when he's emotionally invested in a game. So he'll say things. Chirp. Grind away. Making other players, other teams, even other countries, mad at him — that's what gets his engine going. Like many great NHLers before him — Ted Lindsay, say, or Bobby Clarke (who tried to steal Kesler away to Philly) — Ryan Kesler's body engine runs on bile.

And so there's Ryan saying "I hate them" about Team Canada before the 2010 gold medal game between the U.S. and Canada. *And saying it in Vancouver!* During the second intermission of the same game, Kesler suggested that Canada's goalie, Roberto Luongo, was "fighting the puck." All the Yanks had to do was keep the pressure on him and they'd win. That would be Luongo, his regular-season teammate with the Canucks.

Some Canuck fans wanted Kesler traded right after the game. (Geez, what would they have wanted done with him if the U.S. had won?) Vancouver coach Alain Vigneault understood that Kesler's comments were all

have. Vancouver liked Kesler, but when Philadelphia signed the 22-year-old, third-line center to a $1.9 million, one-year offer sheet in September 2006, the Canucks quickly matched the offer. Injuries scuttled his next season, but with more ice time and responsibilities, he emerged in the fall of 2007 as the kind of premier, play-any-situation center — whether on the penalty kill, power play, or down or up a goal late in games — that hockey GMs go beddy-bye dreaming about at night.

He was a runner-up to Pavel Datsyuk for the Frank Selke Trophy (best defensive forward) in 2009 and 2010, and then won the trophy outright in 2011, scoring 41 goals along the way.

He also leads the NHL every year in driving others bonkers. His best season at shift-disturbing was probably 2007–08, when he drew the opposition into 33 games' worth of suspensions. In October that season, the Flyers' Jesse Boulerice was penalized 25 games for trying to take Ryan's head off. And then, in March, Chris Pronger was thrown out for

"There is one thing you should know and we know about Kes: he'll do anything it takes to win."

about gamesmanship. "There is one thing you should know and we know about Kes: he'll do anything it takes to win," he said. "So you can take all that with a grain of salt. And he really likes French people, so we're all set."

In any case, the head games worked. They always have. Kesler scored goals in both games against Canada in the 2010 Olympics. He also scored the tying goal against Canada in the U.S.'s 2004 gold medal win in the World Junior Championship.

Doing a postseason wrap-up for Fox TV a few months later, Kesler was asked if he watched the Blackhawks beat the Canucks in the 2010 Stanley Cup finals. Everyone else on the panel said yes, of course they had. Not Ryan. "No, not really," he said. "I only watched the final game. I wanted to motivate myself to get up for the next season."

That he did. For about a month in the 2011 playoff march, Ryan Kesler was the best hockey player in the world, leading the Canucks past Chicago, Nashville, and San Jose. In every series, he went up against the other guy's top center — Jonathan Toews, Mike Fisher, and Joe Thornton — and came out on top. His matches against Toews are always exhausting set-tos — two great, defense-first centers who never make mistakes. Watching them is the hockey equivalent of a Wimbledon five-set tennis championship that goes on all morning and afternoon.

The two greats canceled each other out this series. Kesler contributed four assists, but was plus-4. Toews collected one goal and three assists — minus-4. Game, set, and match to Vancouver.

Having escaped the harness of Toews, his game honed to a competitive peak, Kesler exploded against poor Mike Fisher and Nashville. Fisher had outplayed Ryan Getzlaf and Anaheim in the first round, collecting six points. Against Kesler and the Canucks, he was held to a single assist, whereas Kesler was better than fantastic — five goals, six assists, game-winning goals in games three and four. Furthermore, he averaged 25 minutes a night, with 16 hits, 12 takeaways, and six blocked shots. And he won 105 out of 178 faceoff draws.

"Kesler had the all-world series against us. That was one of those dominant performances," Nashville coach Barry Trotz would later sigh. "It didn't matter if I had [Ryan Suter and Shea Weber] or if I had [Bobby] Orr and [Ray] Bourque back there. It didn't matter."

He was great once more against San Jose, incredible in the final match, game five. Chasing defenseman Dan Boyle around the net, he tore his labrum — imagine ripping your leg at the hip — missed only a couple of shifts, then returned to take a faceoff in the Sharks' end with 24 seconds left. He won the draw against Joe Thornton cleanly, took a beating in front of the net as the Canucks pinballed the puck around the periphery, and then neatly deflected a point shot past lunging Shark goalie Antti Niemi with a few seconds to spare.

Vancouver won in overtime and went on to the finals.

Alas, Kesler, shot up with cortisone, was playing on one leg in the final series against Boston. He could only hate himself and the body that let him down now. He set up the only goal in the first game with more last-minute magic — a twirling pirouette at the blue line and a neat set-up of Raffi Torres — but was near invisible after that, a man trapped in a nightmare watching events he could not influence.

Somehow, though, you know Ryan Kesler will use that awful memory as fuel to make other players and other teams miserable somewhere down the road. No one in hockey is better at turning a negative into a positive.

Trevor Linden

WASHINGTON
CAPITALS

 ## Loose Pucks

RECORD: What was that song the Caps danced to in their dressing room after a win during the TV series 24/7? "Beat Dat Beat" by Jersey Shore cast member DJ Pauly D. Inspirational verse: *"It takes me 25 minutes to do my hair / I'm so fresh I got a tanning bed in my house."* Too kissy for your tastes? The Caps also play Stompin' Tom's "The Hockey Song" during games.

RECORDS

MOST HAT TRICKS, CAREER: Peter Bondra, 19

MOST POINTS, ONE SEASON: Dennis Maruk, 136, 1981–82

MOST WINS, ONE SEASON: 54, 2009–10

FEWEST WINS, ONE SEASON: 8, 1974–75 (NHL record)

MOST CONSECUTIVE GAMES WITH A GOAL BY A DEFENSEMAN: Mike Green, 8, 2008–09 (NHL record)

BEST PLUS/MINUS, CAREER: Rod Langway, +117

50-GOAL CLUB: Alex Ovechkin, 65, 2007–08; Denis Maruk, 60, 1981–82; Ovechkin, 56, 2008–09; Bobby Carpenter, 53, 1984–85; Peter Bondra, 52, 1995–96; Bondra, 52, 1997–98; Ovechkin, 52, 2005–06; Mike Gartner, 50, 1984–85; Maruk, 50, 1980–81; Ovechkin, 50, 2009–10

WORKING OVERTIME: Alex Ovechkin has a franchise-record 10 regular-season overtime goals.

DRAFT-SCHMAFT

TOP-10 PICKS, 1989–2009: 8

PLAYERS DRAFTED WHO PLAYED 300 NHL GAMES: 24

IMPACT PLAYERS: Olaf Kolzig, 19th, 1989; Peter Bondra, 156th, 1990; Sergei Gonchar, 14th, 1992; Alexander Semin, 13th, 2002; Alex Ovechkin, 1st, 2004; Mike Green, 29th, 2004; Nicklas Backstrom, 4th, 2006

DRAFT-SCHMAFT RANKING: 17th

LINE CHANGES

THE SOB LINE: Alexander Semin, Alex Ovechkin, and Nicklas Backstrom

"If you want money, go to the bank. If you want bread, go to the bakery. If you want goals, go to the net." — Brooks Laich

SKATE THAT ONE PAST ME AGAIN: The expansion Caps won eight games in 1974–75 and endured a 25-game winless streak the following season. "I slept like a baby. Every two hours, I woke up and cried," coach Tom McVie once lamented.

BRING ON THE ZAMBONI

CELEBRITY FANS: Game show host Pat Sajak, season-ticket holder since 2006

STUMP THE SCHWAB: Which former Cap owns the record for worst plus/minus record in a season? Answer: Bill Mikkelson, minus-82 (1974–75)

CURSED
Broken Skate!

The Washington Capitals became a very good team in the mid-'80s when a big, capable, mostly mean blueline corps — Rod Langway, Scott Stevens, Larry Murphy, and Kevin Hatcher — arrived together. The team's top scorers in 1986–87 were Murphy, Mike Gartner, and Stevens — two of the three were defensemen. The Caps looked to have the New York Islanders beaten in their first-round playoff series, taking a three-games-to-one lead. But you have to drive a stake through a champ's heart. Winners of four Cups in a row earlier in the decade, New York fought back. Game seven was in Washington. The Caps dominated. Still, with five minutes left, they were only up a goal. Then disaster — Bryan Trottier hustled down the right side and got off a weak backhand before Stevens took him out. As goalie Bob Mason slid to cover the open side, a rivet on his skate broke, he stutter-stepped — like a lady breaking the heel of a shoe — and the puck journeyed between a resulting gap in his pads. Tie game. With that, the Islanders caught life, playing better in overtime. Maybe because, unlike the Caps, they were sucking on oxygen tanks between three overtime periods! That's the charge a furious Washington coach,

Bryan Murray, leveled later. Mason kept his team in the game. Kelly Hrudey remained unbeatable — incredible, really — at his end, stopping 73 shots. He was lucky, too. Gartner gave him the dipsy-doodle, sweeping in on net during the first OT, but the puck hopped his stick. The exasperated forward swept air into the empty net. With seconds left in the second overtime period, Greg Smith chimed a blueline slap shot off the crossbar. Finally — too soon for Washington, though — deep into the seventh period, Pat LaFontaine performed a blind pirouette slap shot that found its way through a forest of bodies and went in off the goalpost. "I heard a clank, just dropped to my knees, and that was it," Mason remembered. The Washington netminder received solace from the first player to talk to him. Skating off with his head down, he found a blue sweater beside him: Billy Smith, the Islander goalie who famously never shook hands with opponents. "Greatest game I've ever seen," Smith told Mason, patting him on the back.

"They were sucking on oxygen tanks between three overtime periods!"

FAN-tastic

(Top right) Alberta-born Washington defender Mike Green wears some Great White North headgear to a Caps game. (Bottom) Three Washington hockey head cases.

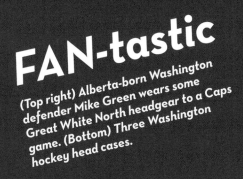

Automatic

American Automatic
Sprinkler

IM Zell

Why Alexander Is No Longer GREAT

"My weapon isn't my shot, it's me." — Alex Ovechkin

It's true. From age 21 to 24, Ovie was hockey's best-ever weapon from the left side. No one in his position had scored as many goals in a season — 65 in 2007-08, and 56 the following year. No other left winger, not even the wondrous Bobby Hull, had performed in such a compelling fashion, hurtling forward, shredding checkers — a runaway train — leaning into a wrist shot so quick goalies could only guess at its destination.

The 6′3″ 235-pound forward scored contract hits as well as goals — went well out of his way every shift to flatten defenders and opposing forwards.

There was no one like him.

Now, not even Alex Ovechkin is like Alex Ovechkin. At 25, in 2010-11, he scored 32 goals. Going into the 2012 NHL All-Star Game, the winger had 33 points, the lowest of any forward in the exhibition match.

"You don't score on 100 percent of the shots you don't take."

What happened? Here are eight reasons (his number!) why Alexander the Great is no longer himself.

"YOU DON'T SCORE ON 100 PERCENT OF THE SHOTS YOU DON'T TAKE."

Wayne Gretzky said that. Certainly, Ovie's old coach — the one people say he got fired, Bruce Boudreau — told him the same thing . . . tossing in expletives for spice. When he was going Great, Ovechkin shot at every chance. Here's a list of the top six shot totals in modern hockey history:

Player	Season	Shots on Goal	Goals
Phil Esposito	1970-71	550	76
Alex Ovechkin	2008-09	528	56
Alex Ovechkin	2007-08	446	65
Paul Kariya	1998-99	429	39
Phil Esposito	1971-72	426	66
Alex Ovechkin	2005-06	425	52

In 2010-11, Ovechkin shot the puck 367 times — still enough to lead the league, but the lowest total of his NHL career. And there was another alarming trend: in '07-08, Ovechkin scored once every 6.8 shots; a year later, once every 9.4 tries in '08-09. By 2010-11, it was a goal every 11.4 shots. Maybe Ovie's greatest mistake was to respond to mounting frustration by giving in and shooting less. Hell, if he'd fired 600 shots in 2010-11, he would have had 52 goals. Changing sports, you don't think Michael Jordan shot more often as he grew older to keep getting his 30 points per game? Gotta want it. Can't be afraid to fail. (See Boudreau tirade below.)

LOVE BOATS AND LOVE HANDLES

"You look kind of fat." That's what Ovechkin said strangers were telling him after pictures of Maxim Afinogenov's July 2011 wedding party — including shots of an evidently overfed Ovechkin in a white tux — reached the Internet. Bad camera angle, Ovie said, laughing off fans' fears. *Hmmm*. The summer before, we saw Alex on a yacht, shirtless, beer in hand, sunglasses upside down, surrounded by bikinis. Then there are the 2009 shots of Alex and Andrei Markov at a strip club, racking up a $10,000 entertainment tab — prior to 1967 expansion, NHL players averaged $10,000–$15,000 a season! Circumstantial evidence suggests Alex is ransacking the temple that God — and the Central Red Army Sports Club — gave him.

FULLBACK FATIGUE

Remember Don Cherry warning viewers that Alex was going to wear out? That no player can run around every shift, playing demolition derby? "Russian machine never breaks," Ovie laughed in response. Not true. Ovechkin is fading like an unplugged electric fan. For the longest time, he played hockey like a football running back. And you know what happens to those guys. Think of LaDainian Tomlinson, Herschel Walker, Eric Dickerson, and Earl Campbell, every one a shadow of their former selves by their late 20s. Washington fans, think of the Redskins' Larry Brown, who last made the Pro Bowl at 24 — the same age at which Ovie last scored 50.

INNOVATE, OR SCORE 25 GOALS

In early 2011, winger-turned-radio commentator Nick Kypreos on *Hockey Central at Noon* said of Ovechkin's unfolding 30-goal season: "He's been doing the same move on defensemen and goalies for years, and the league is onto him — he bull rushes the net, same inside-out move. Alex, figure out some new tricks." It's true. The great ones diversify, improve. Sidney Crosby worked on faceoffs one off-season; developed his shot the next. When Bird humiliated Magic in basketball in the 1984 NBA finals, Johnson worked

on his outside jumper all summer. The next year, he and his Lakers won.

KEEP FLUNKING CHEMISTRY

Linemate Alexander Semin, a great talent, didn't try to speak English for six seasons. Center Nicklas Backstrom never bothered to learn playoff hockey. The Caps lack the forward gear other teams have in the postseason. They're great when everything is going their way, but can never dig their way out of a ditch. Ovechkin is captain, but not The Captain. Neither is anyone else. All of which explains Washington coach Bruce Boudreau's memorable 2011 tirade on HBO's 24/7:

> *Lookit, I have never seen a bunch a guys look so ——ing down when something bad happens. What are you guys, prima donna perfect that you can't ——ing handle adversity? So ——'s not going right. It's not ——ing working the last 10 days. ——, get your head out of your —— and ——ing make it work by outworking the opposition. You kill two ——ing men. And then we stand around and watch as they ——ing score here. ——, you come to the bench like —ing this. [Droops like an old man.] And when the power play's not working, you try and stickhandle. You're looking like this [droops again] and not standing. Outwork the ——ing guy. If you want it, don't just think you want it. Go out and ——ing want it. But you're not looking like you want it. You look like you feel sorry for yourself. And nobody ——ing wants anybody that's feeling sorry for themselves. You got 20 minutes. You're down by one ——ing shot. Surely to —— we can deal with this.*

MISSING MIKE

Wayne Gretzky and Mario Lemieux had their best scoring seasons with Paul Coffey playing offensive defense behind them. Ovechkin's scoring collapse relates directly to all-star defenseman Mike Green's inability to stay healthy.

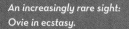

An increasingly rare sight: Ovie in ecstasy.

HE SUCCUMBED TO SOME EXISTENTIAL FUNK AFTER THE RUSSIANS LOST IN 2010 OLYMPICS

Since the Russians got clobbered 7–3 by Canada in the quarter-finals in Vancouver, Alex has been moping as if his dog died. Gone is the continuous joy, the spreading, contagious passion that defined his reckless early play. "What's the greatest thing about playing in the NHL?" a reporter once asked him. "NHL," Ovechkin said. "The NHL?" the reporter repeated. Ovechkin nodded, walking away.

He's not that guy anymore. Doesn't care enough. Someone should introduce him to his old self, the gap-toothed kid who once said, "If you are a great hockey player, you must be a great man."

THE CURSE OF THE BROKEN SKATE

When the going gets tough for the Capitals, the whole team, including Ovie, fall into a Twilight Zone where everything goes wrong, sometimes despite their very best efforts. In bowing out to Montreal in 2010, the Caps outplayed the Habs six of seven games. It's almost like Washington are operating under a curse. It's been that way since Bob Mason's broken skate in 1987. In 1996, Caps lost another four-overtime game to the Penguins. (Bryan Trottier was a Pittsburgh coach that night!) From 2008 through 2011, the Caps were pushed aside by a lower-ranking team every spring. It hasn't been Alex's fault. His postseason totals are above his regular-season average — 50 points in 37 games. What more can he do?

Well, maybe he should take a page out of the Stephen King *11/22/63* playbook, where a determined hero goes back in time to save JFK and America. Forget about pulling up his own bootstraps; Ovie should travel back in time to 1987 and take care of goalie Bob Mason's skates. If he did, maybe we'd be saying that Washington has won a string of Stanley Cups and its greatest player remains the game's greatest and most glorious player.

WINNIPEG *JETS*

 ## Loose Pucks

RECORD: Before the Beatles held our hand, there were rock bands in Winnipeg. Guitarists Randy Bachman and Lenny Breau were jamming in 1959. Bachman started a rock band months later, a group that became the Guess Who. He later co-founded Bachman-Turner Overdrive (BTO). The Jets landed in 1972 and were bigger than Christmas for 24 Manitoba winters. When the team came undone in 1996, Bachman pitched in on a charity album dedicated to Winnipeg hockey. The "B" in BTO changed the lyrics of "You Ain't Seen Nothing Yet" to toast departing Jet Alexei Zhamnov — "That's One Hot Russian." Harlequin gave it up for Teppo Numminen.

RECORDS

MOST HAT TRICKS, CAREER: Ilya Kovalchuk, 11 (Atlanta Thrashers — the Georgia team became the Winnipeg Jets II in 2011)

MOST POINTS, ONE SEASON: Marian Hossa, 100 (Atlanta Thrashers)

BEST PLUS-MINUS, CAREER: Marian Hossa, +21

50-GOAL CLUB: Ilya Kovalchuk, 52, 2005—06 and 2007—08 (Atlanta Thrashers); Stephen Harper, Jets 50-cent piece, 2011 (introduced by the Royal Canadian Mint)

WINTERPEG HOCKEY RECORDS (*Achievements by players who were born or grew up in Winnipeg*):

MOST HAT TRICKS, CAREER: Brett Hull, 33

FASTEST HAT TRICK: The Black Hawks' Bill Mosienko fired three goals in 21 seconds against Lorne Anderson of the New York Rangers on March 23, 1952, the last game of the season. The Winnipegger banged one off the post later in the shift.

MOST SHUTOUTS, CAREER: Terry Sawchuk, 103

MOST STANLEY CUP WINS: Terry Sawchuk, Ab McDonald, and Ted Harris, four each

BEST HEAVYWEIGHT FIGHT: Wayne Gretzky's Winnipeg bodyguard, Dave Semenko, battled Muhammad Ali to a draw in an exhibition bout labeled "Murder in Alberter" in 1982

MOST LAKES: Jonathan Toews, 1. The province of Manitoba named a body of water in Toews's honor after the Winnipeg-born center won a Stanley Cup and Olympic gold medal in 2010.

WORKING OVERTIME: Evander Kane scored a minute into overtime against the Los Angeles Kings on December 29, 2011, to give the remodeled Winnipeg Jets their first extra-period win.

DRAFT-SCHMAFT
TOP-10 PICKS, 1989–2009: 7

PLAYERS DRAFTED WHO PLAYED 300 NHL GAMES: 10

Evander Kane crashes the Montreal bench.

IMPACT PLAYERS: Dany Heatley, 2nd, 2000; Ilya Kovalchuk, 1st, 2001; Evander Kane, 4th, 2009

DRAFT-SCHMAFT RANKING: 27th

LINE CHANGES

American presidents have an emergency hot line that connects Washington with Moscow. The old Winnipeg Jets had a Hot Line that connected Pointe Anne, Ontario (Bobby Hull), to Nynashamn and Ornskolds-vik, Sweden (Ulf Nilsson and Anders Hedberg). The Hot Line was the best thing going in the WHA in the mid-'70s, with center Nilsson setting up 70-goal scorers Hull and Hedberg.

"Brophy couldn't coach a dog in from a snowstorm with a pork chop," superstar meteorologist Bobby Hull, commenting on former Toronto Maple Leaf coach John Brophy.

SKATE THAT ONE PAST ME AGAIN: In 2005, first-generation Winnipeg Jets star Dale Hawerchuk received a request from a Quebec punk band to use his name. "I told them, 'As long as you stay out of jail, go ahead,'" Hawerchuk said. And so Les Dales Hawerchuk were born.

BRING ON THE ZAMBONI

Celebrity fans: Although Neil Young once wrote a great song called "Thrashers" about the breakup of Crosby, Stills, Nash, & Young, he quickly hopped into some Jets duds to appear on *Hockey Night in Canada* when the Atlanta Thrashers moved to his hometown in 2011.

STUMP THE SCHWAB: Who was the last person off the ice when the original Jets left Winnipeg? And the first Jet on the ice for practice in 2011? Answers: Teppo Numminen and Nik Antropov.

The Fighting SPIRIT

Hockey in Cole Harbour, Nova Scotia, didn't begin or end with Sidney Crosby. Way before Sid the Kid made the NHL, Perry Kane had played junior for the Cole Harbour Scotia Colts. He grew up in nearby East Preston, a black community outside of Dartmouth. Family pickup games could take a couple of rinks — Perry had four brothers and sisters along with 100 cousins (his father had 18 siblings). Maritime winters drove Perry to Vancouver, where the hockey player and amateur boxer married a pro volleyball player, Sheri. They named their first child after heavyweight champ Evander Holyfield. (One of Perry's many cousins, Kirk Johnson, boxed for the WBA heavyweight championship in 2002.) Perry wanted Evander to know how to play hockey before letting him join a team, so the pair hit the ice at dawn, when ice time

FAN-Tastic

Mom and son show off their new Jets duds (top left), while another fan (bottom left) goes old school with a vintage Jets uniform — no Winnipeg fan appears to have thrown their jerseys away. (Top right) Spontaneous hockey games broke out in the street when Winnipeg fans learned they were back in the NHL. (Bottom) Other fans carried signs. (Middle) Winnipeg's most famous hockey son, Jonathan Toews, is celebrated in Chicago with, you got it, a Toews truck.

was available. They went at it one on one for two years before dad figured Evander, at eight, was ready for hockey. He also worked with his son in the gym, boxing, increasing Evander's hand speed and competitiveness. It all worked. Evander recorded an assist at age 15, helping the Vancouver Giants to a Memorial Cup in 2007. He made the NHL at age 18 with Atlanta. Kane started sluggishly in Winnipeg, with no goals his first two weeks. But the one-time amateur boxer reacted to Manitoba's first cold snap as if a corner trainer had administered smelling salts. From the last game in October through the end of December 2011, Evander had five multi-goal games. He only figures to get bigger and better. When Evander Kane met Evander Holyfield, the latter sized up his namesake and asked, "How much you weigh?" "Oh, 190 on a good day," Kane replied. "That's good," Holyfield said. "I was [18,] I weighed 149."

"Wipe your eyes, look at the big picture."

Surprise
LANDING

Now, where were we before we were so rudely interrupted? Oh yeah, 1996. NHL hockey in River City was dead in the water. Winnipeg was in the middle of a recession and had a dinky rink, no corporate boxes — the cash cow teats that made Yank arenas so profitable. The city was too small. In fact, it was shrinking. Thirteen hundred citizens disappeared in 1992–93. The Canadian dollar was also shriveling up, worth 65 cents U.S.

At the time, Americans came to Canada to shop — for cottages, companies, NHL hockey teams. The Quebec Nordiques became the Colorado Avalanche in 1995. The Winnipeg Jets took off to Phoenix a year later. The Jets' sale broke 600,000 local hearts. "Wipe your eyes, look at the big picture," fans were told. There were two million more hearts (and wallets!) in

Jets captain Andrew Ladd (foreground) lands his team safely home.

CHICAGO STADIUM REVIEW

25c

BLACK HAWKS CHICAGO

STANFIELD

BRENNEMAN

D. HULL

PAPPIN

ROBINSON

REAY

1964-65 ROOKIES

Hockey karma: St. Boniface Seals rabble-rouser "Tulip Billy" Reay enjoyed a fine NHL career, playing for the Montreal Canadiens from 1946–53, before becoming head coach of the unruly Chicago Blackhawks in the 1960s.

Phoenix. By 2020, there'd be 6.5 million. Phoenix was the new Los Angeles.

Look, it's best for everyone. Phoenix will look after the Jets in a way you simply can't.

The old "get over it, you're not good enough" brush-off. It was the most painful way to say goodbye. Thousands cried in the Winnipeg Arena the night the Jets left. Making matters worse, Phoenix, the franchise's suntanned savior, soon turned indifferent to the old Jets, treating the team like an unwanted toy the day after Christmas.

Hockey didn't work out in Phoenix. Still, Winnipeg hockey fans *knew* — it was clear as a prairie winter night — they weren't getting an NHL team back. No way. No matter how much talk there was of an NHL comeback in Manitoba. Teemu had left the building.

And then, on May 31, 2011, a shaking Mark Chipman, chairman of True North Sports & Entertainment, advised the largest press conference in Manitoba's history — more reporters than there are fans at some Phoenix Coyotes games — that the impossible was happening. "I am excited beyond words to announce our purchase of the Atlanta Thrashers," Chipman said.

Dancing broke out in downtown Winnipeg, right on the streets. Cops and kids threw each other high-fives. Youngsters — adults, too — played ball hockey. *I'll be Teemu Selanne, you be Dale Hawerchuk.* The party lasted the rest of the year. Within a couple of days, Winnipeggers shelled out more than 50 million healthy Canadian dollars for season's tickets (with a minimum commitment of four years). The city was doing okay now. Appropriately, a new airport showed up at about the same time the remodeled Jets did. Real estate was booming around the round, glassy MTS Centre, the Jets' new hangar.

Fans showed up at 5 a.m. to get a good seat for the team's first practice. Teemu Selanne cried on the December night when he returned to Winnipeg.

Sometimes you can go home again.

At Portage and Furby, local artists Michel Saint Hilaire and Mandy van Leeuwen painted a mural depicting the city's winter passion. Here's a companion

piece, nine hockey anecdotes to get everyone caught up in Winnipeg's hockey Jetstream.

NORDIC CONQUERORS, PART ONE

Winnipeg is a rich stew of English, French, Scottish, Ukrainian, German, and Aboriginal cultures. A lot of hard-K surnames went from the Peg into the NHL — Wally Stanowski, Terry Sawchuk, Peter Landiak (Langelle)[1] and Frederick Shirach (Freddy Shero), to name a few. The St. Boniface Seals were as French as the Montreal Canadiens. The tribes all got along, with little overt discrimination, except against the Icelandic. Go figure.

Maybe it was because Icelanders were the last in the census line — the smallest recorded constituency in Manitoba. Two hundred arrived in 1875, settling on the west shore of Lake Winnipeg. There are 35,000 or so today (the largest number of Icelanders outside the home country). Winnipeg's William Stephenson, Ian Fleming's super-spy model for James Bond, was Icelandic. As was the city's best hockey team after the First World War, the Winnipeg Falcons. The "best in Winnipeg" part was hard to prove, though. No other team would play them.

A hundred years ago, local businesses posted signs saying, "Help wanted!" with the catch "Icelanders need not apply." The Winnipeg City League rejected an Icelandic-Canadian hockey team. So Konnie Johannesson, Frank Fredrickson, Bobbie Benson, and Wally Byron, who had all served together, representing Canada and Winnipeg in World War I, started their own league.

The Falcons went on to defeat all civic competition in 1919–20 before traveling to Toronto to capture the Allan Cup. Next, off the Canadian senior hockey champs went to Antwerp, Belgium, with the community's blessing, to play in the 1920 Olympics. A last-minute goal by Romeo Rivers gave them the gold medal, and the Falcons returned to a mile-long parade down Portage and Main.

1 Toronto Maple Leafs superfan John Arnott would holler out, "Come on, Peter," to encourage Pete Langelle when he arrived from Winnipeg in 1939.

"Kid if I had legs like that, I'd walk on my hands."

Having beaten both Toronto and America, the Icelanders were now Winnipeg hockey heroes.

When Teeder Kennedy graduated to Toronto four seasons later, Arnott accommodated his arrival by shouting, "Come on, Teeder."

NICE WORK, JUNIOR

Today, only one Manitoba team competes for the Memorial Cup — the Brandon Wheat Kings. But in the 1930s, 10 teams fought to represent the province in the Canadian junior hockey championship. All that competition made Manitoba the home of wild-west hockey. Between 1931 and 1959, Manitoba teams made the Memorial Cup finals 15 times, winning 10 championships.

The St. Boniface Seals took the silverware in 1938, causing as much trouble as 20 Marx Brothers. Led by Wally "The Whirling Dervish" Stanowski and "Tulip Billy" Reay, the Seals traveled to Toronto to participate in the Memorial Cup, eventually beating the Oshawa Generals four games to two in front of over 15,000 fans, the most ever to watch a hockey game in Canada. Next day, the boys were scheduled to appear at a civic luncheon in their honor. Deciding that such a ceremony would be altogether too dull for their tastes, one of the Seals phoned the hotel hosting the affair and advised the maître d' that the festivities were being advanced from one o'clock to noon.

The team then hurried to the hotel and gobbled their meals, leaving nothing but a few breadsticks for the stuffed shirts who would arrive on schedule. The party continued on the train ride back to Winnipeg, when the Seals locked team coach Mike Kryschuk in a ladies' washroom.

"These guys were the best I ever played with."

THE BEST GOALIE IN THE WORLD

The only goalie to inspire a book of poetry (*Night Work* by Randall Maggs), Terry Sawchuk's life was equal parts heroism and heartbreak. Growing up in Winnipeg's working-class Elmwood district, he was the top goal scorer in hockey leagues in which he played forward and best goalie where he played nets. Neil Young's sportswriter dad, Scott, remembered him as a teenager, "booming home runs in community parks on warm prairie evenings." This was playing semi-pro ball against men.

He didn't go to movies or read books — not even comics. Figured he'd save his eyes for deflected pucks and hanging curveballs. Terry inherited his goalie pads from an adored older brother who died of a heart attack at 17. He made himself the best goalie in the world with haunted equipment, but never quite escaped the accompanying curse. Signing with Detroit Red Wings for a $2,000 bonus in 1947, he converted the check to Canadian dollar bills, hurrying to a motel, where he rolled in paper money as a child would in a pile of crinkly fall leaves. Other nights weren't so good. At the end, which was too soon, the goalie's face was heavy with 400 stitches — pucks and sticks he didn't read in time. He'd suffered a nervous breakdown, car and marital crashes, and died at age 41 from an awkward fall while scuffling with a teammate.

But when he was right, Terry Sawchuk was the best goalie in the world. Coiled and alert, crouching low, dipping his unmasked face to his knees to get a better look at pucks, Sawchuk allowed five goals in eight 1952 playoff games, winning Detroit the Stanley Cup. "He was the greatest goalie I ever saw and the most troubled athlete I ever knew," Detroit hockey writer Joe Falls said.

THE GOLDEN JET RUNS OUT OF GAS

WHA stood not for World Hockey Association, but When Hull Arrived. That was the joke when Bobby Hull landed in Winnipeg in 1972, conferring legitimacy on the NHL's sudden rival. Bobby Hull signed a $2.75 million, 10-year contract to play for the Winnipeg Jets on June 27, 1972. Arriving at the airport, his family was scooped up in a 1934 Rolls-Royce and ferried downtown to a waiting parade that engulfed Wellington, St. James, Portage, and Broadway up to the Fort Garry Hotel. Traffic was dead, but the city was alive, boiling with thousands of hopping, screaming fans. Winnipeg was in ecstasy. Chicago and the NHL were in shock.

That's the story everyone tells about the first days of the Winnipeg Jets. But it's also true that Hull and company weren't exactly a box-office hit. The first time the Winnipeg Arena sold out was when Gordie Howe and his boys appeared with the Houston Aeros in the Jets' second season. Big business hardly kicked in. The five banks bought up a total of 16 season tickets. A few weeks after Hull signed, a Winnipeg lady sent Jets owner Ben Hatskin an invoice for the $2.40 she lost while stalled in traffic the day Hull signed. "It's a real nice city, but as far as supporting a professional team, they leave something to be desired," Bobby Hull told a reporter after his first year with the Jets.

THE WALKING WOUNDED

The first edition of the Winnipeg Jets weren't all superhero models like Bobby Hull. His former Winnipeg junior coach, Ed Dorohoy, took one look at skinny forward Brian Cadle parading back from the shower and said, "Kid, if I had legs like that, I'd walk on my hands."

NORDIC CONQUERORS, PART TWO

Bobby Hull was an old 33 when he arrived in Winnipeg. He'd left his hair, and maybe his heart, in Chicago,

where he'd played 15 seasons. And the new league was hard on a proud old pro. Some teams sounded like drinks — the Cincinnati Stingers, the Miami Screaming Eagles. Franchises came and went — some not fast enough. In New Jersey, the visitors' dressing room was so small teams changed in their hotel. When the Houston Aeros won the first Avco Cup, the team hired circus elephants for a parade. Coach Bill Dineen's animal scooped up some droppings with its trunk and tossed a pound of used straw back into his lap.

That was the WHA at first. Then, in 1973, Jets doctor Gerry Wilson took a sabbatical in Sweden, where he saw — and recommended the club sign — forwards Anders Hedberg and Ulf Nilsson. They arrived in May 1974, reporting immediately to the University of Manitoba's training facility, where Bobby Hull waited. "Bobby, go with the Swedes," the coach shouted before a scrimmage.

Reunited decades later with the two Swedes at a Winnipeg press conference, Hull dissolved as he remembered what happened. "I get a little broken up because . . . I never saw two kids come out of the corner like they were shot out a cannon. And we went on the ice, and bing-bang, it was in the net." Afterward, Nilsson and Hedberg wondered, "*Jag undrar vad Hull tanke?*" ("I wonder what Hull thinks?")

Bobby thought he'd gone to heaven. "These guys were the best I ever played with," he remembered. "God it was fun, even in practice." A reinvigorated Hull, sporting a new bale of hay atop his head, and the two Swedes were the class of the league. They averaged 143 goals a year for four seasons, winning two championships and defeating the Soviets 5–3 at home in 1978 (Hull potted three, Nilsson two). They were hockey's beautiful future — a fast, swirling Canadian-European hybrid. Glen Sather played and coached against the Hot Line, losing too frequently. As a GM, he modeled the NHL's Edmonton Oilers after the Jets, importing Finns instead of Swedes.

Anders and Ulf helped save pro hockey in Winnipeg, although the team was never as successful as it should have been, averaging 8,000 fans most years.

This was a city that grew up on NHL hockey. After the team won its third Avco Cup at home in 1979, fans chanted "N-H-L, N-H-L." When the Montreal Canadiens (owned by Molson) vetoed the addition of WHA teams to the NHL, someone in Winnipeg shot off a gun in the brewery's branch office. The Prairies boycotted Molson beer. When the matter came up for another vote, on March 22, 1979, Winnipeg was admitted to the NHL.

"PICK ME"
Stripped of all their WHA talent, the NHL Jets were pretty terrible at first. But losing has its compensations. The team had first pick in the 1981 draft, when Dale Hawerchuk was the consensus top junior. *Hawerchuk — he even sounded like a Winnipegger.*

Though born in Toronto, Dale was a Quebec celebrity, taking Cornwall of the Quebec League to consecutive Memorial Cup championships. As a pee wee, he helped his team to an 8–1 tournament win in Montreal, scoring every goal (erasing Guy Lafleur's old record). Lots of teams coveted Hawerchuk. But he wanted to play in Winnipeg, so he walked up to GM John Ferguson before the draft and said, "Pick me."

Soon, Hawerchuk was a regular 100-point center for the Jets, leading the team to a win over Calgary in the 1985 playoffs, only to be gaffed and sidelined by a Jamie Macoun spear. "Ducky" helped keep NHL

Nisson, Hull and Heberg.

hockey alive in the 1980s, even if his biggest play that decade was winning a faceoff against Vyacheslav Bykov late in the 1987 Canada Cup. His wingers, Wayne Gretzky and Mario Lemieux (some line), took over after that, scoring the tournament-winning goal.

NORDIC CONQUERORS, PART THREE

Teemu Selanne didn't just show up in Winnipeg. Right before the 1988 NHL draft, the Stanley Cup–winning Edmonton Oilers made a conditional trade with the St. Louis Blues for the ninth pick overall, hoping to snare Selanne away from the Jets, who drafted 10th. All bets were off, though, if Rod Brind'Amour was available when the Blues' turn came around. He was — the Toronto Maple Leafs passed on Brind'Amour, Selanne, *and* Jeremy Roenick to go Philly-tough with Scott Pearson at number seven — and Selanne landed in the Jets' lap.

But he remained in Finland for four seasons, fulfilling military obligations, and was a restricted free

"You just bend over and kiss your butt goodbye."

agent upon coming to the NHL in 1992. The Calgary Flames let it be known they'd pay a million per season for Teemu; Winnipeg reluctantly signed him for three years at $2.7 million. Perpetually sour GM Mike Smith still wasn't a believer, however. "I'm going to be shopping him around for the next couple of days," he said.

That proved an idle threat. Selanne joined the Jets that autumn, fitting onto a line with Alexei Zhamnov and Keith Tkachuk with the same magical ease that Hull had blended with Nilsson and Hedberg. The Finnish Flash scored 24 goals in the team's first 29 games, electrifying the hockey world with his speed and nimble hands. Not only Winnipeg was in love. A televised game between the Jets and Los Angeles (where Jari Kurri now played with Gretzky), drew more than a million early-morning fans in Finland. After Christmas — it was incredible! — Selanne turned unstoppable, blowing past 50 goals with eight goals in three games. The last, in Tampa, came on a penalty shot. Asked to comment on what it was like to face Teemu one on one, Lightning goalie Wendell Young shrugged,

Teemu's team!

"You just bend over and kiss your butt goodbye."
Teemu shattered Mike Bossy's rookie scoring record
(53 goals), finishing with 76.

WAITING FOR A JET PLANE . . .

The first Jets–Winnipeg marriage was a torrid,
dysfunctional affair. Even during the Selanne years,
attendance averaged around 13,000. Yet every time
the team was about to leave, there was a desperate
civic rally — the "Save the Jets" campaign, the "Spirit
of Manitoba" rally, "Operation Grassroots," the
"Blue Ribbon Campaign." Tens of thousands marched,
pouring out their hearts and piggy banks. Everyone
cared, but not enough bought tickets.

Only when the Jets left did the city understand
what it had lost — an old love story, indeed. Grieving,
growing up a little, the city became a better hockey
market. Mark Chipman bought the Minnesota Moose,
herding the minor-league club to Winnipeg. In 2004,
the gleaming MTS Centre sprang up in place of the
old Eaton Centre — a major-league rink at last. Finally,
the cart was before the horse. Significantly, Winnipeg
started acting as if it had a future, not only a past. In
addition to a rink and airport, a new football stadium
for the Blue Bombers and a $310 million Canadian
Museum of Human Rights are under way. By encour-
aging immigration, Manitoba posted a record growth
spurt in 2010–11.

Chipman proved he knew how to play NHL politics,
as well, standing in line to wait for a franchise while Jim
Balsillie threw public tantrums as he tried to bring an
NHL team to southern Ontario. In 2011, Winnipeg got
its team — well, Atlanta's team — and thought about
changing the name to the Polar Bears before returning
to a brand name that had somehow grown bigger in the
product's absence. The Winnipeg Jets were back.

Smart fans spent the day before tickets went
on sale practicing their draw on the Jets' website,
memorizing the progression of links. "We were all a
pack of sled-dogs yanking deliriously at the reins,"
Graeme MacDonald, a Winnipeg investment broker,
told *The Globe and Mail*. Why not? The new Jets

even came with a star number 9 (Evander Kane asked
Bobby Hull for permission) and a ready-made Nordic
hero, Dustin Byfulgien. For Manitoba and its new NHL
hockey team, the new and improved Winnipeg Jets
were truly a matter of love at second sight.

A Winnipeg fan in a homemade jersey, waiting for the Jets to return.

SOURCES

I read three or four sport sections daily, depending on what's going on. Frequent stops include *Hockey News*, *Globe and Mail*, *Toronto Star*, *Boston Globe*, *New York Times*, Montreal *Gazette*, along with the ESPN, WFAN in New York and Sportsnet websites. I also follow several sportswriters pretty well everywhere — Cam Cole, Dan Shaugnessy, Gare Joyce, Stephen Brunt, Michael Russo, Michael Farber, Red Fisher, and Roy MacGregor. I listen to *Hockey Central @ Noon* and *Prime Time Sports with Bob McCown* on Sportsnet 590 in Toronto. And Mike Francesca on WFAN in New York. For just about every chapter in this book, I consulted Andrew Podnieks's invaluable Players and an ancient copy of Dan Diamond's *Total Hockey* — gotta get a new one, mine is falling apart like an old stewing chicken. For old-time players, I always turn to Trent Frayne's hockey book series. Then there is the good old library. For every story in this book, I ransacked the electronic database, searching for items on the topic at hand. That's where I got many of the sources listed below:

Anaheim Ducks: Elliott Teaford and Lisa Dillman, *Los Angeles Times*; David Pollak, *San Jose Mercury News*; Eric Stephens, *Orange County Register*; James Mirtle, *Globe and Mail*; the late John Halligan of the New York Rangers' website; Dick Beddoes, *Famous Hockey Stories*; Trent Frayne, *It's Easy, All You Have to Do is Win*.

Boston Bruins: Jason Gay, *Wall Street Journal*; Dan Shaughnessy, *Boston Globe*; Bob Ryan, *Boston Globe*; Margary Egan, *Boston Herald*; Cam Cole, *Vancouver Sun*.

Buffalo Sabres: John Vogl, *Buffalo News*; Jackie MacMullan, *Boston Globe*; John Connolly, *Boston Herald*; Arnie Stephenson, Canadian Press; Kevin Mio, Montreal *Gazette*; Tim Graham, *Buffalo News*; Mike Heika, *Dallas Morning News*; Jeremy Sandler, *National Post*; Roy MacGregor, *Globe and Mail*.

Calgary Flames: *Hockey Night in Canada*; Eric Duhatschek, *Calgary Herald*; Allan Maki, *Calgary Herald*; Steve Simmons, *Calgary Sun*; Stephen Brunt,

Globe and Mail; Rick Matsumoto, *Toronto Star*; Al Strachan, *Globe and Mail*; Jim Proudfoot, *Toronto Star*; Michael Farber, *Sports Illustrated*.

Carolina Hurricanes: Wayne Scanlan, *Ottawa Citizen*; Jeff Hicks, *Waterloo Region Record*; Chip Alexander, *Raleigh News and Observer*; Frank Orr, *Toronto Star*; Luke DeCock, *Raleigh News and Observer*; Allan Maki, *Globe and Mail*.

Chicago Blackhawks: Paul Patskou; Bob Verdi, *Chicago Tribune*; Neil Milbert, *Chicago Tribune*; Chris Kuc, *Chicago Tribune*; Eddie Gold, *Chicago Sun-Times*; Brian Cazaneuve, *Sports Illustrated*; Jeff Jacobs, *Hartford Courant*; Red Fisher, *Montreal Star*; Dink Carroll, Montreal *Gazette*.

Colorado Avalanche: Adrian Pater, *Denver Post*; *NHL Live*, with Billy Jaffe and Rob Simpson; *The Stick*, by Bruce Dowbiggin.

Columbus Blue Jackets: Paul Patskou; Tom Yawney; Joe Boylan, *Bleacher Report*; Aaron Portzline, *Columbus Dispatch*; Tom Reed, *Columbus Dispatch*; *Hockey News*.

Dallas Stars: Paul Patskou; *Hockey News*; Nick Murphy, *Bleacher Report*; Matthew Sekeres, *Globe and Mail*; Damien Cox, *Toronto Star*; Steve McLean (Rhett Miller interview); *Black Ice* by George and Darril Fosty; *The Hockey Book* by Bill Roche; *Two Solitudes* by Hugh MacLennan; James Duplacey's *The Love of Hockey*; Nancy Dowd's script for *Slap Shot*; Trent Frayne's *The Mad Men of Hockey*.

Detroit Red Wings: Paul Patskou researched all of Gordie Howe's "Gordie Howe hat tricks," as well as all other "Gordies" in this chapter; *Hockey News*; Al Strachan, *Globe and Mail*; John Dellapina, *Bergen County Record*.

Edmonton Oilers: Edmonton Oilers website ("Oil Change"); Greg Harder, *Regina Leader Post*; Vicki Hall, *Calgary Herald*; Josh Wingrove, *Globe and Mail*; David Staples, *National Post*; Jim Matheson, *Edmonton Journal*; Joanne Ireland, *Edmonton Journal*; Terry Jones, *Edmonton Sun*; Cam Cole, *Vancouver Sun*.

Florida Panthers: Michael Russo, Minneapolis *Star Tribune*; Austin Murphy, *Sports Illustrated*.

Los Angeles Kings: Paul Patskou; Paul Hunter, *Toronto Star*; Mark Emmons, *San Jose Mercury News*; Helene Elliot, *Los Angeles Times*; David Cruise and Alison Griffiths, *Net Worth* TV movie script.

Minnesota Wild: Lucy Nicholson, Reuters; Michael Russo, Minneapolis *Star Tribune*; BR Reynolds, Hockey Wilderness (website); Bruce Brothers, *St. Paul Pioneer Press*.

Montreal Canadiens: *Hockey Night in Canada*; Dave Stubbs, Montreal *Gazette*; John Kernaghan, *Hamilton Spectator*; Matthew Sekeres, *Globe and Mail*; Mike Boone, *National Post*; Roy MacGregor, *Globe and Mail*; Pat Hickey, Montreal *Gazette*; Stu Cowan, *Regina Leader Post*; Paul Hunter, *Toronto Star*; Peter Kuitenbrouwer, *National Post*.

Nashville Predators: Paul Patskou; Allan Maki, *Globe and Mail*; George Johnson, Vancouver *Province*; Sandra Sperounes, *Edmonton Journal*; Gayle Fee and Laura Raposa, *Boston Herald*. The Gordie Howe purse snatcher story came from an October, 1973 Associated Press wire story.

New Jersey Devils: Ken Campbell, *Toronto Star*; Kevin Smith's hockey blog; *Hockey Night in Canada*; Tom Gulitti, Bergen County *Record*; Stephen Brunt, *Globe and Mail*; Bill Reynolds, *Providence Journal*; Iain MacIntyre, *Vancouver Sun*; Bill Parillo, *Providence Journal*; Michael Farber, *Sports Illustrated*; Mike Harrington, *Buffalo News*.

New York Islanders: Craig MacInnis, *Toronto Star*; Jim Baumbach, *Newsday*; John Vogl, *Buffalo News*; Roy MacGregor, *Globe and Mail*; Luke DeCock, Raleigh *News and Observer*; John Valenti, *Newsday*; Michael Russo, Minneapolis *Star Tribune*; George Johnson, *National Post*; Peter Botte, *New York Daily News*; Kevin Paul Dupont, *Boston Globe*.

New York Rangers: Ben Shpigel, *New York Times*; *Hockey News*. All research on player performance relating to age by Paul Patskou.

Ottawa Senators: Jamie Fitzpatrick; Ken Warren, *Ottawa Citizen*; *Multicultural Canada*; Wayne Scanlan, *Ottawa Citizen*; Don Brennan, *Ottawa Sun*; Roy MacGregor, *Globe and Mail*; Alicia Siekierska, *Ottawa Citizen*.

Phoenix Coyotes: Ross McKean, *San Francisco Chronicle*; Bill Plaschke, *Los Angeles Times*; Paola Boivin, *Arizona Republic*; Michael Russo, Minneapolis *Star Tribune*; Jim Matheson, *Edmonton Journal*.

Philadelphia Flyers: James Christie, *Globe and Mail*; Mike Jensen, *Philadelphia Inquirer*; Marc Duvoisin and Tom Torok, *Chicago Tribune*; Dave Anderson, *New York Times*.

Pittsburgh Penguins: Bob Blatz Jr., *Pittsburgh Post-Gazette*; Ron Cook, *Pittsburgh Post-Gazette*; *Hockey News*; Damien Cox, *Toronto Star*; Roy MacGregor, *Globe and Mail*; Shawna Richer, *Globe and Mail*; Bruce Arthur, *National Post*; Jeff Z. Klein, *New York Times*; Tarik El-Bashir, *Washington Post*; Sarah Kwak, *Sports Illustrated*.

St. Louis Blues: Jeremy Rutherford, *St. Louis Post-Dispatch*; Dan O'Neill, *St. Louis Post-Dispatch*; Paul Patskou; *Hockey News*; Lionel Chetwynd; *Imperial Esso Films*; *Hockey Night in Canada*; *Great Scott*; Leafs TV; Dink Carroll, Montreal *Gazette*; Red Fisher, *Montreal Star*; Doug Hunter, *Scotty Bowman: A Life in Hockey*; Tom Adrahtas, *The Man They Call Mr. Goalie*; Dick Beddoes, *Globe and Mail*; Allan Turowetz and Chrys Goyens, *Lions in Winter*; Glenn Hall (interview).

San Jose Sharks: Gare Joyce, *ESPN Magazine*; A.J. Perez, *USA Today*; Joe O'Connor, *National Post*; Dave Eminian, Peoria *Journal Star*; Gordon Edes, *Boston Globe*; David Pollak, *San Jose Mercury News*; Harold Kaese, *Sport* magazine; Mike Felger and Tony Massorotti, CBS Boston radio.

Tampa Bay Lightning: *24/7* (HBO series); MSG Network; Chris Johnston, Canadian Press; NHL.com; Paul "Scooter" Barker.

Toronto Maple Leafs: Mary Rogan; *GQ* magazine; Stephen Buckley, *Boston Herald*; Joe O'Connor,

ACKNOWLEDGMENTS

National Post; Iain MacIntyre, *Vancouver Sun*; Damien Cox, *Toronto Star*; Andrew Wig, Sun Media; Mike Sielsi, *Wall Street Journal*; Joe Pelletier, Greatest Hockey Legends blog; Len Broderick (interview).

Vancouver Canucks: Rochelle Baker, *Abbotsford Times*; CTVBC.ca; Elliot Pap, *Vancouver Sun*; Ben Kuzma, Vancouver *Province*; Brad Ziemer, *Vancouver Sun*; George Sipple, *Detroit Free Press*.

Washington Capitals: *Hockey Night in Canada*; Brian Murphy, *St. Paul Pioneer Press*; Eric Duhatschek, *Globe and Mail*; Jim Matheson, *Edmonton Journal*; Reed Albergotti, *Wall Street Journal*; Stephen Wyno, *Washington Times*; Don Cherry, *Hockey Night in Canada*; Nick Kypreos, Sportsnet 590, Toronto; Damien Cox, *Toronto Star*; Charles McGrath, *New York Times*.

Winnipeg Jets: Steve Ewen, Vancouver *Province*; Ed Tait, *Winnipeg Free Press*; Iain MacIntyre, *Vancouver Sun*; Ian Walker, *Vancouver Sun*; Ted Wyman, *Winnipeg Sun*; Dave Stubbs, Montreal *Gazette*; Roy MacGregor, *Globe and Mail*; Paul Waldie, *Globe and Mail*; Kent Youngblood, Minneapolis *Star Tribune*; Randy Turner, *Winnipeg Free Press*; Randy Turner, *Back in the Biggs*.

I would like to thank my family — wife, Jacquie, and kids Harry and Lewis — for their aid and support over the writing/editing of this book. *I'm back if you'll have me.* Thanks also to fellow hockey scouts Kirk and Jodie, who accompany Lew and me to junior hockey games in Brampton. Couldn't do this without my agent, Dean Cooke, and his assistant, Mary Hu. And thanks to the great, entirely professional, and always welcoming crew at Simon & Schuster Canada, especially Kevin Hanson, Alison Clarke, Paul Barker, and the overworked but resolute, Henrik Lundqvist–reliable Brendan May. Special shout-out to project manager Susan Barrable and designer Diana Sullada. I love what you've done here.

PHOTO CREDITS

Photography indicators:
t = top, b = bottom, m = mid / l = left, r = right, c = center

Pg   Photo title: Photographer credit

ANAHEIM DUCKS

11   (t) Ryan Getzlaf, Corey Perry and Bobby Ryan: Igor Ponomarev

12   (t) George Parros: Copyright © 2012 Chasen Ikiri (Inside Hockey)

12   (m, r) Two fans in Duck shirts: Greg Matthews (GregPM/Flickr)

12   (m, l) Corey Perry with Blue Man Group: Ethan Miller/Getty Images Entertainment/Getty Images

12   (b) Hiller playing ball hockey: Train Family

13   Jonas Hiller making a save: Kirby Lee/Image of Sport/US PRESSWIRE

14   Goalie pads: Greg Matthews (GregPM/Flickr)

15   (t) Plante replica mask: Richard Bungay

15   (b) Gilles Gratton mask: Gayle Heran/Flickr

BOSTON BRUINS

16   Tiny Thompson: Photograph by Leslie Jones, 1930. Image provided courtesy of the Boston Public Library, Print Department

17   Chara skating: Copyright © 2012 Cody Smith Photography (Inside Hockey)

18   (m, l) Bruins family fans: Steve Perry (www.phototoart.ca)

18   (b, l) Chara and Thomas on parade: Photo by Robert Dennis

18   (b, r) Seguin deke: Copyright © 2012 Cody Smith Photography (Inside Hockey)

19   (t) Phil Kessel sign: Steven Radcliffe/Flickr

19   (b) Thomas skating by bench: MechaStewartPics/Flickr

20   Tyler Seguin stare: Copyright © 2012 Kevin Burns (Inside Hockey)

BUFFALO SABRES

23   Diving Gerbe: Timothy T. Ludwig/US PRESSWIRE

24   (t) Buffalo fan reaction: Photo by Jerry Vinciguerra (Buffalo, New York)

24   (m) Kissing Sabres fans: Patrick Haney (http://patrickhaney.com)

24   (b) Rick Martin bobblehead: Mike Chrzanowski/2011

25   Gerbe chasing Chara: Greg M. Cooper/US PRESSWIRE

26   Tyler Ennis stickhandling: Ira Tucker (itucker/Flickr)

CALGARY FLAMES

29   (t) Jarome Iginla in Vancouver: Leeanne Barr (lily-loves-photos/Flickr)

29   (b) Jarome Iginla in Vancouver: Leeanne Barr (lily-loves-photos/Flickr)

30   (t, r) Bale of hay: Cory Lievers (http://www.corylievers.com)

30   (t, l) Two women walking: phatmisiek/Flickr

30   (m) Thumbs-up fans: Shicole Stone/Flickr

30   (b, l) Chillin' with Jarome T-shirt: Mike Robbins

30   (b, r) Hard helmet fans: Bryan Birn

31   Al MacInnis statue: Erik Roggenburg

32   Mike Vernon: Andre Ringuette/Getty Images Sport/Getty Images

35   Calgary Herald cover: Reprinted with permission of the *Calgary Herald*

CAROLINA HURRICANES

37   (t) Staal skating: douglasgallery30/Flickr

37   (m, r) Figure skates: iStockphoto (Image #11807212)

38   (t, l) Hartford runner: © Dan Yungk 2009 (XonMus/Flickr)

38   (t, r) Girl in Whaler jersey: John E. Bodnar

38   (b, r) Ring bearer: Don Hazelwood

38   (b, l) Hockey pig: Glenda L. Owens (Raleigh, North Carolina)

39   Staal and Ward: douglasgallery30/Flickr

40   Brandon Sutter: douglasgallery30/Flickr

43   (t) Staal brothers: KC Armstrong

43   (b) Staal and Sutter in suits: © Maureen Lingle 2012 (www.MaureenLingle.com)

CHICAGO BLACKHAWKS

45   (t) Fan wearing Chicago headdress: http://www.flickr.com/photos/vpage/